JAMES BRYCE
AND AMERICAN DEMOCRACY

1870–1922

JAMES BRYCE
AND AMERICAN
DEMOCRACY

1870–1922

EDMUND IONS

LONDON
MACMILLAN
MELBOURNE · TORONTO
1968

© Edmund Ions 1968

Published by
MACMILLAN & CO LTD
Little Essex Street London WC2
and also at Bombay Calcutta and Madras
Macmillan South Africa (Publishers) Pty Ltd Johannesburg
The Macmillan Company of Australia Pty Ltd Melbourne
The Macmillan Company of Canada Ltd Toronto

Printed in Great Britain by
ROBERT MACLEHOSE AND CO. LTD
The University Press, Glasgow

TO

MY PARENTS

WITH LOVE AND RESPECT

Contents

List of Illustrations

Foreword

A study which combines biography with a treatment of the politics and the ideas of a period meets special problems, particularly where the ideas and the politics span fifty years and two continents. To treat certain themes as fully as they deserve would risk losing sight of the central subject of this work, James Bryce and his influence in Europe and America. The biographical element thus dominates the first few chapters in order to establish Bryce in his outlook and disposition. Thereafter, Bryce's travels and experiences in the United States take precedence, together with his interpretations of those experiences. Towards the end the politics and diplomacy of the period receive fuller treatment, when Bryce's influence on his times can be measured.

By casting the work in this form, I trust that the general reader may enjoy it as well as the specialist and perhaps agree that politics and diplomacy can be as exciting as biography and travel. Many historians now show a greater readiness to make their works available to the general reader as much as to professional colleagues. Provided the scholarship is exact, the move must surely be welcomed by all those concerned with education in its widest aspects.

I must record with great pleasure several debts incurred during the research and composition of this book. My principal debt is to Miss Margery (Margaret) Vincenta Bryce, literary executrix of the Bryce Estate. One could not have wished for a more helpful and highly informed guardian of Lord Bryce's intellectual legacy. I owe to Miss Bryce a great many sources, including diaries, journals, family correspondence and other memorabilia, not to mention her acute memory of the statesman during his later years. Another principal debt is to Mr D. S. Porter and his colleagues in the Department of Western Manuscripts at the Bodleian Library. The task of reducing to some semblance of order more than two hundred boxes of Bryce papers, touching every aspect of an astonishingly varied life, proceeds with admirable clarity in Mr Porter's calendar of the main Bryce archive. One hopes that the major task of sorting and assembling the remainder will not be long delayed. I also wish to thank the staff of the Foreign Office Library and of the Manuscripts Division of the British Museum; finally, the Plunkett Foundation for permission to examine their files of Bryce letters, in which the issues of American politics are frequently discussed.

Across the Atlantic, my debts are manifold. I am grateful to the American Philosophical Society for an award which made possible research in American collections in 1963. During the academic session 1965–6 the final research and composition were greatly assisted by a visiting fellowship from the American Council of Learned Societies. For six months at Columbia University I was extremely fortunate to have the counsels of Richard Hofstadter, who kindly read twelve chapters in draft and made fruitful suggestions. I also profited greatly from discussions at Columbia with John Garraty, who has mastered the politics of the period as few others have done, and who made useful suggestions for improving the manuscript. At Stanford University Gabriel Almond not only provided ideal office conditions but, together with his colleagues at the Institute of Political Studies, offered a most stimulating ambience for congenial work. Nor should I omit to acknowledge an earlier, but fundamental indebtedness to the officers of the Harkness Commonwealth Fund who, by the award of a Harkness Fellowship to Harvard allowed me the good fortune to spend two years studying American politics with the late V. O. Key.

Among the many who gave ready assistance in tracing Bryces' geographical and intellectual paths in America, I wish to thank the staff of the Houghton Manuscripts Library at Harvard; the President and Fellows of Harvard College for permission to use the A. L. Lowell and Charles W. Eliot Papers; the curators of the Edward M. House collection at Yale University, and of the Woodrow Wilson collection at Princeton University; the Manuscripts Division of the Library of Congress and of the New York Public Library, and the State Historical societies of Massachusetts, New York, New Jersey, Pennsylvania and Rhode Island. Also the staff of the William L. Clements Library at Ann Arbor, the

Bancroft Library at Berkeley, and the Hoover Library at Stanford for access to special collections. Individual thanks are due to Roberta Sutton of Chicago Public Library; John Buchanan of Cornell University Archives; Frieda Thies of the Johns Hopkins Library; Mary Klausner, Archivist of Grinnell College, Iowa; Frances Goudy of Vassar College Library; Elizabeth Duvall, of Smith College Library, and Clifford Shipton of the American Antiquarian Society. I am grateful to Dr Lyman Butterfield and Stephen Riley of the Massachusetts Historical Society for much hospitality, and to the Rt Hon. Henry Cabot Lodge, Jr, for permission to use the Lodge Papers. Mrs Maitland Beath (née Young) of Comber, County Down, provided valuable information on the Bryce ancestry. The late Mark deWolfe Howe, another acute loss to American scholarship, not only shared his unique knowledge of American jurisprudence, but also gave me copies of unpublished Holmes–Bryce letters.

I am most grateful to my colleagues at York University for kindly allowing me leave of absence in order to complete this study. My debt to my wife, Veronica, is inestimable from any point of view. At every stage of the writing and typing of successive drafts she has provided unstinted help, constructive criticism, and much forbearance.

E. I.

York
August 1967

Introduction

In August 1870 two young barristers set out from England to visit the United States of America. Their journey was not unusual or obviously auspicious; the flow of European visitors to the new world which the American Civil War temporarily suspended had now resumed. The two barristers were also scholars, however, and both had read widely and deeply in history and jurisprudence. Albert Venn Dicey was thirty-five; his companion James Bryce was thirty-two. In 1885, Dicey would produce a learned treatise on Anglo-American constitutional law. In 1888 Bryce would produce his best-known, though not his most learned work, *The American Commonwealth*.

For Bryce, in fact, the 1870 visit to America initiated a lifelong attachment. From his first visit, he was fascinated by American society and institutions, and he returned to the United States as often as a busy professional life in London and Oxford permitted. His interest in the American democracy became an unyielding admiration for the idealism, energy and openness of American society. Over a period of fifty years he interpreted the new world to the old, and in the process helped the new world to understand itself more fully. At the same time, his convictions and his learning made him highly critical of many aspects of American politics and society, and he did not hesitate to speak and to set down his thoughts. He thus became, as an American scholar recently observed, 'the best foreign friend the United States has ever had'.[1]

Bryce possessed a unique set of talents for this long mission, though his present reputation tends to undervalue them. Today he seems one of the less eminent Victorians; in any list of the great luminaries of late Victorian thought and letters, his name has a respectable but secondary place in the shade of great figures such as Gladstone, Acton or Leslie Stephen. Yet during his lifetime he was almost a legendary figure. Henry Campbell-Bannerman remarked of Bryce: 'He is the most accomplished man in the House of Commons. He has been everywhere, he has read almost everything and he knows everybody. There is no man living of which this could be said with less feeling of exaggeration.'[2] In 1913, Harcourt's biographer A. G. Gardiner surveyed the great men of the hour and wrote: 'If one were asked to name the greatest living Englishman, I think it would be necessary to admit, regretfully, that he was a Scotsman born in Ireland.'[3] Gardiner's portrait of Bryce followed. Two years later President Woodrow Wilson told his aide Colonel House that he entirely agreed with Gardiner's estimate.[4] In our own time, Sir Arthur Salter, who knew Bryce and many of the late Victorians personally, remarked in his little book *Personalities and Politics*: 'If I had to choose a single typical representative of the Victorian age I should name one who is not usually among those first thought of for this purpose – James Bryce.'[5]

What Salter and Gardiner partly had in mind, no doubt, was the astonishing range of Bryce's intellectual energies, and it may be that Bryce partly eludes the modern understanding by the very range of his accomplishments. Today we expect a man to be an historian or a political scientist, but not both; a classicist or a sociologist, but not both; a geologist or a botanist, but not both; a Professor of Law or a Cabinet Minister, but not both; an Ambassador to the United States or a mountaineer, but rarely both. Bryce was each of these, all of these, and rather more besides. He leaves us breathless. At one moment we find him lecturing to undergraduates at Oxford on recondite themes in Roman Law, then to historians on the doctrinal controversies of the medieval Papacy; at the next we find him in Caucasia, ascending the vast, unconquered peak of Mount Ararat, leaving his Kurdish guides far below, exhausted and fearful as he vanishes upwards in the mists. In London he dines regularly with Gladstone at Downing Street, where they discuss Liberalism, Toryism – and the light thrown by Icelandic sources on the Homeric question.[6] He departs for America on one of his many long visits and we follow him across the western plains; but he disappears in San Francisco, to reappear in remote Polynesia, filling his notebook with details of the flora, the geology, the language and the social institutions of Hawaii.

Versatility of this order died with the Victorians, and the modern mind is apt to find it suspect. Yet Bryce did not lack the true scholar's gifts. As an undergraduate at Oxford he took outstanding Firsts in Literae Humaniores and then in History and Law. His Arnold Essay on the Holy Roman Empire won the admiration of distinguished scholars throughout the world. His steps turned towards the Bar, but when Gladstone offered him the Regius Chair of Civil Law at Oxford at the age of thirty-two, it seemed that the scholar's life would now claim him for good. It was in that same year, however, that Bryce journeyed to America with Dicey for the first time, and the visit brought a fundamental change to his philosophical and political horizons. Intellectually he became a citizen of two worlds, and he devoted much of his energy over the next fifty years to bringing the two worlds into closer contact with each other. In this task, as a man of action and a man of thought, he was able to deploy the prodigious array of talents which his contemporaries admired in him.

This study traces Bryce's long involvement with American democracy. To understand his intellectual viewpoints as he sailed for America in 1870 we must first discover some of the questions buzzing in his mind; something of his philosophy, his politics and other aspects of his undeclared luggage, so to speak. In Europe, 1870 was a vital year which brought new problems and possibilities. Italian unity was now complete, but the Franco-Prussian War was to make Bismarck's Germany the key to Europe's future. Nationalism and republicanism were the dominant creeds. Federalism also exerted its appeal. In England a lonely Queen, bereaved and often petulant, was unwilling to accept the long political retreat which suffrage reforms would eventually impose on her position. James Bryce was acutely sensible of all these issues as he set out from the old world for his first encounter with America.

For him, travel was always a journey of the mind, and he would linger where he could learn. Bryce undoubtedly travelled more than any historian since Herodotus, and most of his journeys were in the United States. Eventually his innumerable American friends wished to claim him for their own and complimented him with the unique nickname 'Anima naturaliter Americana'. For when his travels, his friendships, his writings and finally his diplomacy in the period before the Great War are set out, Bryce emerges as something more than a friend of the United States. He is found to have played a vital part in the difficult and continuing dialogue wherein the old world seeks to come to terms with the new, and the new world rediscovers its involvement with the old.

I

A Presbyterian Boyhood

James Bryce was born on 10 May 1838 in a modest terrace house in Arthur Street, Belfast. His family roots were in Scotland, and the Bryce line can be traced to small landowners in Lanarkshire in the middle of the seventeenth century. Two of the Bryces fought for the Covenanters at Bothwell Brig in 1679, but after Monmouth's victory, service in the Church, dissenting nonconformity and education became the dominant family traditions.

The grandfather of James Bryce was a Presbyterian minister whose unusual deeds are remembered in church history. The Reverend James Bryce belonged to the Anti-burghers, the faction of the Presbyterian Church which seceded from the parent body in 1732 after refusing to submit to government requirements for an oath of loyalty. The young minister was unusually outspoken, even for an Anti-burgher, and when the elders of the Scottish Church suspended him for latitudinarianism, he moved to Northern Ireland to enter the ministry there.[1]

In Ulster his independent spirit again brought him into trouble with the authorities, for though he now found himself among Anti-burghers like himself, he refused to accept the *Regium Donum*, an apportioned bounty distributed from Westminster in order to pacify separatist elements in the Irish Church. The minister was admonished, then suspended and finally expelled by the Ulster Synod. He then took himself off to Killaig in Antrim and formed his own Church. Some of his flock followed, and before long other congregations were attracted to the eloquent preacher from Scotland, so that he became an unofficial bishop in the area of Killaig.

This record of independence and dissent, a marked characteristic of the Bryces, naturally involved hardship for the minister's wife and family. His five sons often went barefooted and with little food. Happily his wife Catherine, herself of Covenanting stock, was a resourceful and intelligent woman who taught herself Latin and Greek and then in turn taught the languages to her sons and to the children of others in the village of Killaig. At other times she visited the sick and assisted with her husband's pastoral duties in the neighbourhood. It was a hard-working, God-fearing family in which each son was taught the virtues of study, self-improvement and assistance to others. When the five boys grew to manhood, each rose to an outstanding position in his chosen field. The eldest, Reuben John Bryce, became head of the Belfast Academy and a leader of educational and religious life in Ulster. Robert became a physician in Belfast, William a surgeon in Edinburgh and Archibald head of the Edinburgh Collegiate School. The third son, James, father of the author of *The American Commonwealth*, gained high honours in Latin and Greek at Glasgow University before becoming a teacher of mathematics at Belfast Academy. He also became an amateur botanist and geologist of note and produced a scholarly work on the geology of Arran in western Scotland.[2]

Whilst teaching at Belfast Academy, the schoolmaster James Bryce met Margaret Young, the daughter of a local merchant. Margaret had a quick, enquiring mind and after a Protestant schooling she added considerably to her education by wide reading in her father's ample library. When she married James Bryce she had pronounced literary tastes and was a gifted conversationalist. They began their married life in 1836 in Arthur Street, Belfast; a God-fearing couple with simple tastes. Their first-born was named James after his father and grandfather. A second son, born soon after, was named Reuben after his uncle Reuben John at the Belfast Academy, but he died in infancy. A third son, John Annan, was born in 1843, and two daughters, Katherine and Mary, completed the family.

James was thus five years older than his brother John Annan, and at an early age was drawn into the adult world of earnest talk cultivated by his parents and their friends, most of whom were teachers or ministers of the Church. From time to time young James would also encounter his impressive uncles from Scotland or, more regularly, his uncle John, who called frequently despite his many duties as head of the Belfast Academy. The troubles with the Westminster government and relations with the Established

Church were often the subject of family discussions at this time. This was sufficient to raise questions in the mind of the precocious young James, and the earliest anecdote finds him at the age of eight insisting that he sit next to his uncle John during a family outing in order to question him on the British constitution.[3]

In 1846, James Bryce Senior was appointed to a post at Glasgow High School. James and Margaret Bryce made their new home at Blantyre, south of Glasgow, and the education of the two sons continued for the time being at home. At an early age, young James gained from his father an interest in geology and botany and delighted most of all to accompany him on his expeditions into the glens and hills near the coast. With his keen eyes and questing mind, the boy played a small part in the discoveries which his father recorded on the geology and flora of western Scotland. This youthful knowledge, coupled with a marked interest in the methods of natural science, never deserted the future political scientist.

James attended the school where his father taught, and the early training in Latin and Greek which he had received at home soon brought him the first prizes of his academic career. By his fifteenth year, in fact, he had gained from the school all that it could give him, and on the advice of his father spent a year at Belfast to attend lectures at the Belfast Academy, where he incidentally picked up a knowledge of the Erse language from his uncle John.

At the age of sixteen he began three years at Glasgow University, where his father and grandfather had studied before him. Bryce later recalled the zest for knowledge among the students at Glasgow, where the competition for honours and prizes was extremely keen. 'Whenever we had a chance, we talked about our work, discussing the questions that came up, an incessant sharpening of wits upon one another's whetstones. . . . The ambition of most of us would have been to be metaphysicians. That seemed the highest kind of mental exertion.'[4]

The curriculum was dominated by Latin, Greek, Mathematics and Logic, together with Rhetoric. The students thronged the lecture halls to hear William Ramsay and Edmund Lushington orate on the set texts. Bryce was already proficient in Latin and Greek and could translate or compose with ease. Homer was his favourite among the poets, and he could recite many of the books of the *Odyssey* by heart. In his second year, Bryce came close to winning the Latin prize when he was placed *proxime* to the great Latinist Donald Crawford, and one year later, Bryce claimed the prize medal for Greek texts. His father was particularly pleased that his son should have taken the prize he had himself won in 1820. An enthusiasm for the writings of Herodotus and Thucydides was also taking form, and before he left Glasgow, classical history was his dominant intellectual interest.

The professors at Glasgow were held in respect by the students, Bryce recalled, and in some cases regarded with awe. Among the students, however, there was a marked spirit of egalitarianism. Social origins were of little interest or importance:

Some among them earned money enough during the summer to pay their living and fees during the Session in the winter. . . . I remember one stalwart fellow who was one of the best men in the Logic class following the trade of a blacksmith during most of the year. Needless to say this was no social disparagement. Indeed the men who supported themselves in this way were all the more respected.[5]

Bryce did not have to support himself during his years at Glasgow, but his routine was intensely strenuous. Rising at six-thirty, he walked the three miles from his home to the University for his first class at eight o'clock. Often he would walk back home in the morning for preparation and study, then in again for afternoon classes; twelve miles each day. '*Sic fortis Etruria crevit*', Bryce observed.[6] In the evening, he worked hard at his books, or talked with his father on botany, geology, or mathematical astronomy. At other times, he assisted with the education of his younger brother Annan, now at school in Glasgow. During the vacations, the rambles and excursions with his father to Arran and the Hebrides continued.

Bryce was also exchanging letters with two Glasgow friends who had gone up to Balliol College, Oxford, and who told him of their life there. John Nichol and George Luke were typical of the brilliant young men who went on from Glasgow University to further their studies at Oxford. They were guided to Balliol by men like Ramsay and Lushington, who knew that the standards they set at Glasgow equipped the young scholars well for the School of Literae Humaniores.

In 1857, at the age of nineteen, James Bryce decided to try for a scholarship at Oxford. He was the first of the Bryces to attempt this, and Oxford seemed remote, though at the same time challenging. John Nichol and George Luke wrote from Balliol to encourage him, and Bryce's father added his own encouragement. Several Oxford colleges were holding scholarship examinations in May 1857 and early in the month Bryce took the night sleeper from Glasgow for his first glimpse of an English university. At nineteen he was a slim, wiry young man, of medium height, with a shock of brown hair falling across a straight forehead; his earnest expression was emphasised by the deeply set, penetrating eyes of a brilliant Celtic blue. There was an air of agility in his crisp, purposeful walk. *Orandum est ut sit mens sana in corpore sano*: James Bryce embodied Juvenal's maxim to a rare degree when he arrived at Oxford.

2

Oxford

In its visible aspects, mid-Victorian Oxford was a tranquil place. Scholars strolled along quiet streets and on Sundays the university community was gently summoned by bells. At the end of each summer vacation a porter at the Queen's College would emerge to remove the weeds and tufts of grass which had grown between the cobbles in the centre of the High.

If Oxford's outward aspect seemed calm, however, this concealed the bitter controversy which was then rocking the university to its foundations. The Oxford Movement and Tractarianism had divided the university into deeply opposed factions. The main issue concerned the university regulation that members should sign the Thirty-nine Articles to show their allegiance to the Established Church. Urgent protests had prompted Lord John Russell to set up a Commission of Enquiry on the University in 1850. When the report was published in 1854, it pointed out that the religious Tests excluded more than half the population of the kingdom.[1] The reformers took heart and the battle was then fought out in the colleges. Some colleges were prepared to drop the Tests or at least to waive them for Nonconformists and dissenters, but the Oxford Movement had not given up the struggle. High Toryism was deeply entrenched in the university, and many colleges retained the Tests as a condition of membership for undergraduates.

When Bryce arrived at Oxford, he hardly realised that within a few days he would be caught in the crossfire of reformers and defenders of the arcane. John Nichol and George Luke told Bryce of the current storms as he sat with them in Nichol's rooms. Balliol was a centre of reform sentiment, and was prepared to waive the Tests for Presbyterians and Nonconformists whose conscience would not permit them to sign. Bryce promptly wrote to his father that it would be best if he could gain a Snell exhibition at Balliol:

24

'For them, you need sign nothing, nor take any sacrament; they give you £150 a year for five years, and are in Balliol College, which is by far the best college in Oxford for tutors' reputation and liberal and improving society.'[2]

There is no record of an application from James Bryce to Balliol, however, and the likeliest explanation is that, having been born in Ireland and not in Scotland, Bryce was not eligible for a Snell exhibition. He turned instead to Trinity and the Queen's College, where scholarship examinations were to be held in the next few days.

Trinity was a small, scholarly enclave in Victorian Oxford. The President, Dr Wilson, was a high Tory who insisted on maintaining the Tests. His conservatism was endorsed by the elderly Fellows who surrounded him at high table. James Bryce was only partly aware of the attitude of Trinity in the confusing atmosphere of reform and reaction among the colleges; but even as he was writing his papers in the Trinity examination he was summoned to the presence of Dr Wilson and confronted with the rule of subscribing to the Thirty-nine Articles, together with the College rule of attendance at chapel and saying grace in hall. Bryce pointed out that he was a Presbyterian and could not subscribe to the Thirty-nine Articles. The President took a rigid line and told him that he could not become a member of the College without signing. Bryce stood firm. He was told to continue with his examination for the time being.

Bryce wrote to his father the same evening, confiding that if Trinity decided they wanted him, he might agree to attend College chapel, were this insisted on, but that he would resolutely refuse to sign the Articles. 'Whether they will permit it, I still very much doubt', he wrote, 'but if they do it will be a victory gained in the cause of liberty and dissent and help open this College, so it will be a positive good.'[3]

Recalling the President's firm line on the Tests, however, Bryce was not optimistic about the results at Trinity and he took the examination at the Queen's College a few days later. Yet even as he scribbled in the company of the other candidates, he was interrupted by the Vice-President of Trinity, who had been despatched urgently from a College meeting to trace the young Scottish candidate. Outside the hall, Bryce was asked if he would agree to attend College chapel and say grace in hall when his turn came if Trinity consented to waive the Tests in his case. Bryce agreed to the two conditions but stood firm against other College rules of religious conformity. The Vice-President hurried off. Half an hour later a messenger arrived to inform Bryce that he had been placed first at the head of twenty-seven competitors. Bryce went to Trinity and was admitted by the President and Fellows. He later learned that his papers had been considered 'brilliant' by the examiners. So Bryce the dissenter entered Trinity College largely on his own terms, though in a spirit of compromise. His grandfather died in Killaig at the age of ninety that same year, having preached twice on the Sunday before his death.[4]

The victory of the young Scot was quickly known on high tables. Lewis Campbell, a reforming spirit at Queen's, declared it 'the triumph of liberalism'. At Balliol, the reformer Benjamin Jowett noted the victory with relish. Other reformers, including Matthew Arnold, Clough, Froude and Goldwin Smith, also regarded the retraction of Trinity as a victory.

Bryce was entered for Classical Moderations and the School of Literae Humaniores. He threw himself into his work immediately and studied for about ten hours a day much of the time. His physical energy never deserted him, though occasionally he might complain of headaches when he had spent too many hours at his books. Then he would break off and ramble around the meadows beyond Oxford with his friends Nichol and Luke, or swim in the Isis. On the Sabbath Bryce went to church with the utmost regularity and rarely missed the University sermon.[5]

The expected First in Classical Moderations hardly taxed him, and as he worked on for his First in Greats, Bryce began to collect almost every available undergraduate prize in his chosen fields. He took the Gaisford prizes for Greek verse and Greek prose, the Craven scholarship and the Latin Essay prize. His First in Literae Humaniores was pronounced 'distinctly the best' of the two awarded in his year and he then went on to take a First in History and Law. He was awarded the Vinerian scholarship in Law, and in History the Arnold Essay prize. Between these triumphs Bryce found the time to learn Italian, to improve his German and to attend Max Müller's lectures on the principles of Etymology.[6] Such a record of distinction, together with the Presidency of the Union, was rare even in Victorian Oxford. A great future was foretold for the hard-working Scot. Fortunately his success did not go to his head. A. V. Dicey, one of his close friends at Oxford, noted in his diary soon after Bryce had graduated:

The real strength of his character lies, I think, in the happy combination of various qualities, each of which may be found separately as fully developed in other persons . . . his kindness and friendship are beyond praise. He stirs us all up, rushes about like a shepherd's dog, collects his friends, makes us meet, leads us into plans and adventures, and keeps everything going. His life will, I predict, be one of great and deserved success. . . . No one could do otherwise than rejoice should my prediction be verified. His success has never for a moment puffed him up.[7]

Though the President of Trinity still retained a conservative aloofness towards the young scholar, others singled out Bryce for special attention. He was drawn naturally into Jowett's circle of brilliant young scholars. On a reading party at the Isle of Wight in the company of Jowett and a group of Balliol men, Bryce was introduced to Tennyson. Bryce despatched to his mother a long, detailed account of the laureate's study, his appearance, his conversation, and his remarks on the poets of the age.[8] Back at Oxford, Bryce had become, again by a process of natural selection, one of the leading lights in the talented group which formed the Old Mortality Club at Balliol.

The club was formed by John Nichol in November 1856, and the founding members included A. V. Dicey and Algernon Charles Swinburne. The members met on Saturday evenings in Balliol to read essays on 'the more general questions of literature, philosophy and science'. These interests were construed liberally and when Bryce was elected in his first term at Oxford, his paper dealt with 'Gibbon's account of Monasticism and Asceticism'. Unfortunately the minute book does not record its content.[9] His second paper was concerned with education, and Bryce proposed a national system, with all teachers to be given courses of professional training. Here,

Bryce was in advance of the times. 'Some doubts were expressed by members on these proposals', the minute records, 'but all agreed with the speaker that a national system should be nonsectarian.'

T. H. Green joined the group in the Easter term and read a paper on 'Political Idealism'. Green sought 'to oppose views prevalent in the present day regarding the influence of general laws on national and social development. He asserted that society could not be looked at as a mere machine and that the results of such doctrines were highly pernicious, as destroying individual effort and preventing men of virtue and ability from engaging in politics. . . .'[10]

The members of the Old Mortality Club actively influenced each other and almost all rose to eminence in later life. They supported the party of Gladstone and responded to the causes in which the Liberal party was currently engaged. As young liberals, however, they also encountered the dilemmas of mid-Victorian liberalism. They wished to eradicate the social and economic conditions which Chartism had exposed but which successive governments had done little or nothing to correct. The inadequacies of *laissez faire* were not yet self-evident, and no economic theory was available to replace this linchpin of the liberal faith. The classical political economy of Adam Smith and David Ricardo was accessible to the initiated, but Carlyle's 'dismal science' had little currency among these young idealists.

Together with Dicey and John Nichol, Bryce went to Birmingham, Manchester and London to listen to speeches by Cobden and Bright. On the subject of colonies they sided with Cobden and vigorously opposed the concept of Empire. They joined in the debate on slavery in America, denounced the slaveholders, and upheld the cause of Lincoln. At the Old Mortality Club, A. S. Grenfell read a paper in January 1858 condemning the institution of slavery. 'They were', Nichol's biographer recalled forty years later, 'among the first in this country to recognise the genius for democratic leadership that lay behind the rough exterior and Yankee humour of Abraham Lincoln.'[11] In Europe, they admired the spirit of the Risorgimento, and none so passionately as Bryce, who sought to enlist as a volunteer for Garibaldi's army, but was forbidden by the Dean of Trinity on pain of losing his scholarship.

John Nichol, Bryce, Dicey, and the other serious young men who gathered at the select little society on Saturday evenings were for liberty of the individual, for the correction of proved abuses, whether at home or abroad, for the right of self-determination, for the protection of the weak against the strong.

The vital political issues of the day did not prevent Bryce from doing a solid term's work. Many scholars influenced his mind as he listened to their lectures or called on them at their invitation. Jowett, Matthew Arnold, Henry Nettleship and Mark Pattison welcomed Bryce as a young friend and enjoyed the combination of mental exuberance and deep seriousness he showed. Towards the end of his fourth year at Oxford, Bryce was drawn increasingly to the study of history. Here, the two men who influenced him more than any others at Oxford were Goldwin Smith and Edward Freeman. Both extended their personal friendship to Bryce, and their influence can be measured by the voluminous correspondence he maintained with them as long as they lived.[12] Both men deserve particular mention because they helped to direct the young scholar towards the study of democracy and political institutions placed in their historical framework.

In Victorian Oxford, Goldwin Smith was as controversial a character as the place could decently accommodate. Fiercely anti-clerical, he was openly scornful of the Oxford Movement, and had assisted Jowett in the earlier demand to Lord John Russell that a Commission of Enquiry be appointed to enquire into religious and academic freedom at Oxford. Smith was delighted by Bryce's stand against the Tests in 1857. Cast in a patrician mould, he had gone from Eton and Christ Church to Magdalen, collecting the Hertford, the Ireland, and the Latin essay prizes with comparative ease. His anti-clerical views were by then well known and it was generally held that a fellowship at Queen's had been refused him because of his frequent pronouncements against the Tests. No one, however, could deny his wide learning. From the Stowell fellowship in Law, he moved to the Regius Chair of History in 1858.[13]

Bryce was among the many who flocked to the Sheldonian to hear the brilliant controversialist at the height of his powers. In his inaugural lecture in 1859, Smith tilted heavily at the high Toryism of Oxford and at those who would seek to undo the reforms recommended by the Commission of Enquiry in 1852. He also inveighed against the idleness which he observed in many rich young men at the university, and included several admonitions on the proper duties of an aristocracy.[14]

Smith then lectured 'On the Study of History' and expressed his scorn for those who suggested that history is governed by 'necessary laws'. In later lectures, he elaborated his view of history as a moral quest, and argued that historians must bring moral judgments to bear on the historical materials they examine and interpret. Ranke's *wie es eigentlich gewesen* . . . received short shrift from Goldwin Smith. Though he commended the methods of science for 'the habits of methodical reasoning' they could implant in historians, and from which they might gain 'a certain calmness and breadth of view, derived from regions in which there is no partisanship or fanaticism, because there are no interests by which partisanship or fanaticism can be inflamed . . .', nevertheless Goldwin Smith in no way believed that history could or should be a science.[15]

These views were readily accepted by the earnest young Scot in his audience, and there was much else in Smith's complicated and at times contradictory moral universe for Bryce to examine with acute interest. Smith was a liberal, but not a democrat. He believed in the doctrine of progress, and indeed devoted one of his early lectures to the subject. Yet he also believed that an unlimited franchise was a grave threat to progress. He was convinced that new forms of authoritarianism, presenting threats to individual liberty greater than the old threats of unlimited monarchy or 'popish plots', would come from rule by the masses. Despite these views, Goldwin Smith equally rejected and distrusted Carlyle's hero-worship.[16]

The debate on slavery in the United States drew Smith's attention, and he entered the lists as a fierce champion of Abraham Lincoln, denouncing the Southern slaveholders both for the iniquity of the institution, and for their break-up of the union when the 'irrepressible conflict' brought the tragedy of the civil war. He attacked the slaveholders in speeches at Manchester in 1863, and declared his resolve to visit America as soon as possible. He accomplished this in the following year, and stayed for three months. After discussion with Seward, he was received by Lincoln, then travelled to New England, where he met Emerson and the historian George Bancroft. On his travels he formed associations which provided entrées for James Bryce when he in turn visited America six years later. Smith returned from America to castigate the Southern states in his Oxford lectures and in further speeches and articles.[17]

Smith also brought back from America an admiration for many aspects of American society – particularly as he had found it in New England. The absence of aristocracy, pomp and rank, the simplicity and concern for the common good – all made a deep appeal. When the Civil War was over and the American nation had begun to bind its wounds, Goldwin Smith took a major decision. In 1868, Ezra Cornell came to Oxford to prospect for the new university that he was founding at Ithaca in New York, a foundation which was to be free of all forms of religious or political interference. He had a sympathetic audience in Goldwin Smith and in October that year the professor packed his bags and left Oxford to take up the chair of English and Constitutional History at Cornell University.

Among many who were sorry to see Smith leave was his young friend James Bryce. The intellectual debt was considerable. The dissenting, free-thinking side of the nonconforming Smith naturally appealed to Bryce, and the professor's wide learning had been freely available to him. Once Goldwin Smith was settled at Cornell University, the two friends began a correspondence interrupted only by the death of the older man in 1910. Throughout those years Smith was for Bryce an invaluable, if rather dogmatic informant on American politics and affairs.

Edward Freeman was less of a controversialist than the colourful figure whose trumpetings still reached Oxford from distant Ithaca, in New York; but he was also a man of pronounced opinions, especially concerning the historian's muse. Freeman fits well into the tradition of nineteenth-century historians who read widely and did not hesitate to explore different themes in different centuries. From a history of architecture in 1849 he went on to produce a history of the Saracens. His interests ranged from jurisprudence and comparative philology to the history of medieval Europe and federal government. Articles flowed from his pen on eclectic themes.[18]

Freeman lost his fellowship at Trinity because of his marriage, but retained Oxford connections as an examiner in Law and Modern History, and also maintained a voluminous correspondence with his chosen friends. Freeman insisted above all on the unity of history. His wide reading allowed him to see an unbroken stream from the distant past to the present, whilst his breadth of learning prompted a comparative view of constitutional development and politics. When he undertook a study of the Greek models of federal government he had the assistance of his pupil James Bryce, who had by then made his mark as the youthful and brilliant historian of the Holy Roman Empire.

A visit to Germany in 1862 had kindled in Bryce an interest in German history and medieval Europe, and when the Arnold Essay competition approached he decided to attempt an essay on the Holy Roman Empire. He set himself the prodigious task of tracing the changing form and structure of the institution across a thousand years of history. Of course a complete history of the Empire lay far beyond the confines of a prize essay, and Bryce discovered the extreme difficulties of tracing an institution and also the idea of that institution as it evolved over the centuries; but he was encouraged in his task by Freeman. With astonishing insight and penetration, Bryce traced the changing forms of the Roman-German Empire through the complexities of the medieval papacy, the secular controversies of the Middle Ages and the political cross-currents of the modern era up to the demise of the Empire in the nineteenth century.

The essay not only took the Arnold prize, but soon reached a much wider audience. On the recommendation of the examiners, Bryce wrote a revised and enlarged version of his essay during the following year and in 1864 the *Holy Roman Empire* appeared from the university press. Scholarly journals proclaimed a masterpiece. In a long review, Freeman observed: 'He has in truth, by a single youthful effort, placed himself on a level with men who have given their lives to historical study'.[19]

In essence, the work was a study of a social and political institution undergoing change. The theory of the Holy Roman Empire was that of a universal Christian monarchy, and Bryce's interest in the resilience of the Empire and its survival across many centuries underlined his growing interest in the problems of government. His study of the Holy Roman Empire had gaps and shortcomings, as Freeman pointed out in his review; the neglect of the east Roman Empire had to be corrected by additional chapters in later editions. But Bryce was more concerned to portray the spirit of the institution and what it represented to those who experienced it than to provide a comprehensive history. He ended his essay with disclaimers which show his awareness of the complexity of writing on such themes:

That which it is at once most necessary and least possible to do, is to look at the Empire as a whole: a single institution . . . whose outer form is the same, while its essence and spirit are constantly changing. . . . Something, yet still how little, we should know of it if we knew what were the thoughts of Julius Caesar when he laid the foundations on which Augustus built; of Charles when he reared anew the stately pile: of Barbarossa and his grandson, when they strove to avert the surely coming ruin. Something more succeeding generations will know, who will judge the Middle Ages more fairly than we, still living in the midst of a reaction against all that is mediæval, can hope to do, and to whom it will be given to see and understand new forms of political life. . . .[20]

Bryce was ready to play his part in this movement of ideas. Indeed, he devoted the major part of his life to an attempt to understand and interpret political life in its historical and also its contemporary settings.

3

Law and Education

Bryce was elected to a fellowship at Oriel College in 1862 and it seemed to his friends and contemporaries that he was intended for historical scholarship. At that time an Oriel fellowship was an accolade sought by many and gained by few. Only two years later, however, Bryce turned toward a career at the Bar. His decision to become a barrister was not altogether surprising. The profession offered a secure path of advancement to an able person: it combined security with respectability, and for the present Bryce could combine his work in chambers at Lincoln's Inn with tutoring at Oriel College. Albert Dicey was also at Lincoln's Inn and the two were close friends and constant companions.

Dividing his time between London and Oxford, Bryce had his first taste of London life. He was drawn into the salons of eminent Liberals in London. At the homes of men like Dean Stanley, recently translated from the chair of Ecclesiastical History at Oxford, and George Grote, the ageing friend of Mill and Bentham, Bryce met Gladstone, Acton and many of the elder statesmen of the Liberal party. These men undoubtedly turned his thoughts to active politics.

Other aspects of London's social life made no appeal to Bryce. Hostesses were very willing to have the author of *The Holy Roman Empire* as an ornament at fashionable soirées, but Bryce could no more tolerate small talk in 1865 than he could forty years later in the social circuit of Washington when he was British Ambassador to the United States. The only interest he found in those evenings, he confessed in letters to his parents, was that of the natural scientist observing the antics and habits of some curious type of fauna to be found only in the metropolis.

At the same time, he began to weary of the dry-as-dust work in chambers and there is a revealing complaint in his letter describing the daily round at Lincoln's Inn.

Streaming down Oxford Street about 11 every morning to the Inn; then books, very dreary books it must be said, most of them interminable records of minute facts through which it is not easy to trace the course of a consistent and clarifying principle. . . .[1]

Facts were not unimportant to Bryce as a scholar, but he preferred to search for the relations between facts; for their meanings or implications when they were assembled into some coherent order.

Equally, of course, the physical energy and love of the outdoors which his Scottish youth had implanted caused Bryce to chafe in his dusty chambers. During these years he walked in the Rhineland and in Italy with his Oxford friends Henry Nettleship and Dicey. In 1866 he climbed in Transylvania with Dicey's cousin Leslie Stephen, and though Stephen had already established himself as a skilled mountaineer, he later paid tribute to the combination of skill, endurance and daring shown by Bryce in their climbs in the Carpathian mountains.[2]

In London, meanwhile, Bryce continued with his work in chambers with John Holker, who later became Attorney General and a Lord Justice. Holker invited Bryce to accompany him on the northern circuit in 1867 and Bryce welcomed the break this afforded from the tedium of London. At Manchester he was impressed by the different type of person he met: more rugged, self-reliant, less polished than many of the literary men in London and, therefore, much more like the people at home in his youth. Bryce was thus partly drawn into that circle of proud north-countrymen who helped Henry Roscoe to found Owens College at Manchester, and Bryce was delighted when the college invited him to lecture on jurisprudence a few years later.

Another appointment at this time brought him into close contact with the educational life of the country. Bryce was asked to serve on the 1864 Taunton Commission on the condition of schools in England and Wales. For two years he visited scores of schools, took detailed notes of every aspect of the conditions at grammar schools, secondary schools and many church schools, and produced a detailed report on his findings. He deplored the poverty of public education in places like Lancashire and Wales, contrasting their overcrowded and insanitary conditions with those in many private schools. Bryce

35

urged corrective legislation. His report, together with the distinguished contributions of his fellow commissioners, helped to prepare the ground for Forster's Education Act in 1870 and the subsequent Acts of 1880 and 1891 designed to improve primary and secondary education in England and Wales.[3]

Work on the northern circuit, a Royal Commission, law lectures at Manchester and tutoring at Oxford might seem an ample load even for a Victorian liberal, but Bryce was also writing the first of many hundreds of articles and reviews for journals. At the suggestion of Edward Freeman and Leslie Stephen, Bryce reviewed for the *Cornhill Magazine* and *Nineteenth Century*. In 1867, he also contributed an essay in the book *Essays on Reform* produced by a group of liberals.[4] The contributors included A. V. Dicey and Leslie Stephen, and the essays showed some of the doubts, but overall the cautious optimism of these thoughtful liberals towards proposals for an extension of the suffrage. The essays provide, in fact, a very useful insight to the state of the debate on democracy at this time. The opponents of further extension of the franchise were currently warning readers of the dangers of democracy and, in their own phrase, of mob rule. Men like Robert Lowe warned of the dire consequences of opening 'the flood gates', another favourite phrase among those who opposed reform.[5]

In *Essays on Reform* Bryce wrote on 'The Historical Aspect of Democracy'. He examined the cause of decline in nations, taking Greece, Rome and France for his three examples. Much of this essay dealt with Athenian democracy and the Roman republic, with less attention to the case of France. On France, indeed, Bryce was too cursory, and did little more than deplore the state of France under Louis Napoleon. Equally, however, his deep dislike for dictatorship or one-man rule was set out plainly. On Greece and Rome, his hypothesis centred on the 'canker' of slavery, the existence of a rich aristocratic class side by side with slavery, and the moral corruption and decadence which arose from these parallel conditions. The main argument of the piece was that democracy in itself did not bring decline or ruin; rather, 'class government' tended to bring it about. Bryce ended with a defence of democracy and a rebuke of its current critics.

Dicey's essay on 'The Balance of Classes' was similar in its message. There is not, and never was, he argued, a 'balance of classes' in Britain as some contemporary opponents of reform argued. Even if true, their arguments implied a static view of society. It was the essence of society that it should change through time.

The example of American democracy was often used in the debates on democracy and reform at this time. Goldwin Smith was invited to contribute an essay 'On the Experience of the American Commonwealth' and in a mellow mood his essay avoided some aspects of American democracy which had offended him on his visit in 1864. He concentrated instead on the excellence of the American Constitution and the virtues of republican institutions. Smith preferred republican democracy to Tory monarchy. Leslie Stephen had also visited America and took pains in his contribution to the *Essays* to dispose of popular fallacies about American democracy. Like Goldwin Smith, he declared his admiration for the American Constitution.

This admiration for republican institutions among the liberals who contributed to *Essays on Reform* was highly significant. After the death of Prince Albert in 1861, Victoria's personal rule began. An enthusiasm for republicanism can be detected in the lectures of Freeman and Goldwin Smith during the 1860s, sentiments derived not simply from dislike of Victoria and the monarchy, of Toryism or interference by the Established Church, but equally from a genuine interest in the society and institutions of the new world.

Bryce continued to lecture and teach at Oxford during these years, and also lectured on Roman Law and jurisprudence in London during the Law terms. His reputation as a clear yet profound expositor was well known by the end of the decade, and in 1870 Gladstone offered Bryce the Regius Chair of Civil Law at Oxford. Freeman was among those who had urged the candidacy, and Bryce accepted early in 1870.

Before taking up his duties, however, Bryce resolved to do what Leslie Stephen, Goldwin Smith and Albert Dicey's brother Edward had done: to visit and travel in the United States. Albert Dicey was also keen to go. The two friends made plans to travel together for an extensive visit in the summer and autumn of 1870. Leslie Stephen provided letters of introduction to many scholars and men of letters in New England, and the two young barristers sailed aboard the S.S. *Scotia* on 14 August.

4

1870: Journey to America

The S.S. *Scotia*'s crossing that August was one of the smoothest in the captain's memory. Once they had settled in their cabins, Dicey and Bryce scanned the passengers for congenial company. Bryce noted down his observations in a series of letters to his parents, adding to them almost daily throughout the voyage. The boat was full, and most of the passengers were Americans returning from summer trips to Europe. 'Perhaps 60 per cent [were] American', he estimated, 'about 20 per cent English, the remainder Germans, French, Italians'.[1]

Bryce and Dicey were eager to discuss with the passengers their reasons for visiting Europe, or alternatively their expectations of the new world, and their reasons for going to America. But the passengers tended to be uncommunicative and early efforts were not successful. 'Indeed, poor A.V.D.'s efforts met on one occasion with almost a repulse.' On that occasion, however, Dicey's overtures were directed to a lady.[2] Of course the two Britons presented a rather formidable appearance, even though they were in their early thirties. Dicey was tall, extremely slim, with a long, cadaverous face and eyes deeply set under a high forehead; Bryce was of medium height, with reddish brown hair, bushy eyebrows, brilliant, piercing eyes, and he now sported a full reddish beard.

Bryce and Dicey were seated at the captain's table for meals and Captain Judkins, 'a fine specimen of the rather rough and despotic but vigorous and watchful commander, not without a certain gruff humour', occasionally relaxed to tell the two barristers of his many crossings and voyages. Bryce and Dicey conversed at some length with churchmen. There were many Roman Catholic clergymen aboard returning from the Ecumenical Council in Rome that year, and Bryce was eager to hear their views on Papal Infallibility. The Council had held its long and famous debate on the subject in 1870 and already there was talk of a serious split in the Church. Among the five bishops Bryce discovered on board, the most approachable was Dr McQuaid, the Bishop of Rochester, in New York. McQuaid was friendly, talkative and hospitable. He invited Bryce and Dicey to visit him at Rochester should they find time, and they accepted with pleasure. The bishop told them of the debates at Rome and spoke frankly of his own position on the question of Infallibility. 'He was a hearty opponent of Infallibility', Bryce noted. The other bishops on board appeared to hold the same view. Dicey recalled that some of the bishops observed 'that the death of Pius IX might be a possible, and one might say a desirable solution of the difficulty'.[3]

Bishop McQuaid also told them 'a good many curious facts about America', drawing on his own rigorous experience of life in the cities. Bernard McQuaid was born of poor Irish parents in New York and by zealous work among the poor had risen in the Roman Catholic Church to become the first Bishop of Rochester. Bryce liked his combination of humour, compassion and love of life.[4]

However, others on board maintained their reserve, so Bryce and Dicey fell back on their reading. They rose early at six o'clock, walked on deck, spent the next hour until breakfast with their books, and returned to reading for much of the day.

The *Scotia* arrived off Sandy Hook on the evening of Monday 22 August and lay to until dawn. On Tuesday at about eight in the morning Bryce and Dicey stepped off the ship. It was a brilliantly clear day. The sun shone in a cloudless sky as a mild breeze fanned the southern tip of Manhattan at Battery Point. For Bryce, it was a genial introduction to the new world.[5]

They were met at the pier by John Young, a cousin of Bryce on his mother's side, who had emigrated from Ireland and now lived in Brooklyn. After guiding them through the customs and the confusion of the waterfront, John Young insisted that the two friends stay with his family in Brooklyn. They gladly accepted, and in Brooklyn met Martha Young and the two young daughters of the family. At lunch they talked of the voyage and of family matters. But the visitors were eager to see New York, and the Youngs readily understood when they took the ferry again after lunch to visit Manhattan.[6]

The two friends walked out into the hot glare of the August sun and strolled around the streets of lower Manhattan. In 1870 New York's architecture had none of the soaring tendencies it began to assume in the 1880s, but much of the bustle was there. On Broadway, it was difficult to cross between the clutter of horse-drawn carriages and public transport. Dicey and Bryce absorbed every detail of what they observed on the waterfront, on crowded Broadway, and on side streets where refuse lay in the gutter and immigrant children played among the bollards or on the stone steps of the tenement houses.

After cashing cheques at a bank and arranging for further credits during their travels, Dicey and Bryce called on E. L. Godkin at the offices of the *Nation*. Godkin's name was familiar to them as a friend of Leslie Stephen and a man of letters whose offices were a regular port of call for visiting Englishmen. Born in Ireland, a correspondent for the London *Daily News* during the Crimean War and later an amateur historian, Godkin had emigrated to America in 1856 to study law. He helped to found the *Nation* in 1865 and by 1870, despite some financial difficulties, the *Nation* was making its name as a serious journal of discussion on politics, history, literature, and the affairs of the day.[7] To a considerable degree it served in America the purpose of London journals such as the *Spectator* and *Nineteenth Century*. Godkin no doubt had hopes that the articulate men who called on him that hot August afternoon would add strength to his 'English arm', as he liked to refer to contributors from England.

Bryce and Dicey were eager to hear an acute mind telling them something of the new world and to add his advice on the places they should visit and the people they might meet. 'Godkin discourses cleverly on politics', Bryce noted down. From this meeting stemmed a constant exchange of ideas between the two men. Bryce began his contributions soon after his return to England and although duties at Oxford and later in Gladstone's Cabinet reduced the flow, nevertheless when Bryce's articles and reviews for the *Nation* on politics, history, law, literature and society are added up, they amount to almost three hundred contributions over a period of fifty years.[8]

In the late afternoon Bryce and Dicey returned 'very footsore' to Brooklyn on the ferry, which plied where the vast span of the Brooklyn Bridge would stretch its steel cables and iron length twelve years later. At dinner that evening they discussed female emancipation in America. Bryce had heard that the young American female, as she approached the age of courtship, enjoyed much greater freedom from chaperonage than Victorian England allowed. John Young confirmed this and described the American custom of young women meeting young men without the presence of a chaperone. The custom allowed much easier social relationships to develop, the Youngs argued. Bryce was intrigued by this; it prompted his first reflections on the differences between Victorian England and American society. Questions were starting up on all sides.

Bryce had brought along with him a pocket-sized writing book in which to keep a journal from the day he arrived in the new world. He began his journal later that evening, and though much travelling caused some gaps in the record, he made a conscious effort to supply the missing portions in detailed letters to his parents and sisters at home. The journal and his letters help to make the record of his 1870 travels fairly complete, for happily Bryce had the further habit of noting down some of his reflections and conclusions on the experiences of the day.[9]

Dicey and Bryce made their farewells to the Youngs next morning, and came across to Manhattan again to spend part of the day looking at upper Fifth Avenue, where the new wealth of industrialism displayed itself. Manhattan was populated up to the area of Central Park. Above the level of the present Fiftieth Street, open fields and here and there a farm could be seen. In mid-town the opulent, often bizarre houses of the rich appeared, squeezing out the few remaining hovels marooned in a tiny patch of land where chickens and perhaps a goat scraped at the impoverished soil. The newly rich – among them men who had made fortunes in railroads, land speculation and real estate, made New York a divided city. The immigrant poor were crowded in tenements spreading up the lower east side. Some said that New York was like a lady whose neck was hung with pearls but whose feet showed muddy toes peeping out of pauper's shoes. In the *New York Times* on the day Bryce first glimpsed America the employment columns printed twelve separate advertisements from females seeking jobs as chambermaids or seamstresses. In a separate column a 'respectable, Protestant, middle-aged German' sought employment as a coachman and groom in 'a gentleman's place'. The differences between New York and London were not as great as some Englishmen thought, or most Americans conceded.[10]

Returning down Sixth Avenue, Dicey and Bryce took the ferry across to Sandy Hook and the Jersey shore to take the train to Long Branch on the New Jersey coast. Long Branch was at that time a fashionable resort, the summer haunt of Philadelphians and New Yorkers. Hotels were scattered along the sea front behind the dunes, and among summer residents President Ulysses Grant could be found at the house he maintained close to the shore. At this time, in fact, Long Branch was counted as the summer capital of the United States. Philadelphians and New Yorkers anxious to see, to be seen, or simply to bathe or promenade flocked there during the summer months. The houses were decked out in the cast iron trimmings and early Pullman art of the Grant era. A Victorian strictness governed the bathing regulations on the ample beaches: mixed bathing was forbidden and ladies bathed for an hour, when a white flag was hoisted, and gentlemen on alternate hours, when the red flag was up.

Bryce and Dicey chose their hotel on the advice of 'a Scotchman from Dundee' whom they met in the train. Bryce had spent most of the journey firing questions at the Scotsman, and this was the first of a long tally of interrogations by Bryce as he travelled in America. Twenty years later he recalled that five-sixths of *The American Commonwealth* was the result of conversations with Americans in trains, carriages, coaches, on steamboats, in political clubs and conventions, in hotel lobbies, even on top of mountains and at outposts in the wilderness.

At the hotel in Long Branch Bryce found the rooms 'very plain, not to say rough and unfurnished', but with an excellent view of the dunes and the beach. The purpose of the visit was to swim under the hot August sun, and within a few minutes Bryce was plunging into the surf. Bryce bathed as often as he could, and during the next two months he took his 'dip' in a variety of lakes, mountain pools and cold streams from New England to northern Minnesota.

At supper that evening, Bryce talked again with the Scotsman they had met on the train, then strolled with Dicey on the promenade to discuss the journeys they were planning for the next few days and weeks. On the sea front, fashionable couples from Philadelphia and Washington strolled in the evening sun. Here and there young ladies stood chatting and twirling their parasols as they admired each other's dresses. The scene must have been very similar to Winslow Homer's delightful landscape with figures, now in the Boston Museum of Fine Arts and bearing the title 'Long Branch (1870)', a painting whose impressionism and figuring beautifully convey the sensibilities of the time and place.

Next morning Dicey and Bryce went north by train to Newport in Rhode Island. Dicey's cousin Leslie Stephen had urged them to visit the resort. Bryce knew that the atmosphere of Newport would be something special for at that time, perhaps more than at any time in its history, Newport society meant genteel Boston society transplanted for the summer. Most of the charming white frame houses about the point were owned by Bostonians. Some came for the summer only; others, like Colonel Thomas Wentworth Higginson, the Civil War veteran, settled in Newport for the evening of life to write nostalgic novels and pastoral poetry.[11]

Among the notables were Julia Ward Howe, the feminist and pamphleteer, who lived with her husband in a rambling house a little way outside the small town. Mrs Howe had formed, with herself as President and Colonel Higginson as Vice-President, a select little group calling itself the 'Town and Country Club', whose members met at each other's houses to read essays, poems, and occasionally the manuscript of a novel.[12] Bryce and Dicey were drawn into the circle within the next few days. They met Colonel Higginson at dinner and the Colonel quickly informed his friends that two interesting Englishmen had arrived. 'They are very cordial, intelligent and good, very radical and eagerly interested in everything American', Higginson wrote in his diary. Next day he collected them in his carriage to pay a social call on Julia Ward

Howe. Although they found Mrs Howe out, they had plenty to discuss with her husband, Samuel Gridley Howe, who had served as a doctor in the Greek War of Independence before Bryce was born, and since then had become one of the best loved philanthropists in New England. Bryce knew also of his persistent support of the anti-slavery cause, and what was up to now second-hand historical knowledge derived from journals and books became vivid first-hand accounts of the long struggle.

Bryce felt an unusual affinity with these people. In many respects, they were the exact counterpart of the liberals he liked and admired at home. In some ways they were even more radical in their opinions, and certainly more open-minded. They enjoyed good books and dealt freely in ideas on questions of the day such as party politics, the South, or female emancipation. Indeed, in the company of Julia Ward Howe's friends, the issue of women's suffrage and female emancipation could be discussed with much greater freedom than in the salons and clubs of London. In this sense, and in others which he was only just discovering, Bryce found American society more liberal and more relaxed than English society – even that of his chosen friends at home.

Dicey and Bryce were dined at the home of Charles Perkins and his wife. Perkins was a Boston art critic, a devout music lover and a wealthy philanthropist who helped to found the Boston Museum of Fine Arts. He wrote informed works on Italian sculpture and read widely in several languages. Another guest was the painter John La Farge, friend of Henry Adams. With such men, Bryce could find an immediate accord. These men and their wives opened many doors for the two travellers at Boston and Harvard, where they were soon to meet more new friends.[13]

The contacts between men of letters and scholars in New England and in London, Oxford and Cambridge in England were long established. There was a sort of freemasonry from which the present visitors could draw distinct advantages in terms of warm hospitality, but more importantly in frank, informed talk. Almost twenty years earlier, Arthur Hugh Clough – a fellow of Bryce's college at Oxford – had spent eight months in Massachusetts and formed close friendships with Charles Eliot Norton and Longfellow at Harvard. Leslie Stephen had close friendships with the same men.

In turn, scholars and writers such as Ralph Waldo Emerson, James Russell Lowell, Oliver Wendell Holmes Junior and the Adamses travelled to Europe as young men to complete their education. These Americans returned to Europe to renew their friendships, many of which were extremely close and had important literary results. Emerson's long friendship with Carlyle and his meetings with Wordsworth and Coleridge; Longfellow's literary associations with Matthew Arnold and his acquaintance with Froude, Trollope and Kingsley; the friendships shared by James Russell Lowell and Charles Eliot Norton with many writers and statesmen in Britain – all combined to produce a charmed circle: the term should not be shirked. In 1870 Dicey and Bryce followed a path which had been smoothed by many of their countrymen.[14]

This is not to say that Harvard and Newport greeted every visiting Englishman with uncritical warmth. More than they perhaps realised, British visitors received a swift but careful scrutiny the moment they began a conversation. After all, Mrs Trollope had lived in America three years but returned to England to write a petulant, acidulous, and worst of all a condescending tract on the manners of the Americans. Dickens had shown some of the same leanings when he published his *American Notes*. The men and women Bryce met in America were familiar with these works and with the accounts of other travellers which had not flattered Americans, least of all proud Yankees.[15]

Apart from this, the British attitudes to the Southern Confederacy during the Civil War still rankled in many minds. That of *The Times* towards the Yankees had been sufficient to appal the abolitionists of New England, and some British Liberals had displayed a curious mixture of attitudes during the Civil War.[16] Even as they travelled, Bryce and Dicey knew that the *Alabama* claims were being hotly argued in Congress and throughout the northeast. The British-built *Alabama*, together with other British-built raiders in the Confederate navy, had inflicted heavy losses on Northern merchant ships during the Civil War. Powerful voices in Congress now demanded full compensation from Britain. Yankee New England, a centre of abolitionist sentiment during the long controversy on Southern slavery, could not be expected to throw open its doors to every visiting Englishman until he had first shown the direction of his sympathies. The courtesy, the restraint, the gentility and studied good manners of Boston would not allow members of the intellectual community there to show their feelings too obviously; but Bryce was not so foolish as to assume that such feelings did not exist.

At Boston one of their first calls was on Longfellow. The elderly poet was at his summer house at Nahant, north of Boston, and after breakfast on the first day of September the two visitors took a boat from the India Wharf. The *Ulysses* brought them to Nahant at the tip of the promontory by eleven, and they followed the directions sketched for them to go straight to Longfellow's house near the shore. 'Him indeed we found sitting underneath his verandah', Bryce noted, 'reclining in an easy chair, and recognised from far by his goodly face and snow white beard. . . . He greets us cordially, seats us in the verandah by him, and lights the accepted cigar. *Incidet sermo varius.*'[17]

Bryce found the poet 'simple and unaffected, not talking of him-self nor in any way hinting that he is a poet and literary man, but speaking on poetry, when we ask his opinion on Clough, Walt Whitman, etc. with sense, clearness and taste. Clough he seems to like without greatly admiring. . . . Whitman he thinks has true poetical power, obscured by a total want of education and of delicacy of feeling – a complete working man poet . . . Whitman's war poems specially commended. Swinburne has genuine poetry in him – *Atalanta* beautiful throughout . . . Mat.[thew] Arnold's prose more read in U.S. than his poetry. . . .'

Although Bryce had genuine literary interests, he was anxious to talk of other matters. They turned to the subject of university education in America. Longfellow told them that the classics were still in the ascendant in the leading colleges of the east, as at Oxford, but that science 'and the practical arts' were now pressing their claims. In California, they learned, 'literature seems to be taking independent root – tho' of course the people are all immigrants from the Eastern States. A magazine of some considerable merit is now published there, which one ought to see. . . .' The elderly poet told them in some detail of the teaching arrangements and organisation at Harvard. They learned that reform was very much in the air at the university since President Eliot had come to office last year. The full extent and the nature of these reforms became clearer when Bryce and Dicey returned to Boston and Harvard several weeks later, but Longfellow's description helped to clarify the questions Bryce and Dicey asked later at Harvard.

Towards noon Longfellow's brother-in-law joined them on the verandah. Tom Appleton was part artist, part essayist, part poet and a noted Boston wit. Holmes once remarked of him: 'He has spilled more good things on the wasteful air in conversation than would carry a "diner-out" through half a dozen London seasons.'[18] Tom Appleton's wealth, like that of Henry Adams, allowed him to dabble intellectually in this and that. Unlike Henry Adams, he seems to have avoided pessimism.

After lunch Tom Appleton invited the visitors to sail in his luxurious yacht. Bryce greatly enjoyed the fine clear air of the September day as they scudded along close to the shore with a stiff breeze. He was reminded of north-west Scotland and indeed, comparing the two, Bryce felt that the sea, the air, and the beauty of New England exceeded that of the Scottish shores of his youth.

Dicey and Bryce ended their visit to Nahant after tea. They took the evening train from nearby Lynn and arrived at Boston within the hour. After dinner they ended the evening with a stroll on Boston Common, discussing their impressions of the day, comparing notes, and observing the people, the architecture and the streets in the gathering dusk of a warm September evening.[19]

At breakfast next morning they received a call from Oliver Wendell Holmes Junior, a more youthful member of the transatlantic coterie and another of Leslie Stephen's many friends. Holmes had pleasant memories of a visit to London and Oxford in 1866 when he had breakfasted with Jowett and Goldwin Smith in Oxford, with Gladstone in London, and dined with John Stuart Mill.[20] Holmes was now teaching law at Harvard and called to ask Dicey and Bryce to dinner for that evening. Bryce accepted, though Dicey could join them only after dinner, as he had already arranged to make a call on family friends outside Boston.

Accompanying Holmes on the morning call was Arthur G.

Sedgwick, another graduate of the Harvard Law School, and at that time in practice with one of Boston's leading law firms, Chandler, Shattuck and Thayer. Sedgwick was a co-editor of the *Harvard Law Review* with Oliver Wendell Holmes, and both were anxious to have an informed correspondent from the London Bar to keep the *Review* abreast of developments in English Common Law and Chancery. Bryce became their London correspondent in 1871.[21]

When the two visitors left, Bryce made his first call of the day on James Russell Lowell in Cambridge. Lowell, just entering his fifties and busily occupied with editing the *North American Review*, gave a cordial welcome to the younger scholar, and spoke frankly on topics ranging once more from poetry to Anglo-American politics. English support of the Southern secession during the Civil War still affected many Northerners, Lowell assured the visitor. Lowell himself was not without some feeling in the matter. 'He still feels bitterly about England's conduct — & thinks the feeling in the States is generally bitter — no wonder — tho' he expects it to die out in the next generation. He remarks on the desire shown by those who had fought the war to drop everything the moment the war was over, which had struck us already in the reticence of Higginson and Holmes.'[22]

Lowell was a liberal with a very independent mind. Bryce had read and admired *The Bigelow Papers*, where Lowell criticised the American war with Mexico with acid satire and in the Yankee vernacular. He told Bryce that he had a poor opinion of J. S. Mill. 'Lowell thinks England must be in a bad way when J. S. Mill is looked on as a great leader of thought. . . .' This must have come as something of a shock to a young liberal out of Oxford, but Lowell's strong opinions did not end there. 'Does not seem to like Mat. Arnold much. Browning probably our greatest poetical genius if he could be intelligible. He and his wife mutually injured each other's poetry — she tried to get up to his thoughts . . . he became more obscure.' Like Longfellow, like Charles Eliot Norton, Lowell admired English letters; but this did not preclude measured criticism. American letters had long since come of age.

Lowell invited Bryce to lunch with his wife and daughter and their talk continued. The tastefulness and beauty of Lowell's historic, book-filled house set back from Brattle Street profoundly impressed Bryce, and once more he had an opportunity to witness the charm and easy grace of New Englanders in their homes; once more the stiffness and artificiality of Victorian manners in London houses came to his mind. The comparison was unflattering to England.

Returning to Boston, Bryce strolled near the waterfront until it was time to join Holmes Junior at dinner. Holmes had also invited Horace Gray, a justice of the Massachusetts Supreme Court and a future United States Supreme Court judge. They discussed law and legal matters for most of the evening. As the newly appointed professor of law at Oxford, Bryce was anxious to learn more about the law schools in the United States. He learned of the teaching and organisation at Harvard Law School, where Langdell was introducing the 'case method' of legal study to replace the old jurisprudential approach. Bryce questioned, listened, and undoubtedly learned, even if he did not altogether agree with Langdell's method.

Dicey joined them soon after dinner and their talk continued, 'almost wholly on things legal'. Bryce learned a good deal about the state of the Bar in Massachusetts, of the American legal profession and its methods of recruitment, of litigation and the reputations of the judges. It was a long evening of good talk for each of them. In later life Bryce often remembered his dinner with two future justices of the Supreme Court of the United States, for from that evening developed another of his lifelong friendships. The mutual respect between Holmes and Bryce, and their continuous, often intimate correspondence lasted for half a century. No one was more pleased than Bryce when Holmes rose to eminence and became one of the greatest jurists of modern times. No one was more pleased than Holmes when the author of *The American Commonwealth* was fêted by Americans. But on a convivial evening in 1870, Bryce at the age of thirty-two and Holmes barely thirty could hardly foresee such developments. Returning to the hotel, Bryce entered his notes in his journal and slept soundly.

Next day, a Saturday, Bryce left Boston by train at seven-thirty in the morning to visit the White Mountains in New Hampshire. Dicey wished to make more visits, and arranged to join Bryce in

New Hampshire after the week-end, by which time Bryce the energetic hill climber would have worked off enough energy to pause again for further talk with his more sedentary friend.

As the train followed the coast to Portland in Maine, Bryce contrasted the rather bare accommodation of American railroad cars with the cushioned interiors of carriages in England. 'The American cars are pleasanter for short than for long journeys, for one can't lie down at full length, nor ensconce oneself among books and rugs.'[23] However, the American cars had some advantages for Bryce, who liked to get along to the smoking car and combine two of his favourite pleasures – a fragrant pipe and vistas of mountains and valleys: 'The passage thro' the train is a great convenience, especially as one thus gets easily to the smoking car, & from the end platform the country can be well seen . . . one is even allowed to stand on the platform at the end of the car.' Overall, Bryce concluded, 'what with the baggage check system, the power of passing along the cars, the conveniences on board of them, and the better ventilation, the American system is on the whole distinctly better than the European'. This was just as well, for Bryce was due to spend many days and nights 'in the cars' during the next two months.

The train halted for half an hour at Portland, where he lunched with other travellers on their way to the mountain resorts. The journey continued inland along the valleys and lakes of Maine to arrive at Gorham at the northern edge of the White Mountains, and Bryce was reminded continually of the lochs and glens of Scotland. The final destination was Glen House, an inn just below Mount Washington, the six-thousand-foot peak dominating the White Mountains. The final eight miles up the valley was travelled by stage coach. Sitting next to Bryce in the coach was a man whose voice reminded him of Gladstone's and whose face suggested scholarly leanings. Travelling with the elderly man was his son, the two of them clearly off to enjoy the fine air and refreshment of a week-end in the mountains. At Glen House, Bryce learned that they were Ralph Waldo Emerson and his son Edward Emerson. Bryce introduced himself and talked at length with the Emersons during the next two days. By then he had a rich store of impressions of New England scholarship and of the sensibilities of this corner of the new world.

Before breakfast the next morning, Bryce rambled down the stream through a thick wood, narrowly escaped a hornets' nest, and managed to get 'a dip in a sort of shallow pool'. A mountain stream close to the snow line early on a September morning is not to every traveller's taste, but Bryce found it sharpened his appetite and put him in fine fettle for the day's climbing.

After breakfast he was joined by Emerson Junior for a visit to the mountain cottage of William James Stillman, the Boston landscape artist, friend of Ruskin and Rossetti. Bryce had met Stillman at Glen House on the previous evening and when the two visitors arrived the artist made a simple lunch for them, talking meanwhile of his wide travels in Europe. Later they climbed to Glen Ellis Falls, an impressive cascade falling a hundred feet over coloured rocks bordered with rich foliage. By now Bryce was discovering what European visitors are so often slow to discover: that beyond the cities, unspoilt America is an astonishingly beautiful country.

Bryce bathed in a pool just below the falls, and returned with Emerson to Glen House for tea. The evening provided a good opportunity to hear Emerson Senior talk of literature and also of the effects of the Civil War on Anglo-American relations. 'He talks like one accustomed to write, in sentences,' Bryce wrote in his journal, 'and with some precision and finish of language: is quiet and sustained in manner; smiles rather than laughs – is apt to follow out a thread once given into details and illustrations . . . all is judicious, clear, interesting: not noticeably like his written style – less epigrammatic and strained – also, I think, less suggestive. He thinks the effects of the war in calling out heroism and high moral qualities cannot have been bad . . . he does not say politics are any poorer.'[24] Emerson's long friendship with Carlyle was perhaps showing some fugitive influence.

Emerson also talked a good deal about Senator Charles Sumner, who was currently pressing American claims in the *Alabama* case. He had some good things to say on Sumner's behalf, but added: 'When the presidential fever has once caught a man it never leaves him.' The remark intrigued Bryce. He committed it to his journal that evening.

Bryce talked with other New Englanders at Glen House, among them John Woods Brooks of Boston, President of several railroad companies. The Brooks family had recently returned from a tour of Europe, and Brooks remarked to Bryce that he had found the English rather stiff – so much so that the railroad owner took to travelling second class in England and found the passengers much more sociable. Brooks also had scathing things to say of foolish investors in England who readily parted with their money to American railroad speculators. This was the time of great fortunes but also of many bankruptcies. Brooks cited several recent cases to Bryce, and went on to tell him of dubious dealings of the Erie Ring and the stock manipulations of Jay Gould and Jim Fisk.[25]

On Monday some of the guests prepared to return to Boston. A popular custom was to make the return journey by the Connecticut valley inland after first going over Mount Washington. When the coach arrived to take the departing guests up the steep winding track leading to the summit of the mountain, Bryce declined the ride and set out at eight o'clock to walk. Young Edward Emerson offered to accompany Bryce, and made the mistake of 'priding himself a little on his walking powers', as Bryce later confided to his journal. As they walked up the track towards the six-thousand-foot summit a storm descended. Wind, rain and then sleet swept the mountainside. Emerson showed signs of fatigue, and Bryce was forced to halt several times for the younger man. Eventually, Emerson dropped out to await the coach, and Bryce plodded on to the stone hut at the summit.

The coach finally delivered the travellers, some of them soaked through, and after a vain attempt to dry out near the stove in the hut, Bryce fortified himself with the flask of whiskey he carried for such contingencies. Emerson Senior showed signs of suffering from the driving rain and low temperature, and Bryce offered his whiskey flask to the ageing Transcendentalist. There was a show of resistance, then Emerson 'at my insistence takes some whiskey, but is very apprehensive lest he should take too much & it should go to his head. . . .' Young Emerson had meanwhile fallen asleep and was helped to a bunk 'to rest and get to rights'. A roaring fire and an ample lunch improved matters but the rain did not lift.

Bryce talked with Emerson Senior once more and their conversation continued as the party descended in the cog railroad running down the mountainside to the next valley. Emerson's mind

53

ranged freely. He talked of Walt Whitman rather scathingly, seeing him as a conceited, affected creature, Bryce noted: 'Not quite so much a child of nature as might be thought. Edited a paper once, out Ohio or Illinois way for a while.' Bryce decided he must look again at Whitman's verse. Emerson spoke of Wordsworth, whom he had met at Rydal Mount just before the poet's death; of his longtime friend and correspondent Carlyle and also of Coleridge and Matthew Arnold. Bryce realised even more vividly the degree of interpenetration between English and American letters. He did not share Emerson's enthusiasm for Carlyle's heroes, but Emerson's profound understanding of Wordsworth and the breadth of his knowledge provided fascinating shifts of vision for his listener. The perspective of another culture gave Bryce new glimpses of his countrymen and the experience filtered in. Bryce was already a friend of America: now he could become a wiser critic of England and her ways.

When the slow descent to the valley was completed some of the party left by coach for the railroad station in the nearby Connecticut River valley. Bryce had planned to meet Dicey at a neighbouring inn next day and remained behind to climb mountains. Emerson Senior departed, but his son seems to have been fascinated by the wiry professor from Oxford and attached himself once more. Bryce had his bathe in 'a deep green pool' near the inn, then walked with young Emerson until suppertime. Darkness closed about the inn in the silent hills, and Bryce sat by the big open hearth with other guests to listen to 'a Transcendentalist lady . . . who not only talks, but thinks in metaphors'.[26] Perhaps the arcadian setting of the inn, deep in the hills of New Hampshire under a September moon, was suitably inspiring for one of Emerson's disciples. As Bryce's friends so often recalled, he was a very good listener when he was not asking questions. On this occasion, it seemed best to listen.

Bryce spent the next day on a strenuous climb up Mount Lafayette, a five-thousand-foot peak near Mount Washington. Edward Emerson decided not to accompany him this time. This was just as well, for in his zeal to see the sun descending in the west from the vantage of the mountain top, Bryce misjudged his time for the descent. Happily the moon's brilliance lighted his path across the lower ridges of the mountain, but once in the woods above the inn the darkness was impenetrable. Bryce stumbled on and gained the road shortly before supper. He took a quick moonlit bathe in the cold waters of Profile Lake and hurried to the inn to find Dicey arrived from Boston.

Dicey had made visits in Boston and Harvard and there was much to discuss. After supper they strolled down the road in brilliant moonlight, sat on a rock, and talked over their impressions of the last few days.[27] They realised, of course, that New England in general, and Boston in particular, were by no means representative of American life. Now they planned to follow different routes in the mid-west and north-west; Bryce to satisfy his keen desire to see the conditions near the frontier in the north-west, Dicey to follow fairly closely the route taken by his brother and by Leslie Stephen in their travels in the mid-west. Bryce and Dicey would meet again in Chicago to discuss their impressions and compare notes.

Next day, 7 September, they rested, though Bryce punctuated his rest with a swim in Echo Lake and a long talk with another guest at the inn. This man, a Mr Duncan, was also well informed on railroad politics, especially the activities of the Erie Ring and its chief figures, Jim Fisk and Jay Gould. The details of the Ring, its techniques for depressing and artificially stimulating stock according to the required strategy were recounted to Bryce in 'graphic detail' – giving him more insights into the connections between railroads, politics and the corruption of American legislatures.

Bryce and Dicey left at seven next morning in the company of other guests and took their seats on the top of the coach. Three young ladies were already settled there. They were sisters, it appeared, and the daughters of a New York Democrat named Waterbury. 'These young ladies chat very freely & amusingly about themselves, their parents, and things in general. . . . All are fiery Democrats, compassionate for "the poor South" and bitter against Grant & the New Englanders. Much jealousy against Boston. . . .' These remarks, of small consequence in themselves, told Bryce something of the tensions within American society at the time; of the light in which Bostonians were regarded by New Yorkers, especially New York Democrats. He took up the subject he had discussed with his cousins at Brooklyn on the day he arrived in America. The Misses Waterbury 'agreed with most of the points in which American girls' manners are freer than ours, but rather doubt if not the possibility, yet the frequency of correspondence [with young men] where there is no idea of marriage'.[28]

The coach rolled on under a bright clear sky, the young women occasionally laughing at the earnest questions of the bearded professor. At Wells in the broad valley of the Connecticut River the passengers changed to the train, and Bryce used the long journey down to Springfield to talk once again at greater length with Mr Duncan on railroads and politics. At Springfield, Bryce and Dicey changed trains to set out on their respective trips to the west. They travelled to Albany together in the darkness and in crowded cars — neither of which conditions prevented Bryce from interrogating a stranger 'who objects to free schools because he pays for education of people who could well pay themselves, and the poorest class remains untaught. It is admitted however that this class is very small, except in the large cities.' The remarks carried a whiff of the independent spirit of the pioneers. Bryce was impatient to get to the frontier for more of it.

5

North-West Frontier

Bryce parted from Dicey at Albany, and waited overnight for his next train. He would go west via Toronto in order to visit an old acquaintance of his father. The brief overnight stay at Albany was memorable chiefly for 'a wretched inn', but there was the real pleasure of a batch of mail from home, together with a supply of newspapers to enable Bryce to catch up on European events. Bryce read of the downfall of Louis Napoleon in the Franco-Prussian war. He retained his deep distrust of Louis Napoleon, whilst his old affection for the Germany he had known in 1862 still persisted. But his views on the new Germany were to undergo a radical transformation in the next twenty years.[1]

The long, hot journey to Toronto was tiring. Bryce made the promised visit and reported to his father that his old friend was thriving in the Canadian city. The jolting cars and the tedium of travel interrupted Bryce's diary, but his journey can be traced through his letters to his parents and his sisters. A gap of several days in the record of the journey picks up on 14 September with Bryce approaching Milwaukee on a steamer across Lake Michigan. Looking up at the clear night sky, Bryce wrote to his father: 'The rising of the Great Bear towards the zenith apprises me of my progress n.w. wards, and reminds me that I am at least nearer to you in latitude, if further in everything else.'[2] Earlier, Bryce had formed some hope of getting as far as California on his trip, but he now decided against the attempt owing to considerations of time, 'for what would be gained by going there without staying long enough to see California properly?'[3]

The journey across Lake Michigan was occupied with correcting proofs for a new edition of *The Holy Roman Empire*. Arriving at Milwaukee, Bryce returned the proofs to London, then took a hurried look at the city before going on to Minneapolis and St Paul.

He was anxious to get closer to the north-west frontier, but he had promised to meet Dicey at Chicago in a week's time. Already he was beginning to realise the staggering distances involved. The railroad connecting Minneapolis and St Paul to Milwaukee and Chicago had been completed only recently. Bryce thus saw several Minnesota towns at an early stage of their rapid growth. He travelled part of the way by rail, first going west to La Crosse on the Mississippi, then aboard one of the big paddle steamers going upstream to Minneapolis and St Paul.

La Crosse, today a city of 50,000 inhabitants, was barely a township at this stage. Bryce had the impression of 'a half built place, with one main street containing some good houses, stores, and three or four suggestions for streets running off it; then beyond these projected streets each with a dwelling house or two scattered along it – the whole extremely rough and unattractive.'⁴ Early photographs of these young townships of the 1870s show their unfinished streets following the usual grid pattern, with houses scattered loosely around dispersed plots of land, without much pretence to order; the whole settlement conveying a sense of loneliness and even desolation. On this particular morning a fog enveloped the small town. Bryce was not sorry to come aboard the steamer to seek out more subjects for his interrogation of the new world.

He found them soon enough. He was already developing an ability which approached a special genius for detecting the interesting traveller with a tale to tell, or with a special knowledge of the economy or the society of the region. 'On board I had a chat with the Editor of the *Soldier's Record*, published weekly at Madison, Wisconsin, a journal devoted to the interests of the soldiers, urging their claims to office, to pensions and to considerations in every way. Hitherto it has been republican [sic], but henceforth is to be run on neutral principles so as to command wider support. The editor and proprietor expects [it] to be largely bought by the soldiers, avowing coolly enough that he doesn't see any particular principle in the line he is taking, but that he too must make money like other people, and will do it by advocating the claims of those who fought in the late war, thinking there is discontent among them at not having been made enough of.'⁵ This early encounter with a self-appointed lobbyist, capitalising on his own literacy, quickly helped Bryce to understand why the lobbyist often prefers not to become closely identified with any particular party. A lobbyist was a sort of broker, avoiding party affiliations to increase his gains.

Sitting next to the editor of the *Soldier's Record* was a farmer from West Salem in Wisconsin, and Bryce drew him into the conversation. 'An intelligent fellow, who doubts the possibility of running the paper without a political line, but expresses some contempt for both parties or as he prefers to express it, for the wire pullers. Both are equally corrupt, and it is necessary to keep up one to check the corruption of the other and have a change when either party has got demoralised by office.' Bryce detected the note of cynicism, of course, but he was intrigued by this Montesquian view of the dangers of office, especially from a farmer well removed from the colleges and libraries of the eastern cities.

These conversations, stored in Bryce's memory and then entered in his journal, did not prevent him from observing the scenery which now lay on either side as they came to Winona on the broad Mississippi. The fog had dispersed to reveal a low wooded shore on one side, with oak, poplar, birch and maple predominating. Bryce's keen eyes picked out the species. Beyond the other shore, steep bluffs rose, 'with yellowish white rock, apparently limestone, lying in horizontal strata, and sometimes showing fine cliff faces and peaked points, separated by wooded glens, running up a mile or two into the plateau behind'.[6]

A little later his attention was caught by the sight of a huge raft coming downstream 'with two or three huts on it, and about a dozen men directing its course by long steering oars. The logs, all of pine, are firmly lashed together by ropes.' Such a sight, familiar enough to Mississippi travellers, was full of interest and significance to Bryce. It captured a different sense of scale and proportion, such as Europe rarely if ever conveyed. He experienced, as he had already begun to experience across the plains of the mid-west, a new perspective on the relation between man and his environment. Man appeared more puny, yet at the same time more adaptive, more competent, more ingenious in this setting. Men were visibly conquering the wilderness: here was a genial, hopeful reminder from the new world to the old.

At Winona in Minnesota Bryce rejoined the train for the last stage of his journey north to Minneapolis and St Paul, and as the train awaited the ferry, there was barely time for a quick, impressionistic glance at the little town, 'picturesque . . . above the beautiful Sugar Loaf, a limestone cone, rock faced and bare, with a patch of grass on its top'.

In the cars, Bryce buttonholed 'a Scotch stone mason, who left Glasgow five years ago, worked in W. Pennsylvania, and has come lately here to Minneapolis where he complains work is not very plentiful just now. He likes the country and even the people, though at first their ways, their having meals at fixed hours and their coolness and want of civility annoyed him. Prefers born Americans ("Yankees") to any other class – even Scotch or English, as well as Germans or Irish: they are much more off-hand in their dealings. They hire you if they like your looks and then leave you to yourself, while an Englishman grumbles and bothers: they never ask for certificates or recommendations from former employers, as is usual in Scotland, and deal fairly by you, though they will make a sharp bargain if they can. Wages here are from 3 to 5 dollars a day – everyone can get on if he will but work, knows a trade or can do field work. 'Tis the best country for such, and he has never regretted Scotland.'[7]

Bryce had 'some chat also with an Irish Dr Hall and his wife', who were going to St Paul and had arranged to stay at the same hotel as Bryce. The boat arrived at sundown, too late for Bryce to inspect the town, but there was the pleasure of more talk after supper with his travelling companions on the train and other residents who caught the piercing yet friendly eye of the professor from England.

Bryce bathed in the Mississippi at seven next morning – 'stream dark brown, not cold', he noted – then hurried breakfast in order to catch a local train to St Anthony, to see the famous Falls – a sight which his friends in Boston had mentioned and which often figured in Europeans' tales of travel.[8] The train was crowded, but there were the usual compensations en route: 'Car full of emigrants going up country – mostly Scandinavian – as are two thirds of the people one meets all round.'

At St Anthony the Falls proved something of a disappointment.

Instead of a cascade Bryce saw something resembling a mill-race, with sawmills using water power above and below the 'falls'. St Anthony was already a busy little town, still detached from the twin cities growing nearby, but soon to be enveloped by them. Bryce learned from a man in a nearby store that seventeen years before, when he arrived in St Anthony, there was hardly a house to be seen. 'He dilates on the vast Scandinavian emigration [sic]: they are a thrifty, active people, but barbarous in some of their ways, eat meat half cooked, & sleep always in skins, which give them an unpleasant flavour that has communicated itself even to the currency – he makes me smell a bundle of greenbacks which are certainly very strong.'

Bryce did not seem to mind the earthiness of the immigrants as much as the storekeeper, and gladly accepted a ride from 'a friendly Swede' to a fairground about one and a half miles outside the small township. Agricultural produce and implements dominated the fair, but other articles aroused Bryce's interest – including harmoniums and sewing machines. Bryce observed each detail to build up a picture of the local society.

When nothing further remained to be seen or enquired into, he walked about three miles to the Falls of Minnehaha, at that time standing close to unreclaimed prairie beyond the Minneapolis city limits. These falls impressed him much more than those at St Anthony. Bryce walked beyond to the prairie for a small taste of the wilderness. This was what he had come to see. For a few moments he savoured the romance of the American epic, then returned to St Paul (now about six miles distant) in the company of a German whom he met on the way. Bryce quickly elicited the significant details as they walked together, and entered them meticulously in his journal that evening. 'He had been a shepherd not far from Bonn, to the W.N.W. of Coblenz, had had a hard life of it there, brought out his father (who had just then lost sheep by disease) and his wife with him, had settled first at Wisconsin, and was now some fifty miles north of St Paul on a farm of which he had got 50 acres already reclaimed. He insisted much on the advantages of America to a man if he would but work; and on the superiority of woodland to prairie land for an emigrant starting without capital – you get on much more by degrees, don't incur debt for wood for house and implements, on the contrary can make a little off your wood as you cut it, and are less exposed to risk from drought.'⁹

Bryce also discovered more about tensions among the immigrants. 'Doesn't like the Irish – they are unfaithful to promises – nor Scandinavians much, on account of personal habits and turn for small thefts(?)'. Bryce wondered if this was fact or prejudice, but as usual he placed the remarks against others he had heard on the steamer, in the hotel, and at the St Anthony store. In this way, and assisted by his lawyer's ability to weigh the evidence, Bryce carefully built up a picture of American society near the limits of reclaimed land.

This process of weighing the evidence was central to Bryce's method of gathering data from various sources, comparing different accounts, and then moving cautiously to conclusions about the society and its institutional life. He could also, of course, note the more subtle implications of what was said by different individuals. The fact that the German farmer tended to divide other immigrant groups into those who kept their promises or their word, and those who did not, was another way of stressing the vital importance of unwritten, verbal contracts in frontier life, where legal documents and the agencies of the law were not much in evidence. These observations were of the utmost interest to Bryce as a student of law and government. To some degree they threw fresh light on the basis of law in newly founded societies and thus on the foundations of ancient law. The significance was both scholarly and contemporary. Bryce was observing frontier society at the moment when it was developing its institutional framework. At the same time, on a less cerebral level, Bryce exulted in the beauty and the freedom of the barely tamed landscapes upstream. London was a universe away. So indeed was New York.

It was now his last evening at St Paul. After an early supper Bryce strolled around the town and went aboard the steamer *Redwing*. He departed reluctantly, not only because 'one could have pleasantly spent a much longer time in Minnesota', but because he wanted so much to go on to the far north-west beyond the Wyoming Territory, where frontiersmen were clearing the virgin forests to make new settlements. But time would not permit this and he had to go south once more. The next main stop would be Chicago, where he had promised to meet Dicey.

Bryce stayed aboard the steamer *Redwing* for two hundred and fifty miles, until it reached the railroad connection thrusting west from Chicago to meet the Mississippi River close to Dubuque, where the borders of Wisconsin and Illinois meet on the east side of the great river. The journey took almost twenty-four hours, and apart from the pleasures of the view all around, Bryce hardly enjoyed it, for the passengers proved uncommunicative. So far as he could judge, several were returning from fishing holidays in Minnesota, others were going south on business trips to St Louis. Bryce turned for solace to letter writing and *Clarissa Harlowe*, interspersing these pastimes with a pipe and a seat on the top deck. There he could view the valley and the prairies once more as the boat continued downstream to La Crosse in Wisconsin.

The following morning, Sunday 18 September, Bryce was glad to find at least one congenial person on board. This was a Civil War veteran who had fought in the Federal army and was willing to talk with the inquisitive stranger. Their talk was so earnest, in fact, that at one point they were almost left behind. When they arrived at Prairie du Chien, where the Wisconsin River meets the Mississippi, Bryce joined the veteran for a stroll on the shore while the steamer took on more passengers and unloaded some cargo. 'Airily strolling' some three hundred yards from the wharf, they were startled to notice the *Redwing* moving out into the broad reaches of the river to continue downstream. The adventure which followed is best described in Bryce's own words:

We rush to the wharf but in vain – we induce a young fellow to get a skiff – a sufficiently unsteady one, with a big rent in it down almost to [the] water's edge, and row after the steamer which, by the time we are well off in our frail craft . . . is rounding the point of a low island 2 miles off, to run into North McGregor on the Iowa shore. . . . With one pair of oars, we push on; at last [the lad] gives me one: repeated prayers (made whenever the little vessel sways from side to side) to be set ashore are disregarded – he can't swim he says, and though courageous in every other regard dislikes and has always disliked the water – having thrice suffered shipwreck and narrowly escaped.

[Bryce absorbed the relevant details even when close to catastrophe.] The *Redwing* waiting some time at McGregor, we cut as towards her downward course when she leaves it, shout and wave handkerchiefs; the captain, a civil fellow throughout, stops for us and takes us up amid the amusement of the boat.[10]

At five o'clock they arrived at the Illinois border and Bryce left the steamer to join the overnight train to Chicago by way of Freeport and the prairies of northern Illinois. There was little sleep to be had, owing to mosquitoes and the whimpering of a baby in the sleeping car. The train arrived at Chicago at three next morning, and Bryce stayed aboard with most of the passengers until six-thirty, when he made his way to the hotel where he had arranged to meet Dicey. Despite the sleepless night, Bryce had sufficient energy to embark immediately on a busy round of visits to civic officials, scholars, churchmen, and to a young lawyer.[11]

Dicey had partly mapped out some calls they might make and Bryce made further suggestions. Their new friends at Boston and Harvard had added letters of introduction to those they carried from friends in England. In this rapidly expanding city, whose population had increased from 112,000 to almost 300,000 in the past decade, Bryce was eager to see as much as possible of the institutions making up its corporate life. High on his list was the school system, for Chicago was already earning itself a wide reputation for its high schools. Young women teachers, the co-education of boys and girls, and a broadly based curriculum contrasted with the institutional arrangements of much of the English school system at that time.[12]

At breakfast time they received a visit from Robert Collyer, the pastor of a Unitarian church on Chicago's North Side. Collyer was born in Yorkshire in 1823 and started life as a blacksmith's apprentice. He had come to America in 1850 and continued as a blacksmith at Philadelphia before entering the ministry as a Methodist lay preacher. An energetic, self-educated man, his fame as a preacher was the chief reason for an invitation to be pastor of the first Unitarian Church in Chicago in 1859. At the same time he was well equipped to understand the sorts of questions which interested visiting Englishmen.[13]

Collyer took them first to see the vast grain elevator at the

Illinois Central Station. Bryce was once more impressed by the implications of sheer size: 'A piece of mechanism which gives one a lively idea of the vast scale of the grain trade.' Collyer took them on to a book store (in Bryce's words 'finer by far than any in Glasgow or Manchester'), and then in quick succession to the corn exchange, where they saw buyers bidding and out-bidding each other, and finally to a local art exhibition. Bryce noted the vigorous yellows and browns of American landscape painters and contrasted them in his mind's eye with the blues and greens of English painters. The artists' palettes dramatically evoked the bluffs, gorges and valleys he had seen on either side of the brown Mississippi waters during the previous week.[14]

Collyer left them to attend to his flock and they arranged to meet him again the following day. Their next call was on Josiah Pickard, the Chicago Superintendent of Schools, who was proud of the Chicago system and talked with the visitors at length. Bryce was intensely interested in every detail. His work on the Taunton Commission on the Schools in England had given him a lifelong interest in all aspects of the educational process, at all levels. At the same time he was receptive to new ideas and new or experimental forms of education, including the American system of co-education.

He learned that of the 550 teachers in Chicago all but 30 were women, and that the system of co-education for boys and girls worked excellently in the schools and also in the colleges. Pickard told them of similar successes in Wisconsin and in California. They questioned him about the possible moral effects of mixing boys and girls in classes and schools, and were assured that no scandals occurred and work suffered in no way. The superintendent arranged for them to visit a high school and an elementary school in his company next morning. Bryce and Dicey went away profoundly impressed with all they had heard. Next day they saw that Pickard's pride was justified.[15]

In the afternoon Dicey and Bryce called on a young Chicago lawyer named William Furness to learn about legal affairs in Chicago and Illinois. They were interested to hear of the standing of the State Bar in the profession, the reputation of the judges, arrangements between attorneys and clients and how counsel fixed their charges, and went on to a general discussion of law reform in

Illinois. Their informant, a progressive young lawyer from the east, educated at Harvard College and Harvard Law School, gave them his views. Bryce took notes which are reflected in an article on the American legal profession that he wrote soon after his return to England.[16]

In the late afternoon the visitors hurried on to the offices of the *Chicago Tribune*. The editor, Horace White, was out when they arrived, so they talked instead with one of the sub-editors. They discussed the influence exerted by the larger newspapers in growing cities like Chicago, the short supply of writers to the journalist's trade, and the general lack of contributors from the professions, such as young barristers in London provided for London journals. Literary work, Bryce learned, was poorly paid. '$10 is the utmost ever given for an article – it is only by becoming a proprietor that any large income is made by a writer.'[17]

The visitors knew that the *Chicago Tribune* had already earned a name for itself under the vigorous editorship of Horace White. Born in the east in 1834, White had been editor and proprietor since 1867. In 1858, in a famous series of articles, he had reported the Lincoln–Douglas debates for the *Tribune*. Indeed, the *Tribune* had played an important part in the anti-slavery campaigns of Abraham Lincoln and had been instrumental in the founding of the Republican party in the mid-west after 1854. Its journalism was aggressive and fearless. It did not mind offending its readers. People sometimes said of the *Tribune*: 'Its readers swear at the paper even while they swear by it.' It was an early example of the mass circulation newspaper of the future.

Bryce was an avid collector of local and regional newspapers. As he travelled he would mail small bundles of them to his chambers at Lincoln's Inn after he had scanned them as much as time permitted. His scrutinies extended to detailed examinations of the advertisement columns to note what was bought and sold; what was the state of the employment market in terms both of supply and demand; the prices paid for labour; and the style and temper of commercial advertising in the journal.

Bryce was disappointed not to meet Horace White on this occasion, but their meeting was merely postponed: when White returned to eastern America in 1881 to join the New York

66

Evening Post, Bryce's further visits to America provided plenty of opportunities for friendly discussions.

The day was drawing out. Bryce and Dicey made one more visit to complete their rounds. This was to the Presbyterian Theological Seminary – later the McCormick Theological Seminary — to talk with Professor Charles Elliott on general matters relating to education and the Church in mid-western America.

Born in Scotland in 1815, Charles Elliott had emigrated in his early twenties and then rose rapidly in the American academic profession. From Lafayette College in Pennsylvania he moved to become Principal of a small academy at Xenia in Ohio, then professor of *belles-lettres* at the University of Pittsburgh in the 1840s. Now he was professor of biblical literature and exegesis at the Seminary of the Northwest in Chicago. He could thus draw on a wide experience of America in discussing with the two visitors aspects of religious instruction and education in the United States. His Scottish Presbyterian youth provided further perspectives for dealing fruitfully with Bryce's interrogations. Dicey, we must conclude, was content to be a listener on this occasion.[18]

At the end of the day they returned to their hotel well satisfied with their several discussions:

We stroll about the streets till late, discussing the day and comparing notes on American character. Chicago is the handsomest city we have seen in America – the streets are all wide, all straight, all lined with tall, handsome, even stately piles of building; the stores are large and well appointed, there is a great flow of people in all the main thoroughfares, and the suburbs stretch out their lines of villas for miles and miles. . . . The place, it is true, is in parts only half built; between the grand blocks there are often mean houses . . . sometimes open spaces; the river interrupts the traffic awkwardly and is not itself beautiful. But the scale and grandeur and newness of everything makes a strong impression. You feel that those who have built the city have felt it was becoming great, and have been inspired by this spirit to do their best.[19]

Next morning they were once more in the company of Josiah Pickard, looking closely into many aspects of teaching and organisation in the Chicago schools. They visited one of the largest, which combined a high school and an elementary school within its buildings. Bryce noted carefully the size of classes, hours of tuition, ages of the teachers, contents of lessons and the texts used for classics, history, chemistry and mathematics. Where he wanted more information, he asked Pickard or one of the many young men and women teaching at the school. Dicey, long familiar with his friend's questing spirit, patiently followed the energetic inquisition. For Bryce, it was a field day; the pedagogue and the social scientist in him were equally satisfied.

The two friends left Chicago towards midday to return once more to the east. The main line of the Lake Shore and Michigan Southern Railroad would take them to Toledo in Ohio and on to Buffalo in upstate New York, where they would change to the New York Central Line. After stopping off at Rochester to visit Bishop McQuaid and then to visit Goldwin Smith at Cornell, they planned to go on to Boston via the Boston and Albany Railroad.

The train was much roomier than the railroad cars Bryce had met in New England. They spread themselves in comfort and travelled on for six hours to Toledo, seeing no large towns on the way, but gaining once more a sense of the vastness of America as they moved across the plains of northern Indiana to Ohio. The six-hour journey in the cars was well spent, though Bryce's journal for the day is tantalisingly brief: 'Chat with A.V.D. all day long, partly on U.S.; mostly, however, on moral questions.'

At Toledo they had supper, took to their berths for 'an excellent night's rest' and awoke next morning to find the train approaching Rochester near the shores of Lake Ontario. A month had now passed since Bishop McQuaid had urged them to see the New York State Democratic party convention at Rochester if their itinerary allowed it. Their present visit was planned to coincide with this. They walked to Osborne House, the chief hotel of the thriving town, where Bryce had his first close look at the Democratic party of New York in the bustle of the delegates in the hotel lobby. The first impression was not favourable: 'sharp looking fellows, all of them, and some few looking like regular scoundrels. . . .' The Democrats milled around the smoking rooms and lounges of the hotel, clapping each other on the back, holding whispered consultations and here and there caballing in tight little groups.

There was no room available at Osborne House nor at the neighbouring hotels so, not without hope, Bryce and Dicey decided to pay their call on Bishop McQuaid as they had promised. They found him in a 'stately but plain' house in the suburbs 'just beside his cathedral church – a new and in the main tasteful church in 14th century style, pewed throughout. We are shown through it by the Bishop, who admits that the pews are let and only seat holders admitted to the high and 10.30 a.m. mass – the earlier ones, however, are free. The colouring is neat and quiet. All has been done by subscriptions in a short time. Finding there is no room at the hotel, the prelate asks us to share his roof whereto we willingly consent.' They moved in with alacrity and relief. Now they had an elegant base and a hospitable host for their first experience of the American democratic process.

The European student of politics who attends an American party convention – the most fascinating political institution ever invented to suit the ambitions or aspirations of men – usually finds that he must get his admission ticket by some subterfuge. The officials and marshals tell him — usually with complete truth – that every ticket has long been taken up by delegates' wives, children, friends, mistresses, or by the gentlemen of the press. The local press is often the only avenue of hope for the visitor from abroad. Bishop McQuaid piloted Bryce and Dicey to the editor of Rochester's Democratic newspaper, who promised to get tickets. At twelve-thirty they went to Corinthian Hall just in time to hear Samuel J. Tilden call the convention to order. Bryce was fascinated by all that followed. Later he made detailed notes in his journal.

Two factions were present at the convention. The dominant one, firmly controlling the proceedings, was drawn from the machine elements of New York City together with their friends and accomplices from the State legislature at Albany: Tammany Hall had temporarily migrated to Rochester. The minority faction represented a puny effort on the part of a reform group to challenge the Tammany forces. The Convention marked a vital point in the fortunes of Boss William Marcy Tweed, who was already under public suspicion for the graft and embezzlement that accompanied his control of City Hall in New York. Leader of Tammany Hall since 1863, Boss Tweed had used all the devices and stratagems of machine politics to control the offices at the city hall from the mayoralty down, in order to plunder the city treasury.

Subsequent investigations and exposures by the *New York Times* and then by an official investigating committee revealed the enormity of Tweed's dealings in graft and embezzlement. By gross corruption at the polls in New York City, Boss Tweed had succeeded in getting a Tammany puppet, John T. Hoffman, elected Governor of New York State in 1868. That accomplished, Tweed and his Tammany lieutenants set about delivering the city treasury into their own hands by a series of amendments to the city charter, giving them complete control of disbursements and auditing. With Hoffman in the governor's mansion at Albany and Democratic majorities in both houses of the legislature, nothing seemed to stand in their way. Except perhaps the veteran Samuel J. Tilden, chairman of the State Central Committee, who knew enough of the activities of the Tweed Ring to realise that spoils-mongering and plunder had gone too far. At Rochester in September 1870, Tilden was confronted by the Tweed forces. But Tilden was old and almost a lone voice in this particular year of disgrace for the New York Democratic party.[20]

Tilden's opening speech calling the convention to order was given quietly. Bryce took in the details as the old man stood at the podium, 'a veteran with thin prominent wizened features and eyes half sunk in his head'. The speech was short and perfunctory, as the chairman's was meant to be – a mere reminder of the Democratic party's tradition, an invocation of the names of Jefferson and Jackson and the need to bring the great party and thus the nation back to what it had been in those hallowed days of democracy. Tilden was followed by the temporary chairman of the convention, De Witt of Brooklyn, who roused the delegates with an impassioned 'keynote speech'. Keynote speeches usually lack historicity, but that would hardly have disturbed the delegates who thronged Corinthian Hall in September 1870. Then followed the customary roll call and seating of delegates from all over the state.[21]

In the afternoon the convention overwhelmingly endorsed the

party ticket for the offices of Governor, Lieutenant-Governor and Controller in the forthcoming elections. In other words, incumbents loyal to Tammany were left undisturbed. It was less a convention than a gathering of spoilsmen. The reform group from New York City, calling itself the 'New Democracy', was vanquished by the Tammany forces. The convention was, in fact, 'sewn up' and no one recognised it better than Samuel J. Tilden.[22] During the intervals Bryce talked with press men, learning more of the activities of the Tweed Ring than they could safely print in their columns. He also heard more about the Erie Railroad Ring and its doings at Albany and at Washington. Bryce now began to grasp the ramifications of machine politics from city ward through state legislatures to the federal government, wherever bribes could buy votes for land apportionments and franchises. Ulysses Grant was in the White House: the muddy waters had not yet lapped around the Executive Mansion, though Grant's second term was to provide plenty of scandals in the 1870s.

Boss Tweed was much in evidence. He made a short speech, promising his fellow Democrats safe majorities for the party in New York City. Bryce observed the Tammany boss at the podium, 'a fat, largish man, with an air of self satisfied good humour and a great deal of shrewd knavery in eye and mouth'. Tweed kept his word. In the subsequent election Governor Hoffman carried New York City by a majority of 52,000 votes.

Bryce was shocked by much that he had seen and heard at the convention, yet at the same time utterly fascinated. Whatever the morality of the participants and their dealings, this was the very stuff of politics; it was American democracy in action. Nothing he had seen so far intrigued him so much. The full notes in his journal elaborated his sense of shock, but also his fascination. 'The whole thing helps one to realise more vividly the working of their system. . . . Hardly anyone seems to think any principle is at stake in this contest; it is simply for place and power. . . .' Before he left Rochester Bryce's interest in American politics and institutions was implanted for life.

At Cornell University not far from Rochester, Goldwin Smith was eagerly awaiting the visit of his Oxford friends. Dicey and

Bryce took a boat from Cayuga, at the northern end of the long Cayuga Lake, to bring them to Ithaca near the southern end. The convention at Rochester provided plenty of talking points. As the boat came up to the landing stage their friend was waiting to greet them. Goldwin Smith wrung their hands and bore them off with delight to Cornell to meet his colleagues and the President, Andrew White. Smith was anxious to talk with them at great length of their travels, their reactions, of the friends they had met and friendships they had made, of the spectacle at Rochester, of American life and, in more nostalgic vein, of Oxford.

Between their talks Dicey and Bryce explored Cornell in detail, and Goldwin Smith introduced them to the President of the University, Andrew White, who had helped to plan the Charter of Cornell University and had gathered about him a lively faculty. He had served as a New York State Senator from 1864 to 1867 and his experiences as chairman of the New York State committee on education gave him much to say on both politics and education. White talked freely with Goldwin Smith's guests from England and in Bryce's case another important friendship was cemented before the visit ended.

Bryce was especially interested in the Cornell system of combined undergraduate courses in the humanities, the natural sciences and technical studies. As an enthusiastic botanist and amateur geologist he was strongly in favour of bringing to the attention of students of the humanities the principles and methods of natural science. The pastoral setting of Cornell above the great lake also appealed to Bryce. He departed ready to assure friends in Oxford that Goldwin Smith was flourishing at distant Ithaca, just as he carried a vivid set of impressions and ideas on new approaches to university teaching.

On the train to Boston the pleasantness of American life struck Bryce forcefully once again. During the next few weeks, as he remarked later in a letter to his sister, he began to wonder whether, given the choice, he would not prefer America to London or Oxford.[23] The freshness, enthusiasm, friendliness, warmth and charm of his new friends had deeply impressed him. Possibly Goldwin Smith had attempted a small recruiting drive. Of course Bryce had already accepted the Regius Chair of Civil Law at

Oxford, and he put the thought aside; but it was now virtually certain that this first trip to America would not be his last.

From Cornell University, barely three years old, Bryce and Dicey arrived back at Harvard, more than two centuries old. On this visit, they were invited to stay with Charles Eliot at the President's Lodgings. Their visit was timely. At Harvard they encountered a ferment of new ideas and new approaches to traditional studies.

Charles William Eliot was appointed to the Presidency of Harvard in 1869 at the remarkably youthful age of thirty-five. His two famous articles in the *Atlantic Monthly* earlier that same year on 'The New Education: Its Organisation' had proposed an elective system of courses not unlike the system already instituted at Cornell. This would replace Harvard's rigid, English-style syllabus with its set diet of classics and theology. Eliot also wished to reorganise graduate work in a thorough fashion, with the Ph.D. degree to be conferred after rigorous training of the young graduate by course work, examination and dissertation.[24]

The new President, by training a chemist and mathematician, expected to meet some resistance to his proposals for a mixed elective system for students, and even as his English visitors arrived he was in the throes of reform and reorganisation. Nevertheless, Eliot had energy to spare for entertaining his visitors as he told them of his hopes and plans. He was already confident of achieving many of his goals, which also included the sabbatical year for professors. This proposal met less opposition from the faculty than other proposed reforms. Eliot's talk at dinner and in the evenings, when his arduous day of meetings was over, was intensely interesting to Dicey and Bryce. They learned of a great university in ferment. By now Bryce was disposed to take a new, even a more critical look at Oxford on his return.

Apart from the formal organisation of the university, there was much of an intellectual nature to discuss with other scholars. Like Eliot, many Harvard professors had spent two years in Germany before they embarked on their academic careers. The ideas and methods of the German historians had been debated at Harvard as they were at Yale and Columbia. Bryce's memories of a semester at Heidelberg in 1863 to study Roman law and the German language, together with the reputation he now enjoyed as the author of *The Holy Roman Empire*, made his views on historical studies of unusual interest to Harvard scholars. The *dicta* of the German school were by no means embraced in the theological and Anglican atmosphere of Harvard, yet there was great admiration for Ranke, Mommsen, and also for Niebuhr beyond those great names, just as there was a residual interest in the possibility of a more 'scientific' history.[25]

Bryce, always ready to join the search for ultimate and objective truths, with his admiration for the methods of natural science already implanted, insisted nevertheless that the goal of 'scientific history' was a hopeless, even an unworthy quest. The influence of Freeman and Goldwin Smith persisted.

Bryce discussed these matters of common interest with scholars such as the philosopher Francis Bowen, professor of religion at Harvard and almost twice Bryce's age, yet ready to listen with interest to the author of *The Holy Roman Empire*. Another guest at dinner was Ephraim Gurney, the historian whom Eliot appointed as first dean of the faculty for the reorganised Harvard, and who was working closely with the President on every aspect of the new elective system of course work. Eliot and Gurney pushed their plans with the zeal of Puritans. When Bryce returned to Harvard on his second visit to America ten years later, he was to find Harvard transformed from an inward-looking aristocratic college, once designed to prepare young men for the ministry, into a vigorous, outward-looking institution, highly conscious that a famous university must serve the needs of society and the public. This was the measure of Eliot's reforms.

Apart from his interest in historical studies at Harvard, Bryce had a more immediate and practical concern with legal studies and the teaching of law. Here, his friendship with Holmes and Sedgwick opened many doors. He listened to the recently appointed Dean Langdell at the Law School and discussed with his friends Harvard's approach to legal education. They suggested that if time allowed he should take care to visit Yale and Columbia on his return to New York, and Bryce arranged to do so. There was talk of a science of law, but Bryce could not accept the idea of a science of law any more than he could accept the claims of 'scientific' history. Bryce also had reservations about Langdell's 'case' method for the instruction of law students. True, it provided a set of techniques, but he preferred the Institutes of Justinian and the study of jurisprudence to Langdell's innovations. These differences of opinion Bryce aired with Holmes in the years that lay ahead. For the moment, their discussions at Harvard were punctuated by pleasant evenings with new friends.

It was a rare delight when Holmes Junior asked Bryce and Dicey to dine one evening with his father, 'the autocrat of the breakfast table'. Old Dr Holmes had heard of the sprightly visitors from his son and daughter-in-law, and they were duly bidden to the Doctor's table. Bryce found the old man remarkably acute, and full of penetrating wisdom about the differences between the old world and the new. Dr Holmes held that the average, general level of culture in America was now higher than in England, but that the standards for individual excellence, that is to say, the levels aimed at by the really talented, were higher in England. Bryce was inclined to agree:

He stated what is certainly true, that although the average intellectual level of the American population is above (much above) that of the English, the level of high culture and attainment is as much lower; hence an American who can, and this frequently without much effort, get himself into the front rank, stops there, and devotes the rest of his energy to money-making and having a good time; whereas in England, the same man having a higher point to reach to find himself among the first, struggles on, perfecting his powers, eventually makes more of himself and raises still further the general standard. . . .[26]

They talked of other matters, and the urbane Doctor once more made the point which others had made too often now for Bryce and Dicey not to be persuaded of its truth. 'Holmes thought American manners much lighter and easier than English, of whose stiffness and awkwardness he remarked in a way we admitted to be just.' Bryce would take a careful look not only at Oxford University, but also at his fellow countrymen when he returned to England. It would be a keen and critical look, based on quite new perspectives.

It was mid-October. Dicey and Bryce took their last walk beneath the exquisitely coloured autumn trees by the Charles River and in Harvard Yard. They visited Longfellow, now back from Nahant and installed in Cambridge at Craigie House, where many eminent Europeans had been entertained before them. Emerson had invited them to come out to Concord, but time did not permit it.[27] They made their farewells to President Eliot, to Gurney and his charming wife, to Holmes and Sedgwick, then left by train on the morning of 16 October.

Bryce and Dicey had accepted an invitation to Naushon Island, just south of Cape Cod, from the Boston railroad financier John Murray Forbes, a friend of Goldwin Smith. Naushon Island was – and still is – owned by the Forbes family. To get away from business life at Boston, Murray Forbes liked to invite week-end guests to his splendid home on the island.[28]

The train brought the two visitors to New Bedford, where they took the steamer across Buzzard's Bay. Murray Forbes was a generous host. His guests, who arrived in a steady stream, were invited to relax in an atmosphere of servants and good living. The bracing air of Nantucket Sound and Buzzard's Bay had a tonic effect. On this particular week-end Forbes treated his guests to a deer hunt on the island. There was no pack, but the servants acted as beaters. Somewhat to his surprise, Bryce found himself astride a horse galloping alongside his host and precariously carrying a loaded gun across his arm, 'an operation of some delicacy in galloping through the boughs of trees'. When finally the industrious servants managed to flush out a speckled deer, Bryce was given a chance to shoot but did not use it. As the whole affair was not to his liking, it is possible that he deliberately refrained.

The easy hospitality which Murray Forbes accorded his guests tempered Bryce's mixed reactions to the afternoon's sport. Sarah Forbes was a gentle and charming hostess whom Bryce admired. The evening passed pleasantly. Bryce wished to know more about the connections between railroads and politics, as well as the plans and projections for developing the transcontinental railroads of America.

Murray Forbes had immense experience of almost every aspect of the development of the American railroads. He had started his career in a Boston counting house in 1828, and apart from four years in China, his business experience spanned the years of growth and exploitation of the west from Jacksonian times up to the present. He had helped to organise and finance several railroads in the mid-west, including the Michigan Central. Bryce listened intently as his host discussed the prospects for a great northern route across to the Pacific Ocean, to match the network which now joined the east coast with the west along the southern route, by way of Denver and Salt Lake City.

Bryce linked what he heard now with what he had heard else-where, and what he had gleaned from a series of new acquaintances – at Boston, in the mountains of New Hampshire, and on the Mississippi River. In these tales of hope, effort and ambition, there was romance as well as cupidity; the desire to conquer the wilder-ness as well as the desire for personal profit. Here was an American epic, as well as a tangled story full of complex economic and political circumstances. To grasp the significance of this epic was to grasp an essential part of the American myth during the nineteenth century. If he did not know all the details of the saga, Bryce at least began to grasp the importance of it for a proper understanding of the story of America.[29]

Dicey and Bryce returned to New York to make the city their base for a final round of visits in the region. Taking up the advice of Holmes Junior at Boston, they visited Yale to talk with a young instructor at the Law School named Simeon Baldwin. Baldwin was soon to become a distinguished professor of law, then a justice of the state supreme court in Connecticut, and forty years later a famous Governor of Connecticut. A contemporary of Holmes at the Harvard Law School, Baldwin was already an authority on state constitutions, with an intimate knowledge of the strengths and weaknesses of the Connecticut State Constitution. Baldwin was one of many able young jurists who urged a simplification of state and federal law and a general tidying up of the statutes in post-Civil War America. In the 1870s he served as a member of a special commission appointed to simplify Connecticut statutes. On the day he received a call from the two English scholars he placed at their disposal his unusual knowledge of the complexities of the

American legal system, especially in the framework of the two-tiered and three-tiered federal system of courts. When Bryce later decided to analyse and digest the many state constitutions of the federal states for his magnum opus, he turned to Simeon Baldwin to guide him through the maze.[30]

October was nearly ended. Dicey and Bryce had earlier arranged to sail to England on 3 November. They were reluctant to leave, and would have preferred to prolong their visit by at least another month, but the mail from England showed what accumulations of work awaited them at London. Bryce had his duties at Oxford to attend to besides his work at Lincoln's Inn.

The final few days were breathless. Bryce's journal gives out, and there are only brief hints of his remaining visits in eve-of-departure letters to the family at home in Scotland. Eliot at Harvard had urged them to hear Theodore Dwight lecturing at the School of Law at Columbia College in New York. Bryce was impressed by the 'clearness and rigour' of Dwight's lectures on private and company law. They visited Godkin again and talked of Tammany and New York politics. There was a hurried visit to Vassar College for Ladies at Poughkeepsie in the Hudson valley – this again on the advice of Charles Eliot at Harvard, who had furnished an introduction. Bryce wrote to Eliot on 31 October: 'I have been at Vassar College where everything seems to be working excellently, so far as one could judge in a hasty visit.'[31] In New York he had already received from Eliot copies of examination papers from Harvard courses. Bryce was intensely interested and asked Eliot to send him papers from the law examinations when these took place. So began the longest and fullest of Bryce's correspondences with eminent Americans from 1870 to 1922.[32]

November arrived. Bryce finished a letter to his sister Katherine at home in Scotland. 'Were it not for all of you at Boweshill', he wrote, 'I really think I would emigrate hither: there is a sort of freedom and spirit about the place and people which one doesn't get in England. . . .'[33]

The two friends went aboard the S.S. *Abyssinia* on 3 November. A breeze fanned the tip of Battery Point but an Indian summer gave a pleasant warmth to the air. Manhattan slipped astern and the ship rounded Sandy Hook for a ten-day voyage. Bryce and Dicey spent the days discussing their experiences and reading the books they had bought in New York, in Boston, in Chicago. At times they would laugh over some bizarre experience, or discuss some of the things which had surprised, gratified, alarmed, or appalled them in the new world. Both felt that the course of their lives would be affected by these nine weeks in the new world: neither could predict in what manner or to what degree.

Dicey returned to his work in chambers at the Inner Templer to begin laying the groundwork for his monumental *Introduction of the Study of the Law of the Constitution*. In 1882 he joined Bryce at Oxford when he was appointed to the Vinerian professorship of law. Thus a striking similarity in the careers of the two friends continued, for both had taken outstanding firsts in Literae Humaniores; both had won the Arnold Essay Prize; both had been President of the Union; both turned to legal studies and Lincoln's Inn; both returned to Oxford to take up a chair of law. In Dicey's case, All Souls and the Vinerian chair claimed almost all his energies in future years. His further studies in Anglo-American law, in Conflicts, and his great treatise *Law and Public Opinion in England* undoubtedly benefited from his visits to America. Dicey confirmed this much later. Nearly forty years after their return from America in November 1870, the elderly Dicey wrote to his friend as Bryce set out for his eighth extended visit to the new world – this time to become British Ambassador to the United States. Dicey was in reminiscent mood on the eve of his friend's departure for Washington in 1907:

. . . It is curious to think how much in one way or another our journey in 1870 affected both our lives, and I should say on the whole affected them happily. One may pretty well assume that *The American Commonwealth* and probably neither the *Law of the Constitution* nor certainly *Law and Opinion* would have been produced but for this journey. What is strangest to me is that the question which perplexed us then perplexes me still and will do to my life's end: how is it that a people consisting of or at any rate containing so many excellent delightful persons as the United States should still in public life in many respects not rise and perhaps fall below the European Nations at their best. – I hope before your life's end you may be able to analyse still further the condition of the United States. If anyone could properly explain both the virtues and the weaknesses of American democracy, he would render the world a great service. . . . [34]

Viewed in retrospect, therefore, the Dicey–Bryce visit to America in 1870 was auspicious, and for James Bryce it initiated a lifelong involvement.

6

Lessons from the New World

Bryce returned to Oxford to take up the Regius Chair of Civil Law. He gave his inaugural in February 1871 and made it a plea for the study of Civil Law at the university. His reasons were both intellectual and practical. At that time, legal studies at Oxford concentrated on common law and equity – the two systems which had developed side by side out of medieval law. Bryce felt that there was a dangerous parochialism in such studies and he wished to encourage wider horizons. A study of Civil Law, based on the Roman jurists, would prompt a new generation of scholars and lawyers to criticise the concepts and the progress of their own law 'from an independent point of view'.[1] Legal studies could thus move towards a comparative view of English law. This was Bryce's ultimate aim.

To some extent, the lecture was both a progression and an off-shoot from his study of the Holy Roman Empire. He was suggesting that young jurists and lawyers could learn much more from historical studies than they did – not least a sense of the continuity of law from Roman times to the present. But the lecture was also a plea for a more detached and thus a more objective view of English law. In a sense, Bryce was already arguing from another intellectual shore, urging his colleagues and pupils to get outside a narrow and subjective concern with English Common Law. He quoted a continental jurist: 'England sleeps for ever', and added his own gloss: 'She sleeps because her lawyers have allowed them-selves to become as completely isolated as though we were living and legislating for a planet of our own. . . . We do not even care to profit by the experience of a country which speaks our own legal language – the United States – where many problems have been handled by the courts and many experiments have been tried by the legislatures which are full of instruction for us. . . .'[2]

The suggestion that in legal and judicial affairs England could learn from American innovations must have seemed a radical doctrine to the Oxford school of jurisprudence in 1871. Bryce's inaugural was an eloquent plea to Victorians to look outside the confines of an insular tradition. He was already corresponding with Oliver Wendell Holmes at Harvard on matters of common interest. Holmes did not altogether agree with Bryce on the usefulness of tne study of Civil Law for young minds, but he noted a difference between American and English needs. When Bryce sent Holmes a copy of his inaugural the Bostonian remarked candidly: 'It occurred to me that its recommendations may be sounder for England than for us. . . . I think that it would be dangerous to set a student at the civil law here as tending to let him satisfy himself with generalities. . . . The common law training (e.g. in our law school) is to keep him at the solution of particular cases. Just as Agassiz [*] would give one of his pupils a sea urchin and tell him to find out all about it that he could.'[3] Holmes felt that Roman Law was for the mature scholar. The student at law school must first learn how to conduct a case.

Yet the gap between Bryce's approach and the views of Holmes was less, in fact, than this exchange of views suggests. Holmes was already seeking a path that could lead towards a critical examination of many of the broader unwritten assumptions of English jurisprudence. By the 1870s Holmes was finding Utilitarianism increasingly barren: he was searching for some more positive assertion of the moral foundations of society, something which did not rest on texts such as Mill's *Political Economy*, which he considered sterile. Holmes wanted to use the law carefully, prudently and without haste to turn society to new purposes and concerns. The moral foundations of modern society could be shaped and then sustained by judges who dared to be philosophers and sociologists as well as jurists. The method would be a pragmatic meliorism.[4]

For this quest Holmes already valued the aid and counsel of his friend James Bryce. In his letter to Bryce in May 1871 Holmes added: 'Talking of jurisprudence I am going to deliver a University course of lectures on that subject. . . . Can you tell me of any books that will aid me in either French or Latin – I can't read

* Louis Agassiz (1807–73), the eminent Harvard zoologist and geologist.

German? Indeed I should like the name of any very important German book.' The intellectual exchange between Bryce and Holmes during the next fifty years was a two-way process. Each influenced the other to a degree that can be traced in the correspondence which flowed between them from 1871 to 1921.[5] Already in 1871 Bryce was receiving pamphlets and monograph literature from Holmes. Holmes in turn received literature from Bryce. In response to Holmes' earlier request at Boston Bryce sent reports from London to the *Harvard Law Review*. Bryce's report of May 1871 spoke of proposed reforms at Oxford:

Those of you interested in the improvement and extension of the Law School at Harvard may be glad to know that similar steps are being taken at Oxford to reinvigorate long disused law studies of the place. It is proposed to establish two substantial law examinations there – a preliminary or general one in jurisprudence, the history of English law, Roman law and international law, plus a law degree: hopes are being entertained that many young men will thus be induced to lay a wider and more scientific foundation for their practical studies than they can do in chambers in London.[6]

The proposed changes were not of course simply the fruits of the Bryce–Dicey transatlantic trip. Reform had been in the air for several years, and Bryce's predecessor Sir Travers Twiss, together with William Anson of All Souls, were in favour of reform. But Bryce was an able and eloquent member of the reform group, and his inaugural lecture plainly announced his sympathies. He joined with those who sought to divide up the School of Law and Modern History, in order to give the study of law a separate place in Oxford studies.

By hard work, cogent argument, and some persistence, the reformers won their case. The separate Honour School of Jurisprudence was set up during 1872, and the degree of Bachelor of Civil Law also introduced. Bryce had a personal part to play in setting up the B.C.L., which soon attracted able students preparing for a career at the Bar. By the end of the decade legal studies were considerably invigorated at Oxford.[7]

Bryce's lectures impressed both colleagues and students by their range and depth, and despite political duties in London he lectured regularly until his retirement from the chair in 1893. H. A. L.

Fisher recalled how, as a young Oxford don in the early nineties, he once passed the hall of Oriel College on a Saturday afternoon in the summer term 'at an hour when most undergraduates were amusing themselves on the river or the cricket field'. Looking in the hall, Fisher saw an undergraduate audience 'listening to a brilliant speech delivered . . . with a force and animation rare, if not unknown, in Oxford lecture rooms by an alert, wiry, grey-bearded man with clean cut features and flashing blue eyes and an azure neck-tie. The orator was speculating upon the possible effects of English laws upon the immemorial structure of Indian society. . . .'[8]

When he was not occupied with teaching duties and reform of the syllabus at Oxford, Bryce turned to writing and reviewing. Apart from reporting the activities of the English Bar to the *Harvard Law Review*, Bryce wrote on 'The Legal Profession in America' for *Macmillan's Magazine* in London.[9]

The author's perspective was a comparative one. He used his knowledge of the American Bar in order to throw light upon English institutions and experience. The fact that the two systems had common historical origins (except for the unusual case of Louisiana), but that they had diverged to produce different practices, customs and institutional arrangements, gave Bryce a topic for historical research as well as for contemporary comment. He also discussed the subject of legal education in the two countries. Of the American system he remarked: 'The provision for instruction in law is as good, or better, all things considered, than in England, and is certainly more generally turned to account. . . .' He went on to enumerate the eminent men now teaching law at Harvard, Yale and Columbia, 'men of the highest professional reputation, who undertake the work more for the love of it than for the inadequate salaries offered . . .', and included a detailed description of the wide range of courses offered at the Harvard Law School, together with a critical examination of the merits of the course.

The conclusions emerging from Bryce's closely written article were chiefly these: whereas there were relatively fewer men in the United States who took a speculative and philosophical interest in the study of law, yet the average practitioner had a better knowledge of the workings of the law and a wider knowledge of the whole field of law than 'a person of corresponding talents in this country'. The law schools of the United States played a vital role in raising the general standard.

Bryce was again suggesting the novel doctrine that in legal training Britain could now learn from the United States. But it takes more than one zealous professor to change the deeply rooted habits of the British legal profession. Bryce's hopes for wide-ranging reforms in legal training in Britain were never fully realised, though as we have remarked changes were brought about in the Oxford syllabus in line with Bryce's views.[10]

The article in *Macmillan's Magazine* did not mean that Bryce was ready to bend the knee to the American system of legal education or the judicial process there. Two months after this article, he wrote another for the same magazine on 'American Judges'.[11] In this article, the tone is much more critical. The popular election of judges, especially in a system where elections are frequent, is roundly condemned for reasons that are now familiar on both sides of the Atlantic. The results of the system in New York are described, though Bryce is careful to stress that different states showed different standards; that in a state such as Massachusetts, for instance, or Michigan, the bench still included men of the utmost probity and the highest intelligence.

The article is also interesting for Bryce's first critical comments on American democracy. Across many years and in many writings he would modify his views, with now and then a fresh appraisal as new circumstances pointed to strengths or weaknesses he had failed to note earlier. Yet to a considerable degree the underlying essentials of the views he held in 1872 were retained over the next fifty years. Bryce wrote:

There is a notable tendency in any principle or doctrine which has once acquired an ascendancy over men's minds, to go on working itself out in its applications far beyond the limits within which it was first recognised as true, and within which an educated judgment would still confine it. Every serious thinker knows that in politics no principle, however generally sound, can be applied absolutely and universally: it must be kept subject to a variety of restrictions and qualifications suggested by the social and economical conditions of the community wherein or whereon it is to operate. . . .

In the United States the idea of democracy has obtained this sort of sway. The people, whose imagination is in some directions very susceptible, became intoxicated with the notion of freedom, and were ready to go to great lengths in their pursuit of that rather bare and negative conception. The noble idea of the equality before God of all His rational creatures, from which the founders of the Republic started, was soon taken to involve not only equality of all citizens before the law, but also the equality, so far as it could be attained, of their social position and their political rights. From this again the transition was easy to a belief in their equal capacity and worth, the notion expressed by the phrase that one man is as good as another, and a great deal better. . . .[12]

The slight yet deliberate irony of this last phrase provides some clue to the mind of the travelled scholar now replacing the earnest Oxford graduate of a decade earlier. The high moral seriousness is still there, certainly; but not least among the fruits of his travels was a growing realisation of man's follies, foibles and limitations; of his vanity, his selfishness, his occasional hypocrisy, his ability to preach one code of conduct whilst privately following or endorsing another. Bryce devoutly believed that all men are equal before God and before the law: but it was hypocrisy to claim that all men are equal in their abilities – or their worth.

Bryce was liberally endowed with Scottish common sense. He was a realist, but never a cynic. His qualities of humane compassion and wide-ranging observation can be seen in two quite different articles which also came from his fertile pen at this time. The first article he wrote on his return from America was devoted to 'American experience in the relief of the poor'.[13]

This article took up a theme which was of pressing concern to English liberals at this time. More and more evidence accumulated that the Poor Law system, especially the system of outdoor relief, had broken down. The problem of pauperism showed itself at street corners in every city. Bryce began his article thus: 'It is at first sight surprising that there should be anything for Englishmen to learn from Americans in the matter of relief of the poor.' He went on to show that there was a good deal to learn.

Pauperism in America was chiefly confined to the great cities where successive waves of poor and often semi-literate or illiterate immigrants had brought problems not unlike those created by the flight from the land in England. Using the experience of Boston as a guide, Bryce carefully examined the organisations and techniques of aid and assistance which Americans had worked out in the face of these problems. He noted that the provisions of the Massachusetts Poor Law did not differ greatly from English Poor Law, but that the most striking difference was the existence of efficient, well-organised voluntary societies such as the Boston Provident Association and the Boston Ladies' City Relief Agency. These societies, together with others such as the Boston Soldiers' Fund and the Young Men's Benevolent Society, were all housed together in a large building provided rent free by the municipality at a convenient central location in the city. In the basement of the same building was a dispensary and rooms for the city physician, both at the service of the local Overseers of the Poor. Further rooms upstairs in the building were available for other charitable societies that might be formed in the future. Bryce pointed out the many advantages of having various charities in close contact with each other. Both from the point of view of information-gathering and the administering and co-ordinating of all these voluntary activities, the Boston example could surely be adopted by many English municipalities, he urged, and he described in detail the activities of the several charities housed alongside the Overseers. The Boston example was the sort of pluralist solution to a social evil which appealed especially to Bryce's brand of liberalism: half voluntary, half municipally directed, it avoided the taint of state direction on the one hand and the uncertainties of mere voluntarism on the other. Bryce's message was clear and forthright: England's cities could learn from Boston.

In December 1872, in lighter vein, Bryce wrote 'On Some Peculiarities of Society in America'. The article appeared in the *Cornhill Magazine* and was a restrained attack on the stiffness and artificiality of social relationships between young men and women in Victorian England.[14] The author first pointed out that the title of his article (which seems to have been invented at the proof stage by the editor of the magazine) did not mean that American society should be judged 'peculiar' by English people: far from it. Drawing his examples from a number of observed instances – again the direct fruits of his journey to America – Bryce described the much greater freedom of young men and women in America to meet, to correspond, to take up acquaintanceships in a much more casual manner than the tight rubric of the English mores permitted at that time. A young woman in America was free to choose her friends – even her male friends – without needing her parents' express permission. 'It is by no means a matter of course that a girl's friends should be also her parents' friends.' Bryce went on to cite an instance which was probably not autobiographical, though we cannot tell; but there is little doubt his account caused raised eyebrows in the respectable middle-class houses, rectories and libraries where the *Cornhill Magazine* was likely to circulate. Bryce wrote:

You meet her at a party and dance with her, or inquire about the Spanish song she has sung so prettily; she will ask you to call and see her, adding perhaps that she will sing Spanish songs to you all the afternoon. You go to the house and ask for her: she comes down and receives you alone or with her sister. Her mother may or may not appear, probably does not; and you may perhaps keep up the acquaintance for long enough, fall in love with her if you like, without ever being presented to her parents, without so much as knowing them by sight. It is well understood that she is both able and entitled to look after herself and choose her own friends.[15]

And if Victorian mothers and fathers were not sufficiently scandalised by the first few pages of the professor's article, then later passages would make them catch their breath:

Of all American devices for enjoying the delicious autumn, the very pleasantest, and to a European at least the most romantic, is a party in the woods. A group of friends arrange to go together into some mountain and forest region . . . engaging three or four guides. They embark with all their equipments and pass in their boats up the rivers and across the lakes of this great wild country . . . to their chosen camping ground at the foot of some tall rock that rises from the still crystal of the lake. Here they build their bark hut and spread their beds of the elastic and fragrant hemlock boughs: the men roam about during the day tracking the deer, . . . the ladies read and work and bake the corn cakes; at night there is a merry gathering and a row in the soft moonlight. On these expeditions brothers will take sisters and cousins, and their sisters' and cousins' lady friends; the brothers' friends will come too, and all will live together in a fraternal way for weeks together, though no elderly relative or married lady be of the party.[16]

Bryce stressed that these excursions arose simply and naturally from the pleasant, relaxed relations between young men and women in America: that they were a by-product of many admirable institutions and social arrangements; of co-education, of social equality, of the absence of a rigid hierarchy and gradations in society generally — by contrast with social and domestic life in Victorian England. This message for the Victorians was altogether different from the homilies of Mrs Trollope, Charles Dickens and Harriet Martineau.

Bryce left his readers in no doubt which system he favoured. 'Such pleasure in the society of people of one's own age, which no moralist can deny to be one of the most legitimate sources of enjoyment, is in England a good deal cramped by the restrictions which custom has imposed, and a good deal clouded by the idea, so often present to the English youth, of cousins gossiping and parents inquiring into his intentions. . . .' Bryce was convinced that this situation was unhealthy and repressive. He hoped that English society would see the day when 'instead of being driven to suggest half furtive meetings at the Academy or the Horticultural, a young gentleman will ask a lady to come for a walk in Kensington Gardens to-morrow from half-past five till seven'. Bryce would have been surprised, and probably shocked to see how far the pendulum would swing in the twentieth century.

7

1881: America, East to West

Ten years elapsed between Bryce's first visit to the United States and his second. During those years he earned a considerable reputation in several distinct fields, so that when he visited America again in 1881 he was a figure of some renown.

As a lecturer at Oxford, in London at the Temple during the Law Terms, and as a visitor to Manchester, Bryce drew large audiences. Students and young barristers alike enjoyed the combination of erudition and humane discourse. A Bryce lecture or series of lectures invariably began by setting out the first principles of the subject, then staking out the ground in an Aristotelian manner, and then developing the arguments with clear logic. But audiences were constantly reminded by the lecturer that the law was made for men, and not men for the law.

Bryce was also drawn into politics during the 1870s. Gladstone was familiar with his scholarly achievements as well as his work on the Commission on secondary schools. After 1871 Bryce began to receive an occasional friendly summons to Gladstone's famous Thursday morning breakfasts and sometimes to dinner.[1] He was left in no doubt that the Liberal party welcomed men who combined a first-class intelligence with practical administrative ability. Bryce had no great taste and little time for party politics, but there were no objections to an Oxford professor combining a seat in Parliament with his duties in the university: politics was still a part-time occupation for amateurs rather than a vocation for professionals, except for those forming the Ministry of the day. During the next few years Bryce came to accept that as a committed liberal he ought to make his services available to the Liberal party.

He stood for election in the Scottish constituency of Wick Burghs in 1874, but was defeated in a year when Disraeli's 'popular Toryism' made heavy inroads on the Liberal party. The Tory party formed the Ministry which lasted until 1880, when Gladstone's Midlothian campaign brought the Liberals back to power. Bryce again stood for election, this time at Tower Hamlets – a large, sprawling constituency in the east end of London. Tower Hamlets had a poor and politically conscious electorate. Its 44,000 voters included a mixture of Irish, German, Jewish and Dutch elements historically associated with the area behind Aldgate East. Bryce spoke to this audience with insight and sympathy, and had the advantage of being able to address German bakers in their own language. On the hustings he was an eloquent, attractive figure in his tweed cape, with flashing eyes, bushy eyebrows and a generous beard. Bryce defeated three other candidates to take his seat in the new Parliament. Gladstone sent warm congratulations to the new M.P.[2]

One further achievement between Bryce's first and second visits to America deserves notice, for it earned Bryce world renown. During his vacations Bryce continued his travels and climbs in all parts of Europe from Spain to the Alps. In 1876 he carried out a feat which gave him a unique place in the annals of mountaineering and which earned him the Presidency of the Alpine Club some years later.

Accompanied by an old Oxford friend, Aeneas Mackay, Bryce set out for Armenia and the region of Ararat in western Turkey. They planned to make an attempt on the legendary peak of Mount Ararat, 17,000 feet high, and reputed to be the spot where the Ark came to rest. Ararat had never before been climbed. Bryce and Mackay engaged a party of Kurds to guide them to the slopes of the peak, but as they climbed, superstition and fear began to affect the guides. The vast peak loomed above them in the clouds. At 13,000 feet, the guides would go no further. The air was becoming thin and the ascent very taxing, even for the hardy Kurds. One or two were persuaded to go on. Eventually they too refused to budge further. Aeneas Mackay was also fatigued and beginning to suffer from the lack of oxygen. Mackay made camp and remained whilst Bryce pressed on to attempt the final ascent in one day. Mackay watched Bryce vanish upwards in the mists swirling about the slopes of the peak.

A full account of Bryce's ascent that day appeared later in his book *Transcaucasia and Ararat*. The final part of the feat is best given in his own words, with their special Bryceian flavour. Bryce pressed on for several hours in the dark mists:

A violent west wind was blowing, and the temperature must have been pretty low, for a big icicle at once enveloped the lower half of my face, and did not melt till I got to the bottom of the cone, four hours afterwards. Unluckily, I was very thinly clad, the stout tweed coat reserved for such occasions having been stolen in a Russian railway. Suddenly, to my astonishment, the ground began to fall away to the north; I stopped, a puff of wind drove off the mists at one side, the opposite side to that by which I had come, and showed the Araxes plain at an abysmal depth below. It was the top of Ararat. . . .[3]

Thereafter Bryce's name was itself almost legendary wherever mountaineers gathered together to learn of unusual deeds.

Back at London and Oxford, Bryce's correspondence with his American friends was maintained regularly. In letters to Godkin, Eliot and Holmes the topics ranged from party politics and legislative issues in both countries, to the literary scene, and to developments in the high courts. Bryce's monumental series of articles in the *Nation* now began. He commented on Liberal politics and policies, on the Irish problem (in which Bryce's support of Gladstone and Home Rule were clearly set forth), and on other political and historical matters. He occasionally contributed literary essays and reviews of learned works. Bryce's first contribution to the *Nation* was a review of Cleasby and Vigfusson's Icelandic dictionary. Other Bryce contributions to the *Nation* in these years dealt with topics as varied as the revised New Testament, Thomas Carlyle, George Eliot, and Disraeli. Though Bryce never cared to write on any subject outside his competence, Godkin soon discovered that there were few themes in history, politics, literature and law on which Bryce was not extremely well informed.[4]

Following his election to Parliament in 1880 and with further claims on his time beginning to mount, Bryce decided to make another visit to the United States in the summer of 1881. Like all men of ideas, he felt keenly that letters are only a partial substitute for long conversations with chosen friends. Apart from this, the explorer and globe-trotter in Bryce urged him to extend his travels in the new world to the Pacific coast at least. As his plans matured Bryce was invited by Eliot to lecture at Harvard during his visit. Bryce accepted with pleasure.

Bryce would have liked Dicey's company again, but Dicey was now married, had family obligations and a great deal of work in Oxford and London. Bryce sailed alone on the *Britannic* and arrived in New York on 27 August. The voyage was uneventful and Bryce barely enjoyed it. The curious defensive penumbra with which many Atlantic voyagers seemed to surround themselves was again in evidence. No loquacious churchmen like Bishop McQuaid were on board. Bryce fell back on his books and sorely missed Dicey. At times his sombre mood was accentuated by another acute memory. Four years earlier Bryce's father had died in an accident in the Highlands. James Bryce Senior was on a geological excursion in the region of Loch Ness and was examining some eruptive granite when his hammer apparently dislodged loose rocks above his head. He was killed instantly. As the eldest son, James now had the main responsibility for supporting his mother and to a smaller extent his two unmarried sisters. Annan, the second son, was now in business in Burma. Between them, the two sons were able to maintain their mother and Katherine and Mary in fairly modest circumstances in London. Writing to his mother from the *Britannic*, however, Bryce was keenly aware that the light had gone out of her life.[5]

New York was hot under the August sun. The waterfront was thronged with its polyglot community. Among the familiar accents of Irish and German immigrants new tongues could be heard here and there among groups of recent immigrants, including Italian, Portuguese, and the Yiddish of Russian Jews in flight from the pogroms. Along the streets a new and unsightly form of street furniture had now appeared. Telegraph poles and telephone wires festooned the financial quarter and spread an ugly rash alongside Broadway. The first telephone exchange had opened three years earlier. Graham Bell could hardly guess the revolution this would bring to American society before the end of the century.[6]

Bryce again stayed overnight with his cousins at their house in Prospect Place in Brooklyn. Their conversation was dominated by the public anxiety over the assassin's attack on President Garfield

93

on 2 July 1881. According to the newspapers there was still hope that the President might live, but during the next two weeks that hope faded, and Garfield died on 19 September. Bryce called on Godkin at the *Nation* in New York, but the scorching heat of the city ruled out any temptation to linger there and he was anxious to go straight out to the west as soon as he had made a promised visit to Oliver Wendell Holmes at his summer home not far from Newport.

At Newport, Bryce renewed his friendship with Colonel Higginson, a sadder man since the death of his wife three years earlier, but still writing poems and essays. Bryce stayed only briefly but took note of Colonel Higginson's advice that on this trip he should try to see some of the deep south to round out his experiences of eastern and western America. The advice came well from a veteran who had commanded the first Negro regiment in the Civil War, the South Carolina Volunteers. Bryce left Newport determined to return from the west by way of the south so far as time and the railroads permitted.

A little further up the New England coast, he stopped at Mattapoisett to pay his call on Holmes. The two friends settled down to a long talk on matters of mutual interest. Holmes had looked forward eagerly to Bryce's visit. With his usual directness he had paid Bryce a high compliment in a recent letter welcoming his coming visit: 'There are so few men as I was saying to Dicey who have any kind of idealism in their practice that I cling pretty closely to those who have.'[7]

Holmes had sent Bryce copies of his lectures at Harvard and his book on the Common Law, which appeared earlier that year. Holmes wanted Bryce to write 'a magnum opus on the Canon law', and though Bryce never fulfilled this hope, possibly some mild persuasion was attempted at Mattapoisett as the two friends walked by the cove or smoked on the verandah after dinner.[8] Bryce wanted above all to talk with Holmes about the Common Law. In his recently published book on the subject, Holmes made the memorable utterance: 'The life of the law has not been logic, it has been experience.' American jurisprudence had reached a turning-point. As Morton White has observed, Holmes's dictum became 'the slogan for a generation of legal realists' in the United

States.[9] Bryce was reluctant to take his leave of Holmes, who was now, in intellectual terms, closest to him among his American friends. But Holmes and his wife readily appreciated that their guest was feeling the call of the American west. Bryce went west on the first day of September, just as the leaves were beginning to turn for the New England Fall.

Following the existing railroads, Bryce's journey took him from New York west to Chicago, then south-west in a long loop on the Santa Fe Railroad to Denver and Salt Lake City, then across to San Francisco. From there, he went northwards by sea to Seattle in Washington Territory, on to Vancouver, then south again to California, to the Yosemite Valley, then east on the Santa Fe to St Louis, southwards to Kentucky and Tennessee, on to Georgia, then north through the Carolinas to Virginia, to Baltimore, and so to New York and Boston.

He was physically exhausted at times, but his energies always revived for the next stage of the journey. As he travelled, he continued his custom of interrogating friendly strangers in order to learn as much as possible of the patterns of settlement, the forms of the society, the beliefs and institutions of the people who had helped to settle the west. Bryce talked with farmers, miners, railroad workers, engineers, churchmen of many sects and political leaders of the new communities where he now travelled.

At Chicago he rested briefly to change trains, snatched a swim in Lake Michigan, then hastened on to Colorado, in the heartland of America. At Denver he paused to inspect the boom town, whose population had grown rapidly following the discovery of mineral wealth in the area. After talking with various townspeople, he noted down his impressions carefully. Bryce discovered that Denver was a town with a fairly lurid past but likely to have an impressive future:

... till lately the scene of constant murders and outrages but now pretty respectable and blossoming into a local capital. It covers a great area, three quarters of which is intended for the future, with a mixture of hotels and stores five stories high, with plate glass, splendid fixings [sic] and wooden shanties, mostly bar rooms or billiard parlours. It is 5,000 feet above the sea, and therefore very healthy, with a wonderfully dry air, and consequently a sky clear as that of Armenia. . . .

I think of going to a still higher and fresher place, 75 miles to the S.S.W., called Colorado Springs, and thence through the mountains – there is a railway all the way – to the famous mining city of Leadville, and so back to Denver, whence on to California. . . . I continue to find the people very friendly and pleasant when we meet casually. . . .[10]

A few days later Bryce was at Leadville, 10,000 feet up in the mountains and even more of a boom town than Denver. Following the recent discovery of lead carbonate with a high silver content, Leadville's population had soared in a few years from a handful to about 40,000. The main street was an untidy collection of hotels, bars and brothels. Some establishments conveniently combined all three services for the miners and prospectors. Of Leadville's two theatres, the Coliseum and the Comique, or saloons like the Calumet, an historian of the region observed: 'No foul words need be wasted describing them . . .'[11]

Bryce picked his way fairly gingerly among the booted and belted prospectors who lounged outside the bars. Gun law ruled: there was no such thing as a quiet night's sleep in Leadville in 1881 and Bryce departed next morning. It was a universe away from the book-filled rooms of Boston and Harvard but it was just as much a part of America, and salutary for the scholarly visitor.

Returning to Denver, Bryce travelled north to Cheyenne in Wyoming, and then west, across to Ogden in Utah on the shores of the Great Salt Lake. On this thirty-hour stretch in the train, the Rocky Mountain scenery showed its true grandeur, and Bryce chafed at his 'captivity in the cars' as vistas unfolded.

From Ogden, another train brought him south in two hours to Salt Lake City. Bryce was anxious to take a careful look at the fast-expanding centre of Mormon culture and he moved into a hotel for a few days. The descriptions in his letters home are lengthy and detailed at this time:

The city of the saints stands on the last gentle slope of the mountains, just where the plain begins, about fifteen miles from the lake shore. No city in America, perhaps none in the world, covers so large an area for its population. Thirty thousand people are spread

Members of the Old Mortality Club, Oxford, Trinity Term 1860

Standing (from left to right): J. F. Payne (Magdalen), J. W. Hoole (Queen's), T. H. Green (Balliol), James Bryce (Trinity), A. E. Mackay (University); *sitting:* G. R. Luke (Balliol), A. C. Swinburne (Balliol), John Nichol (Balliol), A. V. Dicey (Balliol), T. E. Holland (Balliol and Magdalen)

New York, 1876. View of Manhattan from the New Jersey shore

Harvard Yard about 1876

over an area of more than a mile, each way. Every street is double the width of Prince's St. [*]; every residence stands in its own garden, with a lawn, and trees, mostly fruit trees, so embower it that from a height you seem to look over one huge orchard with only a few high house roofs showing through the foliage. The streets are all bordered by tall trees beneath whose shade one walks: it is only the few principal business streets where there are continuous houses. In these there are some handsome blocks, and of course – one always has this in the western cities – some huge and handsome shops, in front of which the electric light flashes all night. . . .[12]

From physical description, Bryce turned to the society he found in the city. Naturally, the religious life of the community interested him and he knew it would greatly interest his mother in London:

I must not forget to mention the Mormon Temple now building, and the Tabernacle, which holds over 10,000 people. But the society is quite peculiar. Two third are saints: one third Gentiles, a term used here in no sense of fun, but as the ordinary way of describing a Non-Mormon. 'Is he a Gentile?' 'This is a Gentile village.' It includes even the Jews of whom there are enough to build a synagogue. All the local government of the city and the territory of Utah, so far as elected by the people, is in Mormon hands, for they have the majority of votes, but the Governor and superior judges, being appointed by the U.S. authorities at Washington, are Gentiles, and mostly hostile to the Mormons. . . . Hardly any social intercourse goes on between the two parties. The Mormons receive constant immigrants, especially from England, Wales and Scandinavia – they can never convert Irish Roman Catholics, but they lose some by apostasy, people who are carried off by Gentiles, or who get tired of the religious observances. It is hard to learn anything authentic about polygamy: of course many of the women do not like it but what can they do? They are told it is . . . [†] salvation: they don't like to be turned out of the community and have nothing else to betake themselves to. Very often they don't live in the same house with one another, the rich polygamist keeping up several separate wife-houses. The women are mostly very ignorant and superstitious; they are fed on their own literature and kept from all intercourse with the non-Mormon

* Edinburgh?   † Page torn: words indecipherable.

world. . . . I had two interviews with the present head of the Mormon Church, President Taylor, the successor to Brigham Young, a quiet, shrewd slow-speaking deep old Westmoreland man from near Milnthorpe. He struck me as discreet, cautious, sensible, but with less gift for ruling than Brigham no doubt possessed. . . .[13]

John Taylor, a practising polygamist, had become head of the Mormon Church in 1877, following the death of Brigham Young. His active career included founding a Mormon newspaper in New York, serving in the Utah territorial legislature from 1857 to 1876, and thereafter as a probate judge. Bryce was fortunate to manage these two interviews with the ex-judge in 1881, for Taylor was soon forced to direct the affairs of the Church from a hiding place to escape arrest for polygamy.

The long letters continued with detailed observation of the 'Apostles' and chief priests surrounding the President of the Church, men whom Bryce thought to resemble 'English dissenting deacons . . . say Baptists or Primitive Methodists, only sharpened and hardened by American life and by the necessities of their position'. He compared and contrasted the Mormons with other American sects he had observed.[14]

These details were of immediate interest to his mother at home, for the widowed Mrs Bryce was well informed on religious controversy and still read widely. Toward the end of her life Margaret Bryce was even more interested in the struggles of Nonconformist sects, and James Bryce knew that every detail he now set down would be read with close interest.

Bryce often made a long letter to his mother or his sisters serve as a journal, knowing that they would carefully preserve it for his return. The letters show the characteristic elements of Bryce's method of investigation. From his notes on the geographic setting of a city or place, he went on to observe the architecture, the streets and civic institutions. Then he examined in close detail the people who made up the city or the region, observing them from a number of different approaches: as members of social institutions, as political groupings, as members of a church, or simply as men and women with particular jobs – or without them. He noted the physical characteristics of the people, and made comparisons, using similes

98

where appropriate, sometimes drawing on his wide travels and on his knowledge of ethnology. In this way he could build up a composite picture of the geographical, social and usually the political environment. Those facts or circumstances which could not be deduced from simple observation he filled in by interviews, or more often by friendly interrogation of local citizens. Throughout, he used his long historical memory and a prodigious knowledge drawn from fields as disparate as geology, constitutional history, comparative religion, and ethnology. Thus the observations contained in his long and detailed letter from Salt Lake City provided a small foretaste, in structure and form, of the magnum opus on America he published seven years later.

From Salt Lake City, Bryce went west again to get his first sight of the Pacific lapping the far shores of the huge land mass. Here his trail temporarily vanishes. His later letters confirm that he travelled north by boat to Seattle, then returned south again to San Francisco. From there, he journeyed east again, and his tale resumes in a long letter written from a steamer in Chesapeake Bay bound for Baltimore.[15]

He had returned from the far west by St Louis, 'a fine and prosperous town, where I had a pleasant day among very kind people', then through south Illinois to Kentucky and Tennessee, stopping for a few hours at Nashville to take up some introductions. In Georgia, he stopped in Atlanta, then came through the Carolinas to Virginia.

Higginson and Holmes had urged Bryce to visit Richmond, the Confederate capital during the Civil War, where both of the Bostonian Yankees had fought for the Union cause. Bryce knew of the heroism shown by the armies of both sides when Richmond withstood Grant's assaults before the final defeat of the Confederacy, and he stood in thought on the spot where the Confederate Congress had met. 'I mused over human delusions and the changes in this transitory life', he wrote. The tragedy was still fresh in the minds of many to whom he talked in the South. For some the war was not over; it was neither won nor lost: it would continue in men's hearts. For others, there was a genuine wish to put the tragedy in the past where it belonged, and to build a new future.

Even so, after his visits to Richmond and Atlanta Bryce realised that the wounds would take many years to heal.[16]

From Richmond Bryce travelled south-east to Hampton, on the coast. He had heard of a remarkable educational institute there called the Hampton Normal and Agricultural Institute. Founded in 1868 by Samuel Chapman Armstrong and the American Missionary Association, the Institute was a co-educational venture for Negroes and Indians, with a teaching staff composed largely of young women from New England ladies' colleges.

Bryce was fascinated by every aspect of the Institute. The students, the teachers, the curriculum and above all the bold, progressive ideas behind the foundation impressed him deeply. Samuel Armstrong submitted generously to Bryce's many questions. The visitor learned of Booker T. Washington's work as a teacher at Hampton and of another new Negro college at Tuskegee in Alabama. Bryce was highly pleased that his detour to the coast had enlarged his American experience in this way.

The next stop was Baltimore. Charles Eliot at Harvard had told Bryce of a new university there called the Johns Hopkins University. Opened in 1876, it was a non-sectarian institution where social studies formed a central part of the degree courses and where graduate studies and research were also strong features. A medical school, soon to become one of America's best, was also part of the foundation. The university's first President was Daniel Coit Gilman, a graduate of Yale who had wide experience of university administration and teaching. He had left the University of California in order to help found Johns Hopkins, and the spirit of the new university was eloquently expressed in his inaugural address, which included bold statements for those who were about to begin their studies in a decade already feeling the challenge of Darwinism: 'All sciences are worthy of promotion. . . . Religion has nothing to fear from science and science need not be afraid of religion. Religion claims to interpret the word of God, and science to reveal the laws of God.'[17]

Eliot came down from Harvard to speak at the inauguration of his friend Gilman in 1876, and it was probably Eliot who had prompted an invitation to Bryce to deliver a lecture at the young university in 1881. Bryce accepted with pleasure and, hearing that social and political studies were stressed at the university, he chose a number of appropriate subjects drawn from the British scene. They were the Monarchy, the Houses of Parliament, the Established Church, Land, and the Poor. Suiting his approach to the *genius loci*, he wrote to say.that he would attempt to treat the subjects 'in a scientific spirit'. By this, Bryce meant a spirit 'free from tendentious or party feeling' rather than what the modern political scientist would have in mind. He achieved objectivity on this occasion at least to the extent that a young law graduate came up to him after the lectures to say that he could not decide whether Bryce was a Conservative or a Liberal, though he rather thought a Conservative. From an intellectual point of view this was very cheering, Bryce reflected, 'and indeed the lectures were well received and the room crowded'.[18]

For Bryce the visit to Johns Hopkins was thoroughly stimulating. President Gilman became a personal friend, and Bryce formed two further friendships. One was with Basil Gildersleeve, the professor of Greek, and the other with Herbert Baxter Adams, professor of history, in whose company Bryce was to enjoy many long and fruitful discussions in the years ahead. Before Bryce departed, President Gilman obtained from him a promise that he would make a return visit soon. The pledge was soon honoured, for two years later Bryce was again lecturing at Johns Hopkins and also conducting a graduate seminar on de Tocqueville.

En route to Boston, Bryce stayed at New York with E. L. Godkin. Godkin gave several small dinner parties and introduced Bryce to his friends in the literary circles of New York. Later evidence suggests that Bryce first met two important Americans on these occasions – Henry Villard and Carl Schurz. Villard was a complex character, combining the talents of a railroad tycoon with literary aspirations. Born in Germany in 1835, where his name was Hilgard, he came to America in 1853, changed his name, and became a Civil War correspondent for New York newspapers. Like his friend Horace White in Chicago, he had reported the Lincoln-Douglas debates and was an ardent supporter of Lincoln. This brought Villard into New York Republican circles, but his interest in railroad financing soon absorbed his considerable energies. By 1881 he had gained a controlling interest in the Northern Pacific Railroad and was already pushing on with his dream of linking eastern America to the Pacific by the great northern route. This was to be his greatest achievement but also his greatest financial disaster. In 1881, however, his immediate attention was occupied with his newspaper dealings in New York City, where he had advanced from reporter to proprietor.[19]

Villard's financial activities had enabled him to gain control of the New York *Evening Post*, and he extended his empire further by securing a controlling interest in the *Nation* in 1881. Godkin had agreed to Villard's purchase with mixed feelings. Henceforth the *Nation* became a weekly edition of the *Post*, and some felt that a loss of identity was involved. The editor-in-chief of the new organisation was Carl Schurz, like Villard a German émigré. Schurz had fled his native country following his part in the revolutionary risings of 1848–9. After a distinguished Civil War record for the Northern cause, Schurz was successively a United States Senator for Missouri and Secretary of the Interior from 1877 to 1881. He was now the leading German American in the country, and his word was still influential in high places.[20]

Godkin's fears for his own loss of prestige under Carl Schurz, or of interference by Villard, were not well founded. Schurz relinquished his editorship in 1883 and Godkin resumed as editor-in-chief. Villard created a trust for both the *Post* and the *Nation* and formally gave up control over their editorial policies.[21]

These three men, Villard, Godkin and Schurz, combined a knowledge of American politics and affairs which few journalist triumvirates in the country could match. In future years Bryce would often turn to each of these men for an estimate of political, social or economic developments in the United States. He knew that by placing the views of one against those of the other (for Godkin did not agree with Villard and Schurz on some issues) interesting perspectives on American affairs could be gained. And when the fruits of Prussian militarism cast their first shadows not only over Europe but over America, Villard was a valuable informant on the state of opinion in Germany as well as the United States, for he frequently visited Berlin in the 1880s and 1890s. By that time Bryce was a member of Gladstone's Cabinet, and his contacts with Villard and Schurz were not without point.[22]

This background to Godkin's pleasant dinner parties in Bryce's honour as he rested in New York in 1881 is worth noting, for these men not only provided information, but also helped to shape Bryce's views, and thus his interpretations of American politics. Bryce's sympathies leaned towards the Republican party because among its ranks he found highly intelligent, articulate men – many of them, like himself, drawn from the professions. As far as the Democratic party was concerned, the moralistic Presbyterian in James Bryce never completely recovered from the scenes he witnessed among the crude spoilsmen at Rochester in 1870. Bryce wanted to place politics on a higher plane than sordid place-seeking. This gave him a natural sympathy with men like Carl Schurz and the great Civil Service reformer George William Curtis, another of Godkin's associates.

On the other hand it would be unfair to suggest that Bryce merely accepted all that Godkin told him of the iniquities of the New York Democrats. Godkin was a very conservative creature. His contemporaries said that he approved of nothing since the birth of Christ. There were also perhaps deeper, more irrational reasons for his hatred of Tammany, dominated as it was by immigrant Catholic Irishmen, for Godkin was the son of an English Protestant minister and his boyhood in Ireland was spent in the bookish atmosphere of a parsonage. The poor peasants driven to emigrate to the United States as a means of survival in the 1840s and 1850s had nothing in common socially, intellectually or morally with a respectable middle-class editor in New York City.

Bryce realised that if he was to understand America he must keep his eyes and ears open, and not close his mind to facts or political developments which he found unpalatable. When the Republican party split in 1884 over the nomination of the unsavoury James Blaine, Bryce tended to take the side of men like Godkin, Schurz, and George William Curtis. To this extent, Bryce sympathised with the Mugwumps of New York and Massachusetts, the men who put principle above party in refusing to accept the nomination of Blaine as the Republican Presidential candidate. On the other hand, Bryce continued to correspond with Theodore Roosevelt and, later, with Henry Cabot Lodge – both Blaine supporters – on the state of the Republican party, and he respected their views. Bryce would certainly have supported the Democratic nominee Grover Cleveland if he had voted in the United States in 1884. The important point is that Bryce was not against the Democratic party but merely against its worst elements, the machine politicians in the cities. Bryce's early distaste for Tammany Democrats in no way hindered one of the most important friendships of his later years in America – with a Princeton scholar and Democratic governor named Woodrow Wilson who became President of the United States at a vital time in world affairs. In fact Bryce had close personal friendships with three successive Presidents – Theodore Roosevelt, William Taft and Woodrow Wilson – and with scores of political leaders from both parties. This is a sufficient measure of his detachment.

After several evenings with Godkin and his friends in New York Bryce went on to Boston. Eliot had arranged for him to lecture there on subjects discussed in their correspondence. Bryce spoke on 'The Eastern Question' now dominant in British and European politics. After placing the subject in its historical setting – the characteristic Bryceian approach – he related it to nineteenth-century problems and European fears of Russia. The informed audiences from Harvard and Boston presented quite a test for any visiting lecturer. 'The audiences are good and singularly attentive,' Bryce reported, 'you can't tell much as to their sentiments from their manner, for they neither laugh nor clap.' Bryce's doubts were resolved later, when Godkin wrote from New York: 'I was in Boston a fortnight ago and heard nothing but enthusiastic eulogy about your lectures. . . . There is a widespread belief that you are really of American origin. . . .'[23]

Between lectures, Bryce was warmly received by a growing circle of friends. Colonel Thomas Higginson gave a dinner party in his honour, where Bryce was happy to find that Bostonians 'don't at all make of one as a member of parliament, but as a professor of civil law at Oxford, and as writer of the Holy Roman Empire. It has astonished me to meet with such a number of people who have read the book and declared themselves indebted to it.'[24]

After staying with the Eliots, Bryce 'scattered himself', as he described it, to others who had asked him to spend one or two days at their homes, including Higginson and the Holmeses, who were now back in Boston. Apart from these pleasant stays with long hours of good talk on politics, education and the law, Bryce had to run the gauntlet of other Boston hostesses who considered it their duty to introduce an eminently eligible bachelor to marriageable young ladies. But Bryce's busy round of visits helped to avoid most of these blandishments, and when his day was not occupied with calls on Charles Eliot Norton and a last visit to Longfellow (for the poet died the following year) he was browsing in the bookstores of Boston and Cambridge.

One other visit made a lasting impression on Bryce before he departed. Bryce heard from Colonel Higginson – now a leading proponent of female emancipation – and from others at Harvard that another ladies' college had been opened since he was last in America. This was Wellesley, only a few miles beyond Cambridge, which had opened in 1875 and was already noted for its excellent scientific laboratories. The curriculum was entirely non-sectarian. Alice Freeman Palmer had recently been appointed President of the college and probably knew Bryce to be one of the founders of Girton College. Bryce was delighted with all that he saw as he stepped briskly about the laboratories and libraries of Wellesley. He wrote enthusiastically to his sister Mary:

... 450 damsels, all taught by women – not a man anywhere on the premises, tho' one or two come to give stray lectures. ... It isn't quite at the same intellectual height as Girton or Newnham, but still is doing capital work. ... Large grounds with a lake, a chapel, museum, library, pictures hung all over the place ... it made one wish to be a girl of 16 to see such provision for enjoyment as well as teaching. ...[25]

Bryce had never doubted the worth and value of higher education for women, but the visit to Wellesley at least provided valuable ammunition for the pitched battles still to be fought in Victorian England wherever the male prejudice against female education and emancipation existed. For as Bryce knew well, such prejudices were not difficult to find in England at this time.

A break of five or six days in the middle of his lecture series at

Boston allowed Bryce to make a quick visit to Washington, D.C. The first session of the Forty-Seventh Congress had just assembled, and Garfield's successor Chester Arthur was now occupying the Presidency.

Bryce did not lack letters of introduction from Harvard and New York if he should need them, though as a Member of Parliament and a professor of law he had little need of them. President Arthur summoned the visitor for a brief audience and Bryce found him 'a rather shrewd, easy going, fat faced, pleasant man of the world, with nothing in the least remarkable about him'.[26] Bryce now visited several members of Congress in order to glean his first detailed impressions of the machinery of the federal legislature. He was eager to place his impressions of the 1870 convention at Rochester against present impressions of the seat of American government. There was a noticeable contrast. Bryce thought many of the senators he met were extremely able and intelligent. The Massachusetts Senators George F. Hoar and Henry L. Dawes received Bryce, and introduced him to their fellow legislators, besides arranging for him to watch debates in the chambers from the visitors' galleries. The session had just begun, but debates on the floor were desultory. Bryce heard Congressmen engage in early exchanges on the great controversy over silver currency, though the really heated debates lay in the future. Other measures were being introduced dealing with the administration of the Indian Reservations in the west. The attendance was thin in both chambers.

On Capitol Hill Garfield's assassination still dominated the talk. Bryce had the sombre experience of seeing the assassin Guiteau at his trial, and he discussed with members of Congress the bitter lessons to be drawn from the assassination. First among these was the need to reform the spoils system – the evil which had prompted Guiteau (soon to be known in every American history book as 'a disappointed office seeker') to assassinate the President. Men like Senator George Pendleton of Ohio were already determined to bring the spoils system of offices to an end and make Civil Service appointments rest on merit and security of tenure, not on the influence of politicians. Others disagreed, arguing that Presidential patronage, if not Senatorial and Congressional patronage, held the

American party system together. There is little need to speculate on Bryce's opinions of the spoils system, but he undoubtedly learned a good deal about Presidential and Congressional politics as he discussed the problem with members of Congress. The organisation of the Congress interested him, and the rules of debate in the chambers; but like many visitors before and since, Bryce discovered that the best way to learn how Congress actually works is to talk with a cross-section of members of Congress in the privacy of their offices.

Bryce made other calls in Washington before returning to Boston to complete his series of lectures. Henry Adams was holding court at his house in Georgetown. Adams had left the Harvard faculty in 1877, weary of teaching, and had chosen to live in Washington to devote himself to writing. Bryce was invited to dinner to meet some of Henry Adams' companions, among them his close friends John Hay and Clarence King. The evening was not altogether a success. The relationship between Henry Adams and James Bryce presents something of a puzzle, and it is clear that they never sought each other's company in future years. Yet Henry Adams was genuinely interested in history and law, two of Bryce's chief preoccupations. At Harvard Adams had taught Anglo-Saxon law and produced a book on the subject in 1876. Despite this, they do not seem to have struck up a friendship. Bryce did not share Adams' utter gloom on the state of American society and politics, and it is possible that the two men divided on this issue. The pseudonymous novel *Democracy* had appeared in 1880 and it may be that Bryce had heard in the intimacy of Harvard gatherings that Henry Adams was the probable author of the harsh satire on politics and democracy. Or again it may be that the introspective sensibilities of the Bostonian pessimist were not attuned to the sharp, inquisitive, yet cheerful mind of the Scottish scholar who dined with him that evening. Perhaps it was no more than a clash of temperaments, but somewhere among these several possible explanations must lie the reason for a lack of rapport between Bryce and Henry Adams. In later years Adams would now and then refer to Bryce with an odd mixture of respect and aloofness. Bryce, for his part, seems to have had no desire to be drafted into Henry Adams' rarefied circle.[27]

With George Bancroft it was another matter. Bancroft was now over eighty and had settled in Washington to round out a long life divided between politics in America and diplomacy in England and Prussia. His ten-volume history of the United States was an acknowledged masterpiece, even though some readers might ponder the influence of Bancroft's years in Prussia, for the work was very much in the tradition of the German 'scientific' school, and couched in a style that was at times somewhat opaque. Bancroft was soon to revise and improve his massive work, and was already the 'father' of American historiography. His learning was indisputable, and he was anxious to meet the author of *The Holy Roman Empire*. From his personal library, Bancroft pulled out books to assist Bryce in his growing desire to understand more of American history and the structure of American society. He loaned to Bryce works on the American Indian, including monograph literature and reports by the Department of the Interior on the geology and ethnology of North America. In the years that followed this visit, Bryce continued to receive from the ageing scholar valuable books and pamphlets on aspects of American history and society. George Bancroft undoubtedly played an early part in Bryce's first formulations of *The American Commonwealth*.[28]

It was time to return to Boston to round off his lectures and then return to duties in London and Oxford. In the haste of his snatched visit to Washington, Bryce had overlooked an important part of his luggage. In an urgent letter to Higginson at Boston he confessed:

It is a disadvantage of the 'cache' system that one never knows where one has left anything. I am at present anxious to discover a notebook of mine which I thought I had brought from Charles Eliot's but can't find in my baggage. It is done up in paper and string, addressed to me in my sister's hand at New York . . . having been posted from London. It contains material for the lecture I have to give on Thursday . . . I also left on your deer horns in the hall two English newspapers, in one of which there were some things I wanted to keep. . . . I am ashamed to betray the weak side of the cache. . . .[29]

We do not know if Bryce received the notes in time, but the lecturer was not likely to be at a loss for ideas or words. The days and evenings passed quickly and pleasantly. When the time came for him to leave Bryce's friends insisted that his next visit should not be long delayed. Bryce was very willing. At the end of his visit he was genuinely beginning to feel more at home in America than in England. A critic would say that Bryce was reacting to the flattering and comfortable embraces of Brahmin society in Boston, and there is some truth in this. But Bryce had now seen parts of another America, in both the west and the south. If he preferred to talk, discuss, occasionally argue with the many gifted men he knew in New England and New York, this did not mean that his sympathies entirely belonged there, or that he was now an imitation Yankee. In 1881, when he returned from his travels in the west to the cities of the east to give his lectures, Bryce wrote to his mother that he found the atmosphere of the cities rather claustrophobic after a time. 'San Francisco or Salt Lake City for me if I settle out here', Bryce remarked. 'One feels a lamentable want of the freedom of the West when one returns to these Atlantic cities. I feel as if a whiff of Pacific air would do one so much good.'[30]

Bryce managed to get more than a whiff of Pacific air only two years later, when he was at San Francisco once again, only to vanish there and reappear in Polynesia, studying the geology, the flora and the people of Hawaii. For the moment, duties awaited him at Parliament in London and at the lectern in Oxford. He sailed home aboard the S.S. *Germanic* on the last day of 1881.

8

1883: Great Northern Pacific

The year 1883 was a landmark for the American engineering industry. In that year the massive structure of Brooklyn Bridge between Manhattan and Brooklyn was completed: no steel bridge in Europe could compare with it in scale. A less obvious, though in every respect a more significant turning-point was reached when Congress authorised the Secretary of the Navy to construct three steel cruisers: the age of the steel navy had arrived. And the same year saw the completion of the great Northern Pacific Railroad. Henry Villard was the financial architect of the huge project and he wished it to be suitably celebrated when the final spike was driven in to link the Atlantic and Pacific coasts of the northern United States.

Impressive ceremonies were planned to take place at the point where the western section of the track would be linked to the vast eastern section reaching from New York across the mid-west to the plains of Montana and northern Idaho. Henry Villard drew up a list of important guests to be invited from Europe, including some German businessmen who had helped to provide the capital. The final guest list numbered more than three hundred. Ministers and ambassadors at Washington, D.C. were included. Villard arranged for three special trains to carry this great caravan across the American continent so that all America, most of Europe and much of the rest of the world should be suitably informed of the achievement.

Five Foreign Ministers were invited from Washington, including the British Ambassador Sackville-West, and the Imperial German Minister Baron von Eisendecher. From Britain, members of the House of Lords and the Commons were invited, including Albert Grey, the future Governor-General of Canada, and James Bryce. In fact Bryce was earlier consulted by Villard on the British guest list.[1]

Among the thirty or more Germans invited were the historian Hermann von Holst, then at Freiburg University, and the Honourable Max Weber, member of the Reichstag and father of the future sociologist. The American guests numbered about two hundred and fifty in all and included ex-President Ulysses Grant, Carl Schurz, E. L. Godkin, Joseph Pulitzer, dozens of more lowly journalists, and of course many members of Congress. It was an impressive gathering that set out in three special trains from New York on 30 August 1883. The full cost was borne by Henry Villard, who may have paused to wonder how many fare-paying passengers would be needed in future years to recoup the costs of the excursion.

Bryce referred to the outing in a letter as a 'stupendous picnic'.[2] He was less interested in the sumptuous entertainment provided by the host en route than in talking to the many journalists, diplomats and politicians on board. The trains stopped at various points on the route to the far north-west and the municipal authorities at major cities made strenuous attempts to outdo each other in the provision of civic receptions, parades, bands and entertainment. Henry Villard had shrewdly included among his guests the mayors of the cities on the route to the west. Carter Harrison from Chicago and Albert Ames, the 'Boss' of Minneapolis, were among the guests. At Minneapolis and St Paul the twin municipalities laid on separate entertainments and the guests were subjected to an orgy of receptions and civic sideshows.

The journey continued across the north-west through Fargo in North Dakota and on to Bismarck, the state capital on the great Missouri River. Villard arranged for a special stop at this predominantly German town and spoke to the assembled townspeople in their native language.[3] Bryce meanwhile walked busily and inquisitively about the town, also using the German tongue for his talks with the townspeople he met.

On 6 September one of the high points of the entertainment was reached. Near Billings in Montana the train stopped near the Crow Indian reservation. On a lush meadow close to the track the guests saw a row of wigwams, with families and children playing about them. By the side of the track a line of braves was drawn up in full costume. There was an unmistakably contrived air about what followed, as Bryce was quick to detect. At first glance the scene was an impressive one – even if the wigwams and the families had clearly been placed in the meadow only temporarily. The Indian braves presented a striking spectacle as Villard's many guests left the train to receive their greetings:

All were in full costume, their faces, bodies, even their hair painted with ochre and other pigments, red, black and yellow. The dresses shewed a strange mixture of calicoes . . . mocassins of deerskin ornamented with beads in pretty patterns, capes of deerskin covered with rows of elk teeth which serve them for a sort of money, and splendid eagles' feathers stuck in their hair, or sewn into skins to make a long train behind them, or a sort of enormous crest reaching from the head all down the back. . . .[4]

The braves executed various dances for the visitors while the squaws chanted together and seven men beat a vast drum resting on the ground. After this the visitors were conducted around and inside some of the wigwams. Bryce observed the inhabitants keenly. 'The faces were more intelligent than I expected and better also in features and shape – much broader than ours, but with good noses, fairly high foreheads, a large and prominent frontal sinus no doubt, but the whole line of the face from forehead to chin straight and vertical.' Their eyes were soft and intelligent, Bryce was also surprised to discover, and among the womenfolk the expressions sweet and gentle. The discovery was something of a shock. His earliest notions of the Indians of America had been different. The present scene 'brought vividly back to me those days of childhood when I used to masquerade as a Red Indian and had my mind as full of Crows and Sioux and Pawnees as now of politics'.[5] But Villard's spectacle dispelled childhood romance. 'There was something singularly pathetic and solemn in the juxtaposition to this encampment of the trains drawn up upon the line, those emblems and agents of the white man's power. . . . There was a strange impassiveness about their faces, a dignified unconsciousness of our presence, a curious silence and immobility of posture which accorded well with the traditional character of the race and seemed to invest them with an additionally pathetic interest.' Bryce had few illusions about the true significance of the scene contrived for the conquering race beside the railroad track.

*James and Marion Bryce
in the 1890's*

*Charles W. Eliot
(1834–1926), President of
Harvard 1869–1909*

*Abbott Lawrence Lowell
(1856–1943), President of
Harvard 1909–1933*

The trains moved on, through Helena, the Montana capital, and so to Lake Pend Oreille in northern Idaho where, near the little township of Sandpoint, the railroads were to be joined in the final ceremony. On Saturday 8 September the proclaimed 'golden spike' was driven in to link the Pacific and Atlantic oceans by the great northern route across America. In fact no golden spike was used, but the ceremonies were suitably ambitious and oratorical. Villard made a flowery speech and the great Sioux warrior Iron Bull, brought from captivity, stood passively among the assembled guests. A band played patriotic airs and a train obligingly symbolised the object of the vast pilgrimage by travelling over the newly joined sections of track. The crowd cheered, the band played on, and the sweating workmen paused from their toil.[6]

From here, the guests were free to continue on one of several expeditions planned by their host – westward to Seattle and Vancouver, or east and south to Yellowstone, a favourite beauty spot where they would find gorges, geysers, molten mud and other natural wonders to attract the eye.

Villard left the party rather hurriedly at this point. Bad news had reached him by telegraph of the disastrous state of his finances. Before the year was out he was bankrupt, though only for a time: within ten years he emerged as president of the General Electric Company. Villard usually had more than one iron in the fire.

During the long days and evenings of the journey from New York Bryce had talked a great deal with several geologists from the Department of the Interior. He discovered that they were commissioned to make reports to the Government on the area of what is now Mount Rainier National Park. Bryce was delighted when the geologists invited him to accompany them on their explorations of the glaciers on the 14,000-foot Mount Tacoma dominating the region south-east of Seattle.

The small party camped at 5,000 feet and Bryce's considerable knowledge of geological formations – the combined fruits of his father's early instruction and his own travels and reading since then – proved useful to the geologists. As he climbed nimbly among the moraines of the several glaciers on the mountain he savoured the crystal air and once again relished the open spaces of the American West. 'The wild simple camp life, in the open air always, with perfect, untouched nature around one, is very delightful, and makes me understand . . . friends in the west who said they found the civilisation of an Eastern city unbearable after it. . . .'[7]

Bryce was keen to climb to the top of the snow-covered peak, but his companions did not care to attempt it and, with little time and limited supplies available, Bryce had to forgo the expedition. Bryce returned to Portland, the Oregon capital, then travelled back east to Montana, and south to Yellowstone, where many of Villard's guests had assembled for the final sight-seeing before the trek to the east again. Bryce walked briskly about the well-worn paths of the areas near the famous geysers, explored one or two gorges, then decided to go west, rather than east with the main party of guests.

Among the English guests was Horace Davey, one of his London barrister friends, who was also a hardy mountaineer. Bryce proposed an expedition south through the mountains and valleys, many of them unsettled and still wilderness, to Ogden in Utah, where he had stopped in 1881. Davey was willing and they set out among the mountains bordering Idaho and Wyoming, much of it still unmapped. They covered many miles of uninhabited country though their exact route remains a mystery, for conditions were not conducive to keeping a journal. When they finally emerged to comparative civilisation at Ogden, near Salt Lake City, Bryce sent a brief post card to London to assure those at home that all was well with him:

Ogden, Utah, Sept. 27/83.
Have just reached this safely after interesting journey . . . 110 miles of desolate mountains and prairie, carrying our provisions and sleeping in tents. The fresh air is so nice that we almost regret returning to civilisation, tho' it was cold at night on those high plateaux, and the sun and dust have made us brown and horribly dirty and wild looking.[8]

After they had washed and rested at a hotel, Davey took the train eastwards to return to New York and then England. Bryce went west to San Francisco. The city was passing through one of the most interesting phases in its colourful history. The great fortunes made in gold from the fabulous Comstock and Mother Lodes were now reflected in the ornate houses adorning Nob Hill. The local press carried many stories of the flamboyant style of life indulged in by the occupants. As the city's population soared, the casinos, bars and brothels of the Barbary Coast flourished for the wealthy. Beyond the sybaritic life of the millionaires of Nob Hill and the excesses of the Barbary Coast another level of existence could be found among the poorer miners and the unemployed, now feeling the full effects of cheap Chinese labour imported by manufacturers and industrialists to keep wages low.[9]

Whether Bryce walked among the bars and brothels of the old Tenderloin on the Barbary Coast is uncertain. As a social investigator he may have strolled there on one of his daily walks, and certainly Bryce liked to make as thorough an examination of a locality as time permitted. But he left no record of any such visits. As a result, there are gaps in his accounts of the American scene. There were places where the Presbyterian professor did not care to linger. Victorian respectability imposed certain limits on the variety of Bryce's experiences.

The most explosive issues in California politics at this time concerned the importation of Chinese labour. Much unemployment had followed the completion of the great railroads of the Southern Pacific and the Santa Fe. The ups and downs of gold mining speculation had created further uncertainties in the economy across many years. Speculators and investors had tempted vast numbers of immigrants from the east and the mid-west with alluring tales of a Garden of Eden beyond the Rocky Mountains. Meanwhile capitalists had imported cheap coolie labour to man the manufacturing and service industries in the booming cities of San Francisco and Los Angeles.

Dennis Kearney had risen as the leader of the Sandlotters – an organised group of working men who, together with the unemployed, would meet on Sunday afternoons on the vacant sand lots which gave the group its name. The Sandlotters' slogan was 'The Chinese Must Go!' and they heard incendiary speeches from their leader, Kearney, who often spoke with a noosed rope in his hand to symbolise his programme. Kearney urged every Sandlotter to 'own a musket and a hundred rounds of ammunition'. The

Chinese were to be forcibly ejected from California. Capitalists opposing the programme were also promised summary treatment by Kearney's followers.

Bryce was intrigued by the reports he had heard of this agitation. Now he could read of it in the local press. Was Kearney another John Bright, or merely a rabble rouser? Bryce talked with local newspaper editors and journalists. Almost all of them were opposed to Kearneyism. Kearney's militant doctrines and inflammatory speeches were dangerous potions in a city which had seen much violence and lawlessness during its history.

From San Francisco Bryce went north by boat up the Pacific coast. He carried with him a bundle of newspapers and some pamphlets which dealt with the growth of the working men's movements in California. The boat trip gave him leisure to study these social documents. Five years later, he devoted a whole chapter of *The American Commonwealth* to Kearneyism and the Sandlotters in California. In it, he agreed that workers' wages had been depressed by the unrestricted import of cheap labour. As for Kearneyism, however, Bryce's deep distrust of violent or revolutionary doctrines made him unsympathetic to its militant programme. When Kearney wrote to Bryce at length to protest at his account, Bryce printed his submission in the next edition of *The American Commonwealth*, but by then Kearney had left the movement he helped to found and was in business himself and well on the road to riches.

The bundle of California newspapers also allowed Bryce once more to indulge in one of his favourite types of social investigation. He carefully studied the advertisement columns in several journals, counting the number of advertisements for various goods and services. This helped to answer many of the questions which went unasked in San Francisco owing to shortage of time. It also provided some of the raw data which Bryce would assemble later in order to question, confirm or qualify his general impressions. Bryce pored over the materials as the steamer took him up the Oregon coast to British Columbia and Canada.

At Victoria, on the southern tip of Vancouver Island, Bryce quickly set about his investigations and inevitably found himself comparing the city with American cities that he had recently visited. Victoria he found 'sadly stagnant compared with the U.S. towns', with a great deal less movement and enterprise about its streets. 'The people don't get up till 8, nobody in the streets till 9, whereas an American street is alive by 7: and when they are up seem to have little to do but talk to one another at the corners. . . .'[10] But he saw Vancouver, across the broad sound, as a place of promise, and with his eye trained on the future of Vancouver and Seattle he remarked: 'Some day, when Oregon and Washington have become rich and populous regions, the great yachting and hunting ground of the Pacific coast will be here.' Today, Seattle and Vancouver boldly and beautifully confirm Bryce's prophecies.

It must have been at Vancouver or Victoria that Bryce suddenly decided to go much farther west. As he later explained in his letters, it seemed a pity to come this far west and not visit Hawaii. He went south to San Francisco and caught the next boat to Honolulu.

There were several things he wished to see in the Hawaiian Islands. He had an ethnologist's interest in the people there, as his carefully kept journal shows. He took notes on their style of living, their habits, dress, and even their speech – copying words and phrases phonetically into his notebook. He was also interested in the geology of the region, and in the flora of the islands. Again, details were carefully set down.[11]

From the island of Oahu, where he had landed at Honolulu, Bryce took a second boat to the island of Hawaii, about 140 miles away, in order to visit the live volcano at Kilauea. Bryce camped alone near the rim of the crater, from where he scrawled a colourful letter to his uncle William, the Edinburgh physician who shared his late brother's interest in geology and botany. Bryce's letter was headed: 'Oct. 17/83 Crater of Kilauea, Hawaii':

. . . I came up to this marvellous volcano which has two merits above all others in the world, that it is always active and that you can see its operations with the greatest ease. . . . Here in the middle of this stupendous crater . . . are lakes of liquid fire, in which fountains are always playing, throwing up waves and . . . [page torn] of lava twenty feet high, with blue hydrogenous flames bursting out, and sulphurous smoke forming a canopy above. . . .[12]

The sight of a red-bearded professor of law scribbling at the rim of the volcano in remote Polynesia, as sulphurous smoke and blue flames belched into the air, was surely a rare vignette, even in the Victorian age. And as if the daytime eruptions were not sufficiently dramatic, Bryce returned on three successive nights, camping out alone, in order to witness the conflagrations lighting the night sky. Bryce commented: 'Between this and the Yellowstone hot springs, I have had quite a volcanic autumn.'[13]

But time was passing. Bryce had engaged to conduct a seminar within a few weeks at Johns Hopkins University thousands of miles away. He returned by way of New Orleans, where he lost his overcoat, and arrived at Baltimore just in time.

Bryce's seminar was given in the graduate division of the faculty of history. Under the direction of Herbert Baxter Adams the historical seminar had already earned a high reputation in American academic circles. Edward Freeman had addressed it during a visit to America in 1881. Thereafter the seminar bore the imprint of his dictum: 'History is past politics and politics is present history.'[14] Some of the most acute minds in the history of American scholarship were nurtured in the Adams seminar. When Bryce delivered his lectures at the seminary in 1883 and then took the chair for discussions his audience included a young graduate from Vermont named John Dewey; the future historian John Franklin Jameson; and a scholarly young lawyer who had left the Bar in order to complete his Ph.D. at the university. His name was Thomas Woodrow Wilson, and Bryce was to meet him in different circumstances thirty years later. Also present was Albert Shaw, a future expert on municipal government in the United States and biographer of Lincoln. Shaw took careful notes at the seminar and preserved these among his papers.[15]

Bryce asked the graduates to examine Tocqueville's interpretation of American democracy as this was set forth in his classic work *Democracy in America*. Bryce first offered his own comments on the work, with high praise for its brilliant and penetrating observations on American democracy. Hardly any modern book deserved to be put on a level with the work, Bryce remarked: it was to be compared only to Aristotle for lucidity, penetration, and for the subtle analysis and balance of mind shown in its pages. However, if scholars were to extend the horizons of knowledge, great works must be subject to critical examination and discussion. This Bryce proposed to do.

The members of the seminar were asked to submit several of Tocqueville's observations and prophecies to critical examination. Among these were the French scholar's suggestion that the tendency of the Union was towards a centrifugal dispersion of powers, and that the federal government would have progressively less power as the states claimed more. Coupled with this was Tocqueville's comment on the strength of small parties in America, and the tendency for political power to be dispersed among them. Bryce questioned both assumptions. The seminar discussed the opposite tendency, now apparent, wherein the federal government was claiming more and more power, whilst in the party system power was tending to reside exclusively in the two major parties.

Tocqueville had also suggested that the rich in America were discontented and detested the Constitution. Bryce questioned this and argued that the assumption was not justified historically. Tocqueville wrote that the doctrine of the 'sovereignty of the people' became irresistible during the Revolution, and that the colonial aristocracy, or 'higher orders' as he termed them, 'submitted without a murmur and without a struggle to an evil that was thenceforth inevitable'.[16] Bryce argued that the aristocratic elements fought the Revolution in the same spirit as that which attended the Declaration of Independence and the final product of the debates at Philadelphia.

American history provides a rich harvest of moot points. In criticising Tocqueville, Bryce hardly allowed for the Tory and Loyalist elements among the colonial merchants during the Revolution. On the other hand, Tocqueville could scarcely argue correctly that men like Jefferson and John Adams were deeply opposed to the sovereignty of the people.

Tocqueville had also suggested that there was a general absence of free thought and free speech in America owing to the 'tyranny of the majority' – that omnipotence of the majority view which circumscribed the views of dissident minorities. Bryce questioned this assumption also, finding in America a 'decent respect' for the opinions of minorities. The pattern of conformity in modern

American culture has seemed to favour Tocqueville's views, and the McCarthy era gave abundant evidence of the 'tyranny of the majority'. Yet, more recently, movements of protest in America have reinforced Bryce's claim that American democracy does indeed preserve the freedom to dissent. The debate illustrates the difficulty of all attempts to generalise about American society and culture.

On a comparative note, Bryce suggested that Tocqueville had underrated the English element in American institutions, chiefly because he did not know England well and assumed it to be more aristocratic in character than it really was. Hence his supposition that the 'aristocratic elements' hated the Constitution.[17] A further fault was Tocqueville's occasional tendency to ingenuity: that is, to find an explanation, a reason, or a solution for every problem discovered by his penetrating intellect. He left nothing unexplained, Bryce observed; there was a marked tendency to push things to logical or simply tidy conclusions. Perhaps, Bryce suggested, the young French scholar did not fully appreciate at that time the vital difference between things worked out on paper and things working out in practice. Practical affairs, especially in political matters, rarely produce neat, tidy, or logical solutions. They often produce untidy, unfinished part-solutions. Historical and political commentaries should at least reflect these tendencies.

We can detect in Bryce's arguments on Tocqueville the classic distinctions between the Anglo-Saxon and the French mind. Bryce accused Tocqueville of a fondness for abstract notions, a preference for the ideal rather than the concrete. Bryce preferred the safe anchorage of facts; he liked to push forth tentatively and empirically from the known facts and distrusted airy generalisations as much as doctrinaire theories in politics. The difference in approach makes Bryce seem more pedestrian, less exciting, less given to the occasional brilliant, intuitive insight when writing on American democracy. But Bryce felt that American democracy, by its nature, did not lend itself to abstract notions, general theories of society, or assumptions not wedded to facts, and that a work reflecting such assumptions might distort rather than illuminate the truth.

There is little doubt that by 1883 Bryce was clearing the ground for his own study of American democracy. In December 1882 Bryce had written to a Boston friend: 'I have formed the hope, if time can be found, of writing . . . perhaps a little book (this between ourselves, for I know what you make in America of Englishmen's books about you), to try to give my countrymen some juster views than they have about the United States. . . .' He added that he was 'often vexed here at the want of comprehension of the true state of things in America. . . .'[18]

The seminar at Johns Hopkins enlisted the assistance of scholarly young Americans in estimating the strengths and weaknesses of Tocqueville's commentary. It also helped to prepare the ground for Bryce: the graduate seminar often provides the forum for a busy professor's *ballons d'essai*. The immediate fruits of the Tocqueville seminar appeared in 1887, when Bryce published an important article on the predictions of Tocqueville in the *Johns Hopkins Studies in History and Political Science*. The article clearly set out Bryce's admiration and respect for Tocqueville.[19] The young graduates who sat with Bryce also gained much from his lectures, as Albert Shaw later affirmed.[20] One further tribute may be mentioned. At the end of November 1883 the young lawyer Thomas Woodrow Wilson wrote to his fiancée: 'Professor Bryce gave his concluding lecture this afternoon. I have enjoyed the course exceedingly. There are a strength and a dash and a mastery about the man which are captivating. He knows both what to say and how to say it.'[21] Bryce 'studied society alive', Woodrow Wilson went on to remark, and he freely confessed an intellectual debt. Thus the Bryce visit to Johns Hopkins in 1883 instituted yet another long and vital friendship.

Throughout the visit President Gilman and his wife provided Bryce with a busy social life. Mrs Gilman deemed it part of her duty to bring the visiting scholar before the unattached young ladies of Baltimore society. She took him to a wedding at an Episcopalian church, perhaps to get him in the correct mood for the introductions which followed. Bryce recorded the event. Characteristically, he took note of the precise length of the wedding service – comparing it to its counterpart in England – and then detachedly observed the reception which followed: 'The bride and bridegroom stood at the top of the drawing room and all the guests came and shook hands. I was introduced to several bridesmaids and other ladies, some of them decidedly pretty, tho' none could be called beautiful. The whole thing was over in an hour and a half, ending, like all American evenings, with oysters and ices. . . .'[22]

Bryce left Baltimore with his celibacy unscathed, though Mrs Gilman wrote to say that she would marry him yet to 'a Baltimore belle' and also urged him to forget British politics, take a post at Johns Hopkins and settle in America.[23] Bryce was attracted to all four propositions, but he never contrived to accomplish any one of them. He was too much in demand in too many places and he gave of himself too liberally.

At Boston once more, Bryce stayed with the Gurneys, the Eliots and the Holmeses for the remainder of his visit. He had also now formed a friendship with William James, who was hard at work in the department of psychology and philosophy in the reformed Harvard. Bryce was interested in, though never committed to, the radical empiricism of James' theory of knowledge as it was finally elaborated. To a considerable degree, Bryce was an old fashioned moralist. He believed in the Christian God and accepted without question the tenets of his faith. For Bryce, Pragmatism, like Transcendentalism, left too many complicated questions unanswered: neither provided any real basis for the moral law. Besides, his prime interests were now political studies in their historical and constitutional framework. Henceforth, he was so intensely busy with these subjects both in their theoretical and more practical forms that he had neither the time nor, to any noticeable degree, the inclination to dwell on new theologies or epistemologies. There was certainly something of the philosopher in Bryce, and one can find many passages in his works where a philosophical bent is evident, though it is always firmly reined. Bryce did not trust speculative enquiry which did not keep fairly close – at times very close – to everyday observation and experiences.

From Boston he made a quick excursion to Salem in Massachusetts to visit Hawthorne's birthplace, was struck by the many historical associations of the old town and felt a passing urge to settle there. At Harvard again, he delved in the university library, burrowed among the bookshops, and then made his farewells to the

Eliots, the Holmeses and the Gurneys. From New York, where he stayed with Godkin, he made another brief visit to Washington, talked once more with Bancroft, then returned to New York to sail home in the first few days of 1884. Again he was reluctant to leave America. From Harvard Bryce wrote to his sister Katherine, who helped to manage his affairs during his absence, that apart from a backlog of work at Westminster and at Oxford, there was another good reason why he was reluctant to take up his duties again. 'The fact is, I have got a lot of matter accumulated about America which must get somehow into print.'[24] Bryce set to work on the magnum opus soon after his return to London.

9

Politics and Letters

Bryce had given up his practice at the Bar in 1882, for he was already heavily engaged in Parliamentary duties. By a natural process, he became one of the principal spokesmen for Gladstone's policy of home rule for Ireland. When the Government of Ireland Bill was introduced, Bryce defended the measure at the despatch box frequently and at length.

There are two views on Bryce as a Parliamentarian. H. A. L. Fisher held that Bryce bored the House of Commons. Of Bryce's style in House of Commons debates Fisher observed:

... In a speech on Irish coercion he would lay down the general principle that no democratic community ever succeeded in governing another democratic community by force. Then he would stop to ask whether the case of Switzerland and the Sonderbund did not constitute an exception to the general rule, and would stray off the main road to explain to the House why the case of the Sonderbund was not apposite. Now it is highly probable that only five per cent of the honourable members had heard of the Sonderbund, and that even to this small minority the case of the Sonderbund had not suggested itself as an exception to the general rule about democracies. And then, when the Sonderbund had been disposed of, they would be asked to consider another possible exception, the case of the northern and southern States of the American union. . . . [1]

Another view of Bryce in the Commons is that he always attracted members into the chamber when he was at the despatch box. In the smoking rooms of the Commons, the word would be passed that Bryce was on his feet, and members would hurry to the chamber.[2] Members knew that James Bryce would always show a mastery of the immediate facts quite apart from his encyclopaedic historical knowledge. It is certainly true that Bryce was given to long and discursive historical disquisitions to make his points, and this sometimes reduced his effectiveness in the House of Commons. Again, he lacked the politician's capacity to exploit the weaknesses of an opponent's case: there was always a concern to get to the truth of the matter by a judicious examination of both – or many – sides of the issue. Hansard contains many instances of this, and an exchange between Bryce and a famous Tory illustrates the point.

In a major speech on the second reading of the Government of Ireland Bill, Bryce argued at some length against the Tory claim that Ireland desperately needed the overlordship and tutelage in government that only Westminster could provide: that self-government was beyond Ireland's capabilities. In order to refute the argument, Bryce provided several historical examples of granting self-government to dependencies or colonies. One of his examples was that of Iceland in relation to Denmark. In 1874, Bryce pointed out, the Danish government conceded legislative independence to the Icelandic Althing, or Parliament. Since that time, things had gone on 'with comparative smoothness and harmony'. Tory members denied that the case of Ireland was in any way analogous to that of Iceland: Ireland's proximity to England produced a geographical entity. Lord Randolph Churchill jumped to his feet to challenge Bryce:

Lord Randolph Churchill (Paddington S.): What is the distance between Iceland and Denmark?

Mr. Bryce: The noble Lord will find that by looking at the map.

Lord Randolph Churchill: Is it 1,000 miles?

Mr. Bryce: About 1,100 miles; I will make the noble Lord a present of another 100 miles. The distance makes no substantial difference to my argument. . . .[3]

Bryce went on serenely to develop his points, pausing only to read to the House a letter from an eminent Icelander to whom he had written for the latest information. The letter observed, among other things, that 'the relations between the two countries are now incomparably more peaceful than they were before 1874, owing to the recognition by the Constitution of the Icelanders as a people capable of taking care of themselves. . . . A return to the bitter disaffection prevailing previous to 1874 or anything like it is now an impossibility. . . .' The same must be done for Ireland, Bryce insisted.[4]

The Irish question continued to dog Bryce's Parliamentary footsteps, both in the Commons and in the Lords, for the next thirty years, even as it followed Gladstone to his grave in 1898. At times during those thirty years, the Irish problem drained Bryce's physical resources, especially when he served as Chief Secretary for Ireland in the Cabinet of 1906. During all these years Bryce knew that England's relations with the United States were partly and at times considerably affected (especially at the time of Congressional and Presidential elections) by the continued failure to find a just and peaceful solution to Ireland's troubles. American suspicions of the colonial demon at work in all British administrations has lasted well into the twentieth century and it has not yet disappeared. Bryce was often reminded of this as he studied the campaign literature and the election returns from the United States. Speeches were designed, often tailored, for Irish American and German American audiences. As events would show, the Irish problem was no longer simply a problem for the British Liberal party and the Irish people: a large proportion of the American electorate felt themselves deeply involved in the fate of Ireland.[5]

Bryce's frequent duties as one of the chief spokesmen for Gladstone's policy on Ireland imposed some delay on the large book he was preparing on American democracy. The work promised to be further delayed when Gladstone appointed Bryce Under-Secretary for Foreign Affairs in January 1886. Now it seemed that the problems of Europe and the Eastern Question would also cross Bryce's desk in ever-increasing volume. However, Gladstone's Government was defeated in July 1886, and though Bryce survived electorally he was now free of Government responsibilities in the Commons. The work on American Democracy progressed. Such a work was badly needed in Victorian England.

Though some scholars and statesmen were well informed of affairs in the new world – men like Sir George Otto Trevelyan and Gladstone, for instance, or Edward Freeman, Leslie Stephen and

Albert Dicey – there was nevertheless considerable general ignorance about post-Civil War, Reconstructed America. Many Members of Parliament and much of the reading public still imagined America as a predominantly rural country – the America of Jefferson's arcadian dreams, or at most that of President Jackson's rough frontiersman's cult and a plantation society in the deep South. The expanding industrial America, now increasingly urbanised, was outside the comprehension of large numbers of Englishmen. Lincoln was regarded as the ideal American because he had the unvarnished native wisdom of the humble pioneer, born in a log cabin and somehow propelled by events to become the nation's spokesman for a brief hour. The myths and the general ignorance persisted. In 1885, as Bryce was formulating his study, Dicey remarked to his friend on a recent article in a journal where an English commentator 'has the air of a discoverer when he cites verbatim passages from the Constitution of the U.S.A. . . .'[6]

The prevailing ignorance tended to breed an air of condescension towards America among sophisticated Englishmen. Americans were quick to detect it and resented it intensely. Informed journals in London could still be patronising towards the United States, when they did not assume proprietary airs. In 1883, Andrew White of Cornell wrote to Edward Freeman at Oxford, discussing the Irish problem in British politics and deploring the attitude of *The Times* in exhorting Americans to be loyal to the mother country on this issue. White pointed out that this persistent *de haut en bas* attitude infuriated Americans. He recalled the intense bitterness felt towards *The Times* by many of his colleagues and friends during the Civil War, 'when that journal sent men commissioned to prepare falsehoods regarding everything on the Federal side, holding Lincoln, Seward, and all our leaders up to contempt. . . . This is not likely to be forgotten, as long as anyone who was then able to read shall remain among us. . . .'[7]

Such a letter from the President of Cornell University underlined some further problems that Bryce would encounter in writing a commentary on American democracy. He wished to give a balanced, yet critical account without risking misunderstanding on either side of the Atlantic. Bryce had no intention of simply praising the

127

United States in all its aspects. He knew how worthless such a tract would be. There were many institutions and practices in America – especially in its political life – which Bryce deplored, and he intended to speak his mind.

Further problems were presented by the sheer magnitude of the task. The United States was now so huge, so complex, so swiftly growing and so many-sided a federal republic by comparison with the small nation states of Europe, that to portray all of it in the round was clearly an impossible undertaking. But what should be ignored? Which aspects should be left out completely and which adverted to only briefly in order to present a balanced portrait and analysis of American democracy? Bryce now possessed not only a considerable knowledge of American history and geography, but a fairly wide experience of its institutional life, its universities and schools, its courts of law and judicial system at all levels, its variegated social life, and its highly diverse political institutions at the national, state, and local level. He knew that his problem was not what to include in his commentary, but what to leave out.

In the end, he included what seemed to him essential for a complete understanding in depth of American democracy. The study contained an historical explanation of the sources of American constitutionalism and the political system; a detailed description of the workings of the political system at all levels from the national government to the town meeting; an analysis of the strengths and weaknesses of the system; and a final section examining American social and economic institutions. At the same time, and with scholarly precision, Bryce constantly sought to compare and contrast the Greek, Roman and other European models which had partly inspired American institutions, but which had been transmuted by the American experience.

The result was a work of 116 closely written chapters, with 16 appendices on such topics as the federal constitution, state constitutions, lobbying, political conventions, and the Supreme Court. Nineteen of the chapters were devoted to the diverse social, economic and educational institutions of the United States – including the universities, the position of women, the American Bar, Wall Street, the railroads, and the temper of the west. Throughout,

Bryce's capacity for minute observation was revealed, together with clear, orderly analysis of the strengths and weaknesses of existing institutions.*

When the three-volume work appeared from the press towards the end of 1888, it was reviewed in almost every distinguished journal and newspaper in the English-speaking world, as well as in many continental scholarly journals. It is not possible to give here a complete survey of all the reviews but on balance they amounted to a paean of praise for the author's vast industry, and for a penetrating analysis of American democracy in its historical and contemporary institutional settings. The work was beyond doubt a milestone, just as Tocqueville's great work fifty years earlier had been a milestone.

Gladstone read it with his customary care and wrote to its author: 'It is, I think, a great book. It is an event in the history of the United States, and perhaps in the relations of the two countries.'[8] Freeman, Acton and Dicey added their praises both in reviews and in letters to Bryce. Understandably Bryce was anxious to discover American opinions of the work as soon as it appeared in the United States.

The reviews soon appeared, and after them scores of letters from Bryce's personal friends in America. The congratulations of friends are not necessarily good guides for assessing a scholarly work, but a letter from Theodore Roosevelt to Bryce is worth noting. Roosevelt was a competent judge, as his many essays and reviews and his own historical work on the War of 1812 already testified.[9] Moreover, his voracious reading was combined with active participation in politics in New York and he was not particularly friendly toward England at any time in his life. His chief characteristic was a proud and vigorous Americanism.[10]

Roosevelt and Bryce had met only briefly, and no firm friendship had been cemented, though Roosevelt had consented to read a number of the chapters on American politics in proof and had given the author his comments. Now that he had read the whole book, Roosevelt wrote:

* For a more detailed description of the structure and content of Bryce's *American Commonwealth*, see Appendix I, p. 299.

My dear Mr. Bryce,

You must by this time be tired of hearing your book compared to De Tocqueville's; yet you must allow me one brief allusion to the two together. When I looked over the proofs you sent me I ranked your book and his together; now that I see your book as a whole I feel that the comparison did it great injustice. It has all of Tocqueville's really great merits and has not got, as his book has, two or three serious and damaging faults. No one can help admiring the depth of your insight into our peculiar conditions, and the absolute fairness of your criticisms. . . . [11]

In several passages Bryce had not spared his criticism of aspects of the American political scene, especially the effects of the spoils system. Indeed, throughout the work, Bryce did not disguise his conviction that in America the profession of politics had come to a low ebb, and that radical reforms coupled with more active participation by good citizens was urgently needed.

Among the many reviews which appeared in American journals, one of the most interesting is Woodrow Wilson's. When *The American Commonwealth* appeared, Wilson 'pounced upon it with a kind of passion', one of his biographers records. [12] Wilson had just been appointed professor of political science at Wesleyan University in Connecticut. Few men were better qualified to appraise Bryce's work than the author of a scholarly work on Congressional Government which was already recognised as a classic. [13]

'This is a great work, worthy of heartiest praise,' Woodrow Wilson began his review in the *Political Science Quarterly*. [14] If Mr Bryce's work was possibly inferior to Tocqueville's in the 'illumination of philosophical conceptions', the review continued, this must not be counted a disparagement, for Mr Bryce had set himself an altogether different task. 'De Tocqueville came to America to observe the operation of a principle of government, to seek a well-founded answer to the question: How does democracy work? Mr Bryce, on the other hand, came, and came not once but several times, to observe the concrete phenomena of an institutional development, into which, as he early perceived, abstract political theory can scarcely be said to have entered as a formative force. . . .'

The reviewer went on to examine the work in detail, finding fault with some of Bryce's interpretations, and regretting that the volumes did not contain rather more on the historical bases of American democracy. But Wilson's final remarks convey the overall impression that the work had made on an acute American scholar:

... Mr. Bryce has given us a noble work possessing in high perfection almost every element that should make students of comparative politics esteem it invaluable. If I have regretted that it does not contain more, it has been because of the feeling that the author of *The American Commonwealth*, who has given us a vast deal, might have given us everything.[15]

In another review, given originally as a paper to one of the most illustrious of American learned societies, the professor of Public Administration at the University of Chicago began thus: 'Bryce's "American Commonwealth" is a unique work. It is not only a comprehensive account, at once intelligent and intelligible, of the political institutions of one great nation by a member of another; but it is also the best of all such accounts, either in our own or other literatures.' In the thirty-three pages of review which follow, the Chicago scholar Edmund James found several faults and mistakes of emphasis in the author's wide-ranging analysis, but at the end he returned to his opening statement and observed that 'it would be little short of a miracle' if some mistakes had not crept in: 'It is only remarkable that there are so few. . . .'[16]

Although the scholarly community seized on Bryce's work, the volumes were soon being read in much wider circles. In 1890 Bryce received a letter from an admirer in Indianapolis telling him that the Plymouth Institute in that city was holding courses on American government, attended by many of the townspeople. The text used was *The American Commonwealth*.[17] In the years that followed, Bryce continued to receive further notes or to hear tell of similar occurrences. The enormous demand for the work proved without doubt that it was circulating well beyond the confines of the academy. Translations were made into French, Italian, Spanish, Portuguese, and Russian.[18] Within the universities, of course, its success and popularity was most marked wherever history and government were studied together. Jesse Macy, a professor of political science in Iowa, wrote to Bryce in November 1889 to say that already *The American Commonwealth* '. . . is made the starting point for nearly every discussion on the American government. It seems to me by far the most important book that has been written on our government. I base my opinion more on the profound impression which I know the book to have made upon those who have read it than upon the remarkable chorus of praise with which it was greeted by the reviewers.'[19]

Henceforth in America, Bryce's name was greatly extolled. Many American people began to assume a proprietary claim on his name, where they did not automatically assume he was an American citizen. The cognoscenti invented the term 'Anima naturaliter Americana' to refer to Bryce.[20] As Gladstone had foreseen, the publication of *The American Commonwealth* proved to be an important event in the relations between the two countries.

1888: 'The American Commonwealth'

Bryce liked to remind those who praised his volumes on American democracy that five-sixths of the contents came from conversations with Americans and one-sixth from books. More precisely, a good deal of the factual material and data which went into the work was sent to Bryce by friends in America, following his interrogations and conversations during his American visits.

In some cases, scholars and men in public affairs took the trouble to carry out minor pieces of research to arrive at the correct answers to Bryce's questions or requests for help. Like the young Tocqueville in 1834, therefore, Bryce benefited greatly from the willingness and generosity of busy men who paused from their own tasks to assist an inquisitive European.[1] Bryce duly acknowledged the assistance of these friends and acquaintances in the preface to the work.*

In London and Oxford, Bryce's friends and colleagues had also fertilised his ideas and even helped to shape the work. Among those whose influence can be directly traced were Lord Acton and the Cambridge scholar Henry Sidgwick. Of the two Sidgwick was the greater influence. Born in the same year, 1838, Sidgwick and Bryce had many shared interests and a marked intellectual rapport. The two men corresponded frequently on subjects touching political economy. Sidgwick consulted Bryce for his work *Principles of Political Economy*, published in 1883, and Bryce turned to his Cambridge friend at an early stage when formulating his projected book on American democracy. In 1885 Sidgwick replied thus to his friend's enquiry:

My general view is that we want just now an answer to these questions. How do the political institutions of America work?

* For details of the assistance Bryce received from many eminent Americans, see Appendix II, p. 300.

How far is the theory on which they were constructed realised? So far as it is not realised, what are the causes? How far are the effects bad? How far are the failures in the working due to causes peculiar to the history of the United States or its economic conditions? What is the relation of the peculiar characteristics of U.S. *Politics* to the *social* characteristics? How does the division of functions between Federal Government and State governments work? Are there any great difficulties caused by the multiplicity of State governments as regards development of law or administration of justice? . . .[2]

A glance at the contents of Bryce's completed work shows how important was the influence of Henry Sidgwick in helping to shape it. Sidgwick was a careful and sagacious counsellor over a long period. When Bryce produced a third major work in 1901, *Studies in History and Jurisprudence*, he dedicated it to the memory of his Cambridge friend, who had recently died. In the dedication of the book Bryce freely recorded his debt to Henry Sidgwick, 'with whom I had often discussed the topics it deals with, and in whom I had admired, during an intimate friendship of nearly forty years, a subtle and fertile mind, a character of singular purity and beauty, and an unfailing love of truth'.

The influence of Lord Acton on *The American Commonwealth* is more conjectural. Bryce and Acton encountered each other frequently in Parliament or at the Athenaeum and corresponded with each other on historical matters. When Bryce arranged a meeting of historians in the summer of 1885 to found the *English Historical Review*, Acton was one of the principal advisers, and it was Acton's learned article on the German Schools of History which gave the *Review* an auspicious start.

Acton knew of Bryce's projected work on American democracy as early as 1884, and was soon lending Bryce books from his vast personal library. When Bryce went abroad to take holidays in Switzerland and Austria, Acton invited him to use his library and study at Tegernsee. He assured his younger friend that he looked forward to the finished work 'with more interest than almost any of your future readers, and I shall be very glad when we have an opportunity of again talking it over'.[3]

Bryce did, therefore, discuss his book with Acton, though the precise nature and extent of Acton's influence is difficult to gauge, as it took place in conversations at the Athenaeum or at Bryce's house in London.

Acton reviewed *The American Commonwealth* in the *English Historical Review*.[4] The reviewer gave unstinted praise for the vast industry shown in the work and for its undoubted scholarship, but among the plethora of recondite allusions and the snippets of German, French, Latin and Greek aphorisms with which the great historian sprinkled his review, a note of disappointment appeared. Clearly Acton had hoped for much more on the sources of American constitutionalism. Perhaps Acton had hoped for some extended treatment of the sources of American liberty, as part of the grand theme which occupied him for so many years, but which was never fully to be expounded from his own pen. There was in any case a difference of opinion between Bryce and Acton on the sources of American liberty. Bryce argued that the Revolution was essentially a continuation of the spirit that could be traced through English Common Law back to Magna Carta and even beyond it. For Acton, the American Revolution was a complete break with the past even though he felt that the Declaration of Independence had its origins 'in the forests of Germany'.[5] Döllinger's influence on Acton persisted.[6]

Bryce and Acton did not subsequently agree, though they discussed this difference of interpretation in a friendly fashion.[7] The two men had a profound respect for each other and Acton continued to consult Bryce on matters as various as the duties of the Regius professorship at Cambridge (to which Acton was appointed in 1895), Liberal party politics, the German historians, and American historians who might contribute to Acton's great project, the *Cambridge Modern History*. Bryce, in turn, was always eager to listen to the older man's advice on historical matters, and on the internal problems of the Liberal party.[8]

The considerable amount of help Bryce received from American and from English friends in gathering materials for *The American Commonwealth* naturally affected the content of the work. More significantly, however, its tone was also affected by the willing assistance of many respectable, Protestant, middle-class scholars and reformers.

Two of the most notable chapters were actually written by Americans ardent for reform in politics, though Bryce arranged this especially to prevent the pirating of the work by American publishers, who at that time were not constrained by copyright laws except where the author was an American citizen. Thus Volume I contained a chapter on municipal government in the United States written by Seth Low, the famous reform mayor of Brooklyn, a graduate of Columbia College and later its President. Seth Low's zeal for reform was fully displayed.[9] In Volume II, Professor Frank J. Goodnow, an expert on administrative law and municipal government at Columbia, wrote on 'The Tweed Ring in New York City'.[10] This particular chapter was to have a history of its own in future editions.

Frank Goodnow had not hesitated to describe in detail the enormities of the Tweed Ring during its spoliation of the city treasury. The exposures printed in the *New York Times* in 1871 and further disclosed by a reform administration had brought to light an astonishing amount of graft, corruption and malfeasance in office. Despite this, Frank Goodnow's strictures on one member of the Ring were so extreme as to be libellous. Oakey Hall, Tammany's appointee to fill the mayoralty in 1869, was described by Goodnow in terms which prompted Hall to threaten a libel action against the author of *The American Commonwealth*. This involved Bryce in much expense and tedious correspondence. Many legal complications ensued, owing to Goodnow's position as a contributor to the volume and the status of the evidence referred to in Goodnow's chapter. The affair dragged on for ten years, though Hall never dared to bring a court action. Finally he dropped his threatened suit. Meanwhile, however, the notable chapter on 'The Tweed Ring in New York City' was omitted by Bryce in the second edition of his work. The chapter reappeared later in rather different form, under a different title, from Bryce's own pen.[11]

The Oakey Hall affair underlines the chief bias in Bryce's famous work. One of the weaknesses of *The American Commonwealth* is that it is partly a tract for the times. The many chapters on municipal government, city charters and on politics at the 'grass roots' level – both urban and rural – reflect the issues and concerns of America in the 1880s. That decade, together with the one preceding it, saw the high tide of machine politics in American states and cities. Bryce's preoccupation with these problems was very much in tune with that of educated reformers, the men and women of old immigrant stock who dominated the professions in cities such as New York, Boston and Baltimore, and who were appalled, but also afraid of what the newer immigrants – notably the Irish – had done to corrupt American politics. Their views were understandable when frauds, peculation, bribery – the whole gamut of corrupt practices – were periodically exposed by 'reform' administrations in American cities.[12]

In another sense, however, their views were partial. Even Bryce might have paused longer to wonder why there was an astonishing consistency in the pattern of machine politics which he described in such detail, in cities as widely separated as New York and San Francisco, Minneapolis and Atlanta, Chicago and New Orleans. This pattern of machine domination could not be entirely explained by the schemings of a few dishonest men. There was, equally, a tradition of acquiescence, of apathy even: some corporate guilt embraced the 'good citizens', as they liked to call themselves, as much as the machine politicians. Again, the phoenix-like ability of the urban political machines to rise again and take control of former 'reform' administrations required explanation. Among the important factors were the many positive activities of the machines in providing a crude, yet often efficient welfare system for poor, newly arrived immigrants. A job, a bag of coal, a loan, or 'assistance' before a sympathetic judge (who perhaps owed his own appointment to the machine) were tangible benefits whose meaning and value could be fully appreciated only by an immigrant newly landed in a strange land. If the machine sought, bought, or otherwise required the immigrants' votes at the next election – and took care to see that the political debt was honoured by 'assistance' at the polls – then the machine was acting merely as a broker, even if it was rarely an honest broker.

Bryce's account of the machines was one-sided and unhistorical. He made frequent reference to the efforts of 'good citizens' to oust the machines, whilst those who controlled the machines were invariably 'fellows of the baser sort . . . without a trace of morality'. Bryce's reactions to all that he heard and witnessed at the Rochester

Democratic Convention in 1870 had gone deep – too deep for dispassionate historical and political analysis. In fact Bryce had borrowed, to a considerable extent, the judgments of his genteel friends at Boston and in New England. Modern scholarship has substantially amended the old view of the urban political machines. Indeed, one can argue that, far from being a deviation from the trend of American democracy in the nineteenth century, the machines were very much in tune with its spirit and were simply a stage of development, rather than a distortion of American democracy.[13]

Another criticism of *The American Commonwealth* in its original version must be Bryce's neglect of the South. One searches the chapters of the first edition in vain for any treatment of the social and economic conditions which have rightly claimed so much of the historian's attention from that day to this. Of course, Bryce did not care to write on any subject where he felt his knowledge to be deficient, and it certainly was deficient on the subject of the American South at this time. Neither his travels nor his reading had equipped him to comment on the complexities of Southern history. Nor had he any illusions on the enormous amount of work which would be involved in attempting to unravel the history of slavery and the plantation system up to the Civil War. However, the absence of any chapter on the Reconstruction in the South was less excusable.

It can at least be said that Bryce was acutely conscious of these lacunae in the first edition of his work. In preparing a new edition in 1894, he included two chapters on the Southern states. They were entitled 'The South Since the War', and 'The Present and Future of the Negro'. The first of these chapters was an historical account of the period 1865 to 1877 approximately, with some references to the earlier history of the South. On Southern Reconstruction, Bryce gave no praise to the quality of the post-war Southern legislatures but equally deplored the activities of the 'carpetbaggers' who arrived from the North to further their own interests rather than those of the defeated Southerners or the newly enfranchised Negroes. Following this, a discussion of the relations between the old planter class, the poor whites, and the Negroes led into the chapter on the Negro.[14]

Bryce's views on the Negro were characteristic of liberal opinion at that time. There was first of all sympathy for the Negro's social and political aspirations; but the modern reader will also detect a note of Victorian paternalism in the account. Thus Bryce described the Negro in general as 'by nature affectionate, docile, pliable, submissive. . . . He is seldom cruel, or vindictive, except when spurred by lust.' Bryce noticed other characteristics – the Negro's fondness for music, his simplicity, his ability to work hard for small rewards.[15]

The twentieth-century Negro may find the portrait which emerges somewhat condescending. Yet Bryce was reporting the facts as he observed them; he was not offering any theories on the differences between races. His views also reflect the limitations of ethnological and anthropological studies at that time.

His chief concern in this long and thoughtful chapter on the Negro was to take up the social problem of white dominance over the Negro, together with the immediate political problem of securing the vote and thus, eventually, political and social equality for the Negro. Various proposals were currently being canvassed for securing justice for the Negro, and Bryce examined each in turn. He rejected the suggestion that federal officers backed by federal troops should give protection to Negro voters in the South. Bryce was convinced that coercion was least likely to cause recalcitrant Southern whites to alter their views. He also rejected, however, a proposal that the Fifteenth Amendment to the Federal Constitution be revoked and the states allowed to decide separately the basis of the franchise. Bryce had no illusions about the true intentions of white Southerners who proposed to abolish the Fifteenth Amendment. Nor did he agree that the states should be allowed to determine other suffrage requirements, such as property qualifications or poll taxes.

Bryce was, however, attracted to the idea of a literacy test, and this fact is worth noting for the clue it carries to Bryce's political views. Provided it was justly administered and in no way abused, and always provided that immediate steps were taken to augment – or rather, to commence – the proper education of the American Negro, Bryce regarded a literacy test as the best solution to the problem. To Bryce, the franchise was not a natural right: it should not be automatically conferred. The vote was a precious asset which should be earned, if only to convince the voter that it must be used carefully and thoughtfully. Bryce had already noted the effects of giving the vote to all, irrespective of their literacy or honesty, in the corrupt administrations of many American cities. A suffrage carelessly granted was a suffrage to be carelessly used and possibly abused. The voter had obligations as well as constitutional rights; he should at least know what were the purposes and the possible effects of his voting. Democracy relied upon an educated electorate. It was the old dilemma which John Stuart Mill had failed to resolve.[16]

Bryce's deep commitment to education for its own sake and also as an instrument of democracy prompted his arguments on Negro suffrage. Apparently it did not occur to him that white supremacists could easily abuse literacy tests; that they could delay and frustrate the cause of Negro education by their control of local school systems; that lip service to such proposals cost little; that indeed it would eventually become a convenient method of denying the Negro his political and civil rights.

Yet Bryce certainly recognised the vital importance of positive action to improve the status of the Negro. The lack of social contacts between white and coloured, the frequency of lynchings, and widespread insistence on white dominance in the South all promised future troubles. 'In this situation there lie possibilities of real danger' he warned: social and political equality must be admitted in principle and eventually secured.[17]

In the fourth edition of *The American Commonwealth* Bryce added yet another chapter entitled 'Further reflections on the Negro problem', and repeated the warning, besides drawing attention to the neglected subject of racial antagonism in the Northern cities. Bryce's appeal was to reason and sanity, against the primitive fears among Southern whites (and many of their Northern cousins) that Negro fecundity would soon swamp the white man in North America. Bryce disposed of the argument with census data, showing that the white population was increasing faster than the Negro over the whole Union, and even throughout the South. Bryce was one of the first social scientists to use census data to expose irrational arguments and to destroy a racialist myth: the youthful idealism of the Old Mortality Club and loyalty to Abraham Lincoln's cause never deserted Bryce in his mature years.

In sum, therefore, though *The American Commonwealth* began with important omissions, Bryce corrected many of them in the three editions that followed the first. However, one bias of the work persisted. Historically, Bryce's standpoint was largely that of a highly educated Protestant American living in the 1880s. Added to this were the austere assumptions of a Scottish Presbyterian, who believed in democracy and equality in all things spiritual and temporal, but who at the same time set high standards of conduct for his fellow mortals. Bryce would have acknowledged this, but would have seen little reason to apologise for his viewpoint. He saw nothing wrong in historiography which carried within itself an insistence on high standards of social conduct. He was acutely conscious of the fine line which divides a social order and the rule of law from anarchy and barbarism; of the thin crust which civilisation has imposed on the forces of the jungle. It was this consciousness, as much as any personal moral tone, that caused Bryce to excoriate men like Boss Tweed and all who corrupted the body politic. For Bryce was also a man of broad historical vision, who could see trends, and thus appreciate how soon political institutions can decay through misuse by the few and indifference by the many. This awareness was at the core of *The American Commonwealth*.

The work is too large, too compendious, too densely packed with description, comment and analysis in the 1,400 pages of the first edition in 1888 or the 1,700 pages of the fourth edition in 1910, for any short discussion of its contents to do it full justice. It is easy to detach a chapter here or a section there and submit it to rigorous examination in the light of subsequent research and thus to new historical interpretations and re-interpretations. As Woodrow Wilson stressed in his review, the work deserves to be judged as a whole. Judged as a whole, *The American Commonwealth* remains a rounded and faithful portrait of the strengths and weaknesses of American democracy in all its complex, often contradictory and paradoxical elements.[18]

II

Marriage and Travel

By 1889 Bryce was famous in two continents as a scholar, a traveller and a man of affairs devoted to liberal causes. He was also still a bachelor. Bryce's younger brother Annan was now married and so were most of his friends. The happy domesticity of the Diceys, the Freemans or, across the Atlantic, the Eliots, the Holmeses and the Gilmans, reminded Bryce that he lacked a helpmeet.

After the death of his father in 1877, the need to provide for his mother and to some extent for his two unmarried sisters caused Bryce to put aside thoughts of marriage for some years. But with the long toil on *The American Commonwealth* completed, followed by a recuperative voyage for a holiday with his brother in Burma, Bryce was newly reminded that he had reached his fiftieth year.

During his visits to Manchester in the 1880s Bryce often visited the home of Thomas Ashton, one of Manchester's leading citizens. Thomas Ashton was a Liberal and a Free Trader who used the wealth he earned as a successful merchant and millowner to improve the educational and cultural life of the city. Owens College and later Manchester's Victoria University owed much to his benefactions. He helped to found the Hallé orchestra and bequeathed to the city art gallery a notable collection which bears his name today.

Thomas Ashton's daughter Marion shared her father's devotion to good works and liberal causes. Both at home and on civic occasions she often met her father's friend James Bryce, whose law lectures at Owens College drew large and appreciative audiences. Marion Ashton also possessed beauty, charm and intelligence. In April 1889 her engagement was announced to Professor James Bryce, M.P. They were married in July. It was a perfect match and their married life was one of great felicity.

On her mother's side, Marion was descended from the Gairs, a

New England family of Scottish extraction. In 1826 Samuel Stillman Gair, a merchant banker, returned from Boston to Liverpool, where he raised the family which included Marion's mother.[1] James Bryce was proud of his wife's New England extraction, and lost no time in taking his wife to meet his American friends. Their warm congratulations arrived with every mail. When the engagement was announced Charles Eliot had written from Harvard: 'You have had an eventful year. To issue the best book ever written on a great subject of perennial interest, and to win a wife also within six months is a remarkable combination of achievements. The first makes you famous, the second happy. May the happiness be even more lasting than the fame.'[2]

The opportunity to take Marion to see America came in the summer of 1890. The couple sailed on August 10 for a trip that would take them from New York to Boston, then across most of Canada, back to Chicago, south to Kentucky, and so back to New York.

As they sailed to New York, Bryce recalled his first visit to the new world exactly twenty years earlier. In a letter to his mother he wrote:

So long it seems now since I went out first with Mr Dicey, the year of the great war, we wondering what was happening on the eastern frontier of France and not yet sure that Germany would prove the stronger. What changes! Who expected that Bismarck after 20 years would fall beneath an emperor then a boy of ten. For myself, I didn't think then of parliament, or of writing. Life seemed to stretch illimitably in front.[3]

Now, with his wife by his side, most of the voyage would be spent reading and chatting, Bryce took up Dean Church's essays on Dante and Wordsworth, and also an account of the Celtic legends. But their wish to be left undisturbed was hardly realised, for the distinguished passenger was too well known to the Captain and other voyagers. Bryce was asked to take the chair at a concert in the main saloon. 'Very hot it was', Bryce wrote. 'The singing was not bad – one professional aiding the amateurs: but the comic business was as usual inexpressibly stupid.'[4] One is reminded again of the unbending side to Bryce's character. He was incapable of enjoying the broad humour or risqué banter which could amuse others, and it is inconceivable that he ever told, or heard with enjoyment, a smutty story. Bryce upheld the standards that a devout grandfather had implanted in the family. This puritanical quality in Bryce prevented him from investigating, and thus perhaps understanding more sympathetically, the seamier sides of American life. He wished to elevate the condition of the poor and the un-educated, but never to join in their cruder pleasures. To this extent, it deserves repeating that part of the American experience would always lie beyond his immediate understanding.

The Eliots were at their summer house in Maine. Eliot had hoped Bryce might get across before the summer recess at Harvard in order to accept an honorary LL.D. degree, but this had to be deferred. Eliot's stature had grown with the influence of the uni-versity he had done so much to reform. 'The University keeps gaining force and influence at home and abroad', he informed Bryce in 1889. 'The same mail which brought your welcome note brought two letters from Tokyo, one thanking me for selecting a law professor for the Imperial University, and the other saying that Kentaro Kaneko, Secretary of the Privy Council, who drew the new Constitution for Japan, attributes his success in great measure to the training he received in our law school.'[5] In Boston Bryce heard of a vigorous, expanding and outward-looking Harvard. Eliot's vision was already realised.

In Maine in the late August sunshine of 1890, the Bryces spent a quiet, restful week. The Eliots' summer home was on Mount Desert Island, then an unspoilt retreat. By day, Bryce clambered about the shores, discovering rare flora and lichens in his rambles. Marion Bryce followed where she could, or rested with a book. In the evenings they walked by the sea and relaxed in the unhurried atmosphere of the Eliots' house, where there was little formality and where other friends, mostly scholars, would drop in casually or join them for dinner.

At the end of their week in Maine, the Bryces sailed north to St John in New Brunswick. There they began a train journey across Canada by way of Quebec, Montreal, Ottawa, Winnepeg, and as far as Vancouver on the Pacific coast. Bryce thus completed what he had long wished to do – a journey from coast to coast across the great northern neighbour of the United States. What he saw, noted down and remembered was of some importance twenty years later, when he was involved with intricate diplomacy in Washington as British Ambassador.[6]

Returning from Vancouver, the Bryces left the Canadian Pacific Railroad to join the Northern Pacific across the border in Montana, bringing them south to Yellowstone Park, where Villard had regaled his guests seven years earlier. The park gave them a much needed opportunity to escape the tedium of the railroad cars, and Marion Bryce marvelled at the geysers, the gorges, the waterfalls, and the magnificent views of the mountains which her husband had promised her.

Bryce's old habit of quizzing strangers on trains was now curtailed. Marriage brought an access of respectability, apart from felicity. He was now less free to roam up and down the jolting cars or to seek companions in the smoking car. Hotel life brought him more *ennui* than before, and now that he had passed his fiftieth year, the raw manners of the far west could even irritate him slightly:

On the whole, tourist for tourist, the American seems preferable to the average English sportsman in Scotland, or the average Cook's ticketer in Switz[erland]. I am naturally trying to see how far my former impressions of men and manners were correct: and on the whole, tho' sometimes disposed when one encounters the bluntness or incivility of hotel clerks or table maids anxious to assert their indifference to guests, to modify one's favourable view of republics as schools of breeding; still on the whole I come back to thinking that . . . the level of intelligence is certainly higher than in England or France and though there may be less external polish there is not less kindliness or less willingness to help upon occasion. . . . We are now leaving the mountains, which is always a sad moment for me, to return to the cities of men. . . .[7]

They travelled to Chicago, by way of Montana and St Paul, Minnesota. Eliot had written from Maine to two of his acquaintances in Chicago on Bryce's behalf, and the Bryces were brought into the company of Eugene Field, a whimsical journalist of New England stock who edited a column in the *Chicago Morning News* (renamed the *Chicago Record* in 1890). They also met a group of Chicago bibliophiles who shared Field's serious interest in book collecting. The other new acquaintance was William Mackintire Salter, an Ethical Culture preacher, who had come under the influence of Felix Adler in 1879 and had studied theology at Harvard, Yale and Columbia during an egregious career in and out of the Church.[8]

Bryce was reminded of the extraordinary cultural diversity to be found even in a young city like Chicago. When Eugene Field was not writing a whimsical and satirical column in the *Chicago Record*, or discussing rare finds with fellow bibliophiles, he devoted himself to serious study of his favourite author, Horace, on whom he wrote a minor work. At other times Field was composing poems which today belong to the canon of American literature, even if they did not appeal to a wide audience during his lifetime. Again, when Salter was not examining his soul afresh with the studied introspection that led him from one divinity school to the next in America and Europe, he devoted himself to Nietzsche, of whose writings he had a specialist knowledge.

After talking with these men and their friends, and with other mid-westerners like Robert Collyer and Professor Elliott at the Theological Seminary at Chicago, Bryce could hardly accept the notions of some eastern Americans that Chicago was isolated from the mainstream of American culture. He admired intensely the educational achievements, independent spirit, and the legitimate pride of mid-westerners. To this extent, James Bryce continued to understand America better than many informed Americans.

The Bryces made a quick trip to Grinnell in Iowa, where they met the founder of the community, Josiah Grinnell. Bryce had heard of the co-educational, nonsectarian college for which Grinnell had given land and endowments, and which was also to bear his name some years later. Josiah Grinnell had sacrificed his pastorate in Washington, D.C. by preaching an anti-slavery sermon in 1852, and had forthwith heeded the famous words of Horace Greeley, 'Go west, young man, go west.' Grinnell had worked and prospered in the west, and now the fruits of his labours were present for everyone to see. Bryce counted it a rare privilege to meet the ageing founder of the city and its nonsectarian college: there was, after all, some affinity in the careers of the Reverend Josiah Grinnell and the grandfather of James Bryce. Among the fifteen honorary degrees Bryce was to receive from American universities, few touched him more than his degree from the small college in Iowa which he toured in 1890 in the company of its founder.

From Chicago the Bryces travelled to Toronto to visit Goldwin Smith. Smith, who had married a wealthy Toronto heiress, now made his home in Canada and was applying his polemical gifts to the subject of Canadian-American relations. Smith wanted to see a commercial union between Canada and her great neighbour. Indeed, in the long debate on closer ties and, possibly, a federation of states throughout the North American continent under one Republican form of government, Smith sided with the federalists.

This was a subject on which Bryce could not agree with his friend. They discussed it but could find little common ground. Bryce wrote somewhat sadly to Edward Freeman on Smith's views and the increasing pessimism which now seemed to engulf their old friend. Smith had turned his back on his homeland finally and completely.[9]

From Toronto the Bryces went south to Kentucky in order to observe the fairly rare political phenomenon, historically speaking, of a state constitutional convention. The 1890 convention at Lexington in Kentucky proposed sweeping changes to the state constitution. New articles were designed to introduce the secret ballot, the registration of voters, and amendments to the constitutional revision procedure. The final product of these deliberations was to increase the length of the constitution from 9,000 to 21,000 words. It testified to the patience, and the mental stamina of the delegates.[10]

Bryce heard the debates with keen attention, taking notes for revisions to the appropriate chapters in *The American Commonwealth*. The long speeches and laborious detail of the convention proceedings may have seemed boring to some observers, but to Bryce they were an intriguing witness to the difficult process of formulating democratic institutions. Bryce did not endorse Napoleon's dictum that constitutions should be short and obscure. The constitutional convention at Lexington in 1890 heartened him as much as the party convention at Rochester in 1870 had depressed him.

James and Marion Bryce left Kentucky to go on to the historic town of Richmond in Virginia, where letters of introduction brought them a good deal of Southern hospitality, then on to South Carolina, where Bryce energetically observed various local elections whilst Marion parcelled up the books and pamphlets which always multiplied in her husband's luggage. In South Carolina, Benjamin Tillman was standing for Governor as the Farmer's Alliance candidate against the Old Bourbon Democracy. It was now 29 October and the campaign was at its height. Bryce thus witnessed the groundswell of Southern Populism, but before the elections took place and the Tillman victory was declared, the Bryces had departed. Bryce wished to see the final stages of Congressional mid-term elections fought out in New York, where Tammany was once more in the ascendant.[11]

In New York there was much to discuss with Godkin and Seth Low, who had just been appointed President of Columbia University. New and violent doctrines were in the air. Four years earlier, the Chicago police had used bullets to disperse an anarchists' meeting in Haymarket Square. The strikes of the early 1880s in the railroad and mining industries had featured much violence and bloodshed. Henry George's *Progress and Poverty* had now circulated for a decade. In Europe and America the followers of Marx and Engels were propagating a sanguinary crusade against all the assumptions of nineteenth-century capitalism. The term 'bourgeois' was acquiring fresh connotations. Labour was now organising. At the end of 1886, the American Federation of Labor was formed at Columbus in Ohio by some twenty-five labour groups. Samuel Gompers, the first President of the organisation, was already speaking from strength.

Bryce and Godkin had discussed these matters often enough in their letters across the Atlantic. Each kept the other informed of the state of things in their respective countries: neither saw any easy answer to the challenge which socialist doctrines presented to liberals on both sides of the Atlantic.

As a member of the Liberal party, Bryce was wedded to Free Trade and *laissez faire*. Thus he could never accept the Tariff on the one hand, nor socialist theories on the other. As a genuine liberal he saw the urgent need to improve the condition of the working classes in America as well as in England. He sought this not as a means of forestalling violence and revolution, as some Victorian capitalists did, but because of its indisputable, self-evident rightness. But improvements must come by peaceful and orderly means. Bryce utterly rejected violence as a means of obtaining economic or political ends. This made him a gradualist. Theories of working class revolution were abhorrent to him not because he rejected the aspirations of working men, but because he was convinced that the overturn of the social order would result in instability and the increased likelihood of continued violence. Ordered society necessarily entailed a compact with the past, and one did not have to swallow Burke whole to accept the point.

Bryce rejected Marxist theories of the inevitability of revolution, just as he rejected other speculative theories of history. This general opposition to doctrinaire theories in history or politics tended to spill over into an opposition to theories in the economic sphere. Thus Bryce would not accept that there could be a theory of labour, a theory of wages or a theory of employment. Like his fellow liberals, he clung to *laissez faire* at home and free trade abroad. But the 1890s brought fundamental challenges to the old assumptions. Populism was rumbling in the mid-west.[12]

The Bryces sailed home the day after the close of the poll in New York City. To the dismay of reformers like Seth Low, Tammany had risen again, phoenix-like, from the defeats of the 1870s. The hope that the local elections would also bring a reform administration to the city was dashed; Tammany's hold on the votes of the immigrant poor was demonstrated yet again. New York politics were back in the control of the Irish bosses. Bryce arrived home just in time for the new session of Parliament at Westminster. The Irish troubles dominated the domestic scene.

12

Anglo-American Discord

The connection between Ireland's struggle for independence and Anglo-American relations in the age of imperialism was not self-evident to many Englishmen during these years. Yet there was a connection, and Bryce's close contacts with many Americans, added to his own knowledge of the American political system, constantly reminded him of it. Bryce was corresponding regularly and at length with Godkin, Seth Low, Charles Eliot and Oliver Wendell Holmes during these years. Political scientists and historians in the mid-west were also regular correspondents. Contentious political issues such as Ireland and also election results in the two countries usually prompted an exchange of views and information between Bryce and his American friends.

When Gladstone was defeated over the Irish Land Bill in 1886, Godkin wrote to Bryce: 'I have never known anything short of a great war watched with as much eagerness as this struggle. . . . You must remember that the crisis is of immense interest to Americans because reconciliation of the Irish with England will have a marked effect in American politics. . . .'[1]

Godkin's letter of course reflected his preoccupation with the voting patterns among the immigrants in New York City – principally the Irish and the Germans, but also the newer immigrant groups such as the Italians and Slavs. These groups now represented a very considerable voting power. In metropolitan areas such as New York, Brooklyn and Boston, and increasingly in cities such as Jersey City, New Haven, or Philadelphia, they formed a majority of the votes cast. Thus at the times of Presidential elections every four years, and of the Congressional elections every two years, the urban immigrant vote was now the dominant factor in the populous eastern states.

To most ordinary Americans, Ireland's struggle for independence and home rule closely resembled the struggle of the American colonies more than a century earlier. That struggle had resulted in independence only after a bloody revolutionary war. The differences, in terms of policies, issues and ideas, which informed observers might see between Ireland's struggle and the struggles of the American colonists were not obvious to the immigrant voters of New York, New Jersey, Massachusetts, Ohio or Wisconsin. Ireland's present struggle was seen as a continuation of the old struggle against British colonial rule. Again, the liberating movements of the nineteenth century had prompted hundreds of thousands of Europeans to leave their native land in order to escape persecution or oppression. In this sense, America was certainly the land of the free and the home of the brave. England's denial of political independence to the impoverished, struggling Irish was thus seen as a denial of the most deeply cherished American ideal.[2] Godkin was therefore not guilty of exaggeration in his letter to Bryce in 1886. Ireland's struggle continued to be watched with the closest attention by millions of Americans. At the same time, political leaders, political managers, indeed anyone who wished to influence the vote at election times with the well tried recipe of 'twisting the lion's tail', proved beyond doubt that it was a vote-getter.

There was dramatic evidence for this in the American Presidential elections of 1888. The candidates were Grover Cleveland (the incumbent Democratic President) and Benjamin Harrison for the Republicans. The choice of Harrison, an obscure ex-Senator in law practice in Indiana, made it virtually certain that Cleveland would be returned to power. Cleveland was a popular President who had conscientiously attended to his duties and was untainted by the scandal and corruption identified with previous incumbents – notably the Republican President Ulysses Grant.

The Republicans adopted the Tariff as the main plank of their platform in 1888. The Tariff was a complex issue and ordinary voters were confused by it more than they were attracted to it. Only when the issue was put forward in terms of 'America First', chauvinistic appeals did it begin to earn support, though Harrison was hardly the candidate to personify vigorous, nationalistic appeals of this sort. As the campaign mounted in October, Cleveland's lieutenants felt confident of victory. However, in the closing weeks of the election, the Republicans injected into the campaign the Sackville-West incident.

It was the principal hope of the Republicans in this campaign, as Professor Allan Nevins has shown, to arouse prejudice against Britain and thus against Cleveland's Democratic administration.[3] Cleveland was held to have acted much too leniently, if not supinely, in a current dispute with Britain over fishing rights in North Atlantic waters. Again, Cleveland's opposition to the Tariff was portrayed as an un-American timidity in the face of Britain's sea power and her expanding empire.

As the election campaign developed, a California Republican named George Osgoodby devised a plot to dramatise these charges against Cleveland. Posing under the pseudonym 'Murchison' and purporting to be an Englishman recently naturalised as an American citizen, Osgoodby wrote to Sackville-West, the British Ambassador at Washington, asking for his advice on how to vote in the coming Presidential election. Sackville-West fell into the trap. In a careful, detailed reply, the British Ambassador reviewed the platforms of the two parties and the two candidates for the Presidency. He concluded that Cleveland and the Democrats were most desirous 'of maintaining friendly relations with Britain' and that Cleveland was likely to 'manifest a spirit of conciliation' in dealing with the Atlantic fisheries dispute if he was returned to the Presidency.

The Republicans carefully withheld the letter until the campaign was at its height. When it was released, the press took it up as eagerly as the Republican managers had hoped. The outcry against Sackville-West's interference was immediate and widespread. Cleveland was extremely embarrassed by the affair. When Prime Minister Salisbury refused to recall Sackville-West over the shoddy incident, Cleveland felt compelled to dismiss the Ambassador in order to save face. But it was too late to repair the damage. The publication of the letter had been timed to a nicety. After Sackville-West's dismissal, the leading Republican, John Sherman, stirred his audiences with charges that the Cleveland administration had always been 'pro-British'. Sackville-West had been 'given the shake', Sherman observed to his audiences: 'Now all that remains for you to do is to give Mr Cleveland the shake. . . .'[4]

Cleveland was defeated in the election. It was an amazing upset.

He did manage to retain a plurality of the popular vote, but with greatly reduced margins. He failed to win New York, with its heavy voting power in the Electoral College, and this loss brought his defeat when votes were counted in the College. Thus Benjamin Harrison, one of the least distinguished Presidents in American history, was the victor. As Cleveland's biographer has noted, there was no national decision against Cleveland's Tariff policy in 1888; rather, 'various special factors played a decisive part in swinging the electoral vote against him'. The Sackville-West incident, by its shrewd timing, its enormous publicity, and thus its marked effect on the immigrant voters of the populous east coast, was an important factor in Cleveland's defeat in 1888.[5]

The 1888 Presidential election revealed several important tendencies in American domestic politics. Latent but strong feelings against England existed in the electorate. These feelings could easily be aroused at election times, and sections of the American press were ready to dramatise them, not least because of their appeal to readers. The dependence of Presidential candidates on the urban immigrant vote was demonstrated. The particular importance of that vote for a Democratic candidate was also underlined when Cleveland was defeated for the Presidency.

The significance of these factors was impressed on James Bryce as he discussed them with his American friends in the many letters they exchanged. The Sackville-West incident revealed depths of feeling among Americans against England which surprised even Bryce. It dispelled easy assumptions of a natural Anglo-American alliance. It showed that at election times especially, the attitude of Presidential candidates towards England, or towards issues which had a direct bearing on relations with England, were potentially explosive. This lesson was to be learned again in future elections. Indeed, the next occasion came only a few years later.

In 1892, Cleveland regained the Presidency when the nation was in a more temperate mood and could judge the abilities of the two candidates and the policies they represented. During the following three years, however, the Venezuela incident erupted in Anglo-American relations. In 1895, with a Presidential election year once more approaching, the crisis came to a head.

Britain's dispute with Venezuela over the exact boundary line between British Guiana and Venezuela had simmered for years. Venezuela had broken off diplomatic relations with Britain in 1887. The United States offer to arbitrate was repeatedly refused by the British Government. By 1894, even the patient Cleveland was irritated by Britain's continued refusal to accept the good offices of the United States. Stripped of diplomatic niceties, Britain was saying that Venezuela was none of the American government's business. Feelings grew sharp in the United States in 1895. The Republicans could once more make capital out of Cleveland's apparent reluctance to force the matter. In June 1895, Henry Cabot Lodge wrote an article in the influential *North American Review* under the title 'England, Venezuela and the Monroe Doctrine'. The article can be regarded in retrospect as an important turning-point in the history of the Monroe Doctrine.[6]

Cabot Lodge first traced what he termed a number of territorial 'aggressions' by England in the history of Venezuela. With the aid of a somewhat obscure map, Cabot Lodge argued that England had been guilty of a gradual encroachment on Venezuelan territory, with the undoubted aim of taking over the Orinoco River and the rich mining districts to which it gave access. The article progressed from pugnacious phrasing to straightforward bellicosity:

All that England has done has been a direct violation of the Monroe Doctrine, and she has increased and quickened her aggressions in proportion as the United States have appeared indifferent. The time has come for decisive action. . . . If Great Britain can do this with impunity, France and Germany will do it also. These powers have already seized the islands of the Pacific and parcelled out Africa. . . . The American people . . . are ready to fight to maintain the Monroe Doctrine and their rightful supremacy in the Western hemisphere. . . .[7]

Senators and Congressmen in both parties could read such an article with great relish. President Cleveland once more faced the charge of abject submission before England. He was challenged to act.

What followed has been fully recorded and documented by diplomatic historians. In July, Cleveland's Secretary of State Olney despatched a surprisingly bellicose note calling on England to accept arbitration under American auspices in the Venezuela dispute. The final wording by Olney was slightly more belligerent than Cleveland's agreed draft, and may have contributed to the long delay in the reply from London. Olney's note contained the famous sentence: 'Today the United States is practically sovereign on this continent, and its fiat is law upon the subjects to which it confines its interposition.'[8]

Salisbury's Conservative government had come to power only in July, following the defeat of Rosebery's Liberal government. Gladstone had retired in the previous year. Salisbury's reply was delayed for more than four months, despite repeated requests from Olney and representations from Bayard, the American Ambassador in London. As it happened, Salisbury's attention was taken up with the Eastern Question, whilst events in South Africa also gave him much to think about during the late summer of 1895.

Olney had made it clear that the British reply was needed in time for President Cleveland's Address to Congress at the beginning of the new session in early December. Salisbury's reply arrived a week too late: the British Foreign Office had mistaken the dates of the Congressional terms. Thus Cleveland had received no reply to the July note when he spoke to Congress. He insisted on the applicability of the Monroe Doctrine and again called for arbitration of the dispute – this time in even more decisive terms.

When Salisbury's two notes were finally received, they contained a firm though cautious insistence that arbitration was not appropriate to the present dispute. The notes also argued – again in careful, precise, and pacific language – that the Monroe Doctrine could not be applied to the Venezuelan dispute. To seek to apply the Doctrine as Olney had done implied a 'novel prerogative' on the part of the United States.[9]

Cleveland's famous message of December 1895 followed ten days later. Its language was unmistakably belligerent. England was warned that the United States would now proceed unilaterally to discover the exact merits of the opposing claims. With the agreement of Congress, a commission would be set up; eminent adjudicators would investigate and report on the territorial claims.

This was a 'take it or leave it' posture by Cleveland. A closing passage in his message observed: 'In making these recommendations, I am fully alive to the responsibility incurred, keenly realising all the consequences that may follow.' Congress overwhelmingly endorsed the President's proposal. Intense diplomatic activity followed. Thomas Bayard, the American Ambassador in London, and Paunceforte, the British Ambassador in Washington, sought a detente, but it soon became clear that Cleveland and Olney would not yield.

In the autumn of 1895 James Bryce was on a long visit to South Africa. He did not return until the end of December, by which time jingoist feelings were much in evidence, both at London and Washington. He quickly learned of the developments which had led to Cleveland's message of 17 December. The tone of the President's message surprised him, and Bryce wrote immediately to Godkin to inquire what he knew. Godkin had followed the controversy closely and wrote in confidence to Bryce, telling him that Cleveland's bellicose stand had been prompted partly by the need to steal the thunder of the jingoists in Congress. Republicans had repeatedly accused the President of feebleness abroad and of continued submission before England's expansionist policies. Thus, Godkin went on, when Cleveland heard that Republicans in the House of Representatives were about to introduce a resolution aimed at forcing Cleveland's hand in Venezuela, he 'determined to be beforehand with them and steal their thunder. As a political move it was most effective, for they rallied to him promptly. . . .'[10]

Once more then, American party politics had produced international repercussions. But Bryce's attention was particularly caught by what Godkin went on to observe:

Now let me say something more, *which you will not quote*. The opponents of Jingoism and of Cleveland's performance are the businessmen, clergy, professors, and the like of the eastern coast. The hatred of England in the west and south-west is rabid, bitter, and ferocious and would welcome war tomorrow. There are a few newspapers here and there . . . which condemn Jingoism, but the great mass are frantically for war. . . . The children have been taught in all the schools for twenty-five years to hate England and to believe that we can thrash her, and that we did so in 1812. They do not know why they should fight England except that she is 'grabbing and insolent'. They resent English contempt for American manners and customs, and envy her greatness and think America ought to make as big a figure in the world as she does. . . .

A generation has come into the field which has, since it left school, been fed on a very vile and silly press. . . . It knows nothing of Europe and knows nothing of any history before 1776. It does not read books at all. It is made perfectly drunk by the knowledge that it is 70,000,000 strong. . . . It has a curious Chinese contempt for the rest of the world and thinks it can do without Europe. . . .

I am sure that all this evil will be encouraged by any sign of weakness on your part. Much of the abuse of you . . . is due to a popular belief that England will not fight. . . . So I am sure a firm policy clothed in conciliatory language, but copious in argument and explanation is the best one for you. . . .[11]

Bryce told Godkin that he would have his remarks conveyed 'to the proper quarter . . . of course, without mentioning my authority. . . .'[12]

Bryce also wrote to Theodore Roosevelt, the influential friend of Cabot Lodge and now rising fast in the Republican party. In his letter he drew attention to the fact that whereas all reports spoke of a jingoistic war fever in the United States, no such feeling existed in Britain. Bryce wrote:

I confess myself astonished at four things:

(1) The apparent existence of ill-will towards Britain in a large part of your population. What in the world is the reason? There is nothing but friendliness on this side.

(2) The notion that we want to interfere with American rights or with the balance of power in the New World. Nothing further from people's minds here. Our hands are more than sufficiently full elsewhere.

(3) The sympathy with a corrupt military tyranny like that of Venezuela, a government which our Foreign Office has found it not possible to deal with. . . .

(4) The total want of all ordinary diplomatic courtesy and decorum shown by Cleveland and the State Department. . . .

As to the Monroe Doctrine, I have never been able to see how it applies at all to such a case as this: if the U.S. are going to assume a protectorate over all Central and South America . . . that is another matter. Then all countries will know whom they have to deal with. But the U.S. has not done so – and certainly that is not the Monroe Doctrine. – This by the way, however. The subject is too big for a letter. . . .[13]

This was plain speaking from a friend. Bryce and Roosevelt had exchanged many letters during Roosevelt's six years as a Civil Service Commissioner in Washington, though none on matters as delicate as the present one. In the same letter, Bryce went on: 'I should like immensely to come over and talk about 1,000 things with you. . . . But you really must not go to war with us – for how then should we be able to come and go and have our talks?'

Bryce was writing to Henry Villard at the same time. Again he stressed in Britain the complete absence of any unfriendly feeling against the Americans. '. . . So we are astonished at all this fury, especially over a trumpery question which not one man in ten in the House of Commons has heard of, and which does not touch any material interests the U.S. have. The idea of "making the Caribbean an English Lake" (according to Lodge) is quite a novelty to us. . . .'[14] Bryce was also in touch with Carl Schurz and Seth Low. Other letters went from Bryce to his friends at Harvard, Cornell, and Baltimore. Then he sat down and swiftly wrote an article for the *North American Review* to take up the subject that Cabot Lodge had introduced in his article six months earlier. The editor printed it promptly in the February 1896 issue of the journal. At this time, few American journals carried the weight of the *Review*: no journal circulated among a more influential readership.[15]

Under the heading 'The Anglo-American Imbroglio', Bryce's article set out to convey the British feeling on the Venezuelan dispute.[16] After first calling for a calmer and more peaceful spirit of compromise and negotiation, Bryce pointed out that in Britain not one man in ten thousand knew anything whatever of Venezuela. This was not to deny its importance in principle, but merely to place the matter in perspective if, as some voices in America seemed to be saying, the matter was about to become the *casus belli* of a major war. An honourable way out must be found which would not require submission or capitulation by one nation or the other. This was the dominant theme of the article.

Bryce spoke candidly to his American friends. He argued that the Monroe Doctrine as it had been known up to the present could not be applied to the Venezuela dispute, and that proponents of such a claim were merely dressing up *Realpolitik* in spurious appeals to history and national honour. 'After reading what has been said by Mr Olney and others in America', Bryce continued, with an obvious reference to Cabot Lodge's article, 'the Monroe Doctrine seems to have no more application to this particular case than a dogma of religion or a proposition in mathematics.' Bryce developed his argument with references to President Monroe's original statements and historical examples of the doctrine since that time. His central point was that the present application of the doctrine was quite different in its implications from the doctrine as it was understood by other nations. The case of American intervention against France in Mexico in 1867, and the American ultimatum to Napoleon III, of which Cabot Lodge had made much in his article, could not be applied to a quarrel between Britain and Venezuela, two sovereign states, in an area far removed from the borders of the United States.

Bryce was frank, but there was a cautious, undogmatic element in his choice of phrases. He made liberal use of expressions such as 'seems to be', 'would appear to be' – the cautious phraseology, in fact, of the scholar who appreciates that truth is rarely the prerogative of one side or the other in a complex dispute involving national honour. Bryce chose his words with extreme care, therefore, having in mind Godkin's timely warning on the war fever still rampant in many areas of the United States. Again, Bryce fully appreciated that Britain's increasing isolation in Europe made it all the more necessary not to bring about her isolation from the United States, especially over such a bagatelle as a swampy tract of land south of the Orinoco River in a distant continent.

For the remainder of his article, Bryce turned from argument to constructive suggestion. There must be no more bellicose statements across the Atlantic; no further use of 'the language of menace'. The first and sole concern of the United States and Britain must be to seek justice. 'Justice first', Bryce stressed: all else was subordinate. A full review of the facts of the case must precede, and not follow, postures by either side. Bryce pointed out that the official American position was formulated merely on the basis of protestations from the Venezuelan authorities. Yet Venezuela was demonstrably a military tyranny with no pretensions to democratic rule. As for Britain, Bryce concluded: 'Everyone desires that an honourable way out of the difficulty be found. If the same temper prevails on the other side of the ocean – as we trust and believe it does – that way will be found.'[17]

The article was sane, pacific, forthright where it argued against the Olney–Cabot Lodge positions, and finally constructive. There can be no doubt that it was read widely in influential circles.

For the British side of the case, of course, formal diplomacy was in the hands of Salisbury and his advisers. Chief among them was the erstwhile Liberal Joseph Chamberlain, whose imperialism was in a rampant mood over the treatment of the 'Uitlanders' in the Boer republics of South Africa. Chamberlain was for as few concessions as possible, but knew that war between the United States and Britain must be avoided at all costs.[18] Emboldened by his current popularity at home, and to some degree by his pride in a Bostonian wife, Chamberlain made a visit to the United States to attempt to intervene personally with Olney. His trip was fruitless. Olney and Cleveland stood firm. Chamberlain even required the special protection of two detectives during his American visit, following a threat of assassination by the Fenian organisation of America.[19]

Cleveland had been infuriated by the delayed British notes of December 1895. Their entire tone, as careful scholars have noted, 'suggested the influence of minds less flexible' than Salisbury's.[20] Yet Salisbury realised that a war with the United States must be avoided at all costs. Cleveland and Olney also knew that Britain was increasingly isolated in Europe, preoccupied with the Eastern Question and Russia, and divided at home over the Irish problem. Cleveland could afford to stand firm. In the end, Salisbury climbed down, and ensured that the Foreign Office co-operated with the American investigatory commission by supplying all the necessary documents, maps and records from official sources.

Cleveland's commission began its work early in 1896, chaired by Supreme Court Justice David Brewer. The four members included two of Bryce's old friends: Daniel Gilman of Johns Hopkins and

Andrew White, now a diplomat and recently returned from his post as Ambassador to Russia. The two university ex-presidents were in close touch with others who had supported the move for a thorough investigation of the facts in the dispute between Venezuela and Britain. These included Charles Eliot, Seth Low and Carl Schurz, each of whom had publicly deplored the belligerency of Olney's 1895 note and Cleveland's message.

With the commission at work, assisted by co-operation from the British Foreign Office and, perforce, the Venezuelan authorities, war fever died down in the United States. Diplomatic negotiations continued separately for the setting up of an arbitration tribunal, and by November 1896 agreement was reached. The tribunal was composed of two justices of the Supreme Court and two English jurists. The umpire was to be the Russian jurist F. de Martens. The American investigatory commission set up by Cleveland produced voluminous findings for the guidance of the arbitral tribunal. Daniel Coit Gilman thoroughly examined the claims of Venezuela and Britain with detailed maps and much historical research. Andrew White worked closely with his friend. The investigatory commission finally submitted seventy-five maps and fourteen volumes of evidence to the tribunal.[21] In October 1899, the tribunal declared its decision, which favoured the British case and conceded most of the British claims in the disputed territory.[22]

Cleveland did not profit from his vigorous diplomacy. In 1896 the Democrats nominated William Jennings Bryan as their candidate when the Democrats split over the issue of silver currency. In the November elections the Republican William McKinley won the Presidency. McKinley had promised an even more 'vigorous' foreign policy, which his supporters took to mean high tariffs at home and the annexation of undefended territories abroad. McKinley did not disappoint them. Within twelve months the United States was fully committed to the doctrines of imperialism and expansionism.

13

The Quarrel Contained

Bryce made his fifth extended visit to the United States in August 1897. There were many friends and acquaintances he wished to see for discussions – Godkin, Villard, Carl Schurz, Theodore Roosevelt, and Senator Henry Cabot Lodge. Charles Eliot was at his summer house on Mount Desert Island in Maine and urged Bryce to come to Maine as soon as possible. Daniel Gilman of Johns Hopkins and Seth Low were there, Bryce learned, together with 'many other persons on the island whom you have met at former visits to this country'.[1]

Bryce went to Maine immediately; there was much to discuss, especially with Gilman, who was resting there away from intensive work for the American commission on the Venezuela boundary. Gilman, Eliot and Seth Low jointly deplored the belligerency of Cleveland's and Olney's notes. But Bryce wished to talk of much broader matters than the Venezuela dispute between England and the United States. The dispute had revealed widespread and deep animosities against England. A rash of anti-British articles had appeared in the United States in 1896.[2] Another guest at Mount Desert Island was Charles Kendall Adams, the President of Wisconsin University, who was closely in touch with the state of opinion in the mid-west. Bryce questioned his companions on a number of related topics. What was the strength of anti-British sentiment in the United States? What caused it? What sustained it? How could it be modified or, better still, eradicated? What were the overall aims of American foreign policy?

The scholars who joined Eliot at his home to talk with Bryce spoke frankly. Bryce already knew that the spirit of imperialism was abroad in the United States. It was also entrenched in the Senate. To expansionists like Henry Cabot Lodge and Theodore Roosevelt American imperialism was necessary; Anglo-American understanding merely contingent. The United States might prefer to dispense with all alliances if its power became invincible. There were still good reasons for avoiding 'entangling alliances' with the nation states of Europe. Americans would never wish to be drawn into a major war merely for the purpose of deciding one of Europe's intermittent quarrels. A formal alliance with Britain would certainly reduce America's freedom of decision.

Bryce was opposed to imperialism for many reasons, but chiefly because it increased the likelihood of future wars. He had already witnessed for himself its tendency to bring major powers into collision with each other in the search for colonies. On his trip to South Africa in the autumn of 1895, Bryce had seen the evidence in the Transvaal. The Jameson raid and the Kruger telegram merely confirmed his forebodings. With expenditures on armaments now increasing in Britain and Germany, the possibility of war at some future date was already a real one.

In Bryce's view, the decision of the United States to join in the scramble for colonies was not merely a denial of her history, with the splendid example it provided to the colonialist powers of the old world; it also invited the possibility that she would at some time in some place confront the naval and military might of either Britain or Germany, and possibly other nations too. The Venezuela incident provided a timely warning: Latin America was one possible tinder box. Africa was another. In the Far East, the need for an agreed policy on trade with China was becoming daily more urgent.

The other side of the argument, of course, was that if the United States did not promptly and firmly claim certain 'spheres of interest', she would soon be left behind in what was now a world-wide scramble for markets and dependencies. The remorseless logic of Mahan's writings on the influence of sea power became more plain each year as the British, the German, the French and what remained of the Spanish navies plied between their foreign possessions. As followers of Mahan, Theodore Roosevelt and Henry Cabot Lodge were simply facing brute facts in declaring that if the United States did not promptly stake out its spheres of interest in the Far East, the Pacific archipelagos, and the Caribbean area, then these would soon be claimed by Germany or Britain. Worse, they might be claimed by both in a naval confrontation.

As Bryce's friends correctly predicted, imperialism and expansionism transformed the American role on the international chess board. On the one hand, she was much more likely to be a contestant in rival claims to spheres of interest – especially in the Far East and in the Pacific; on the other hand, she was less likely, at this juncture, to plunge into a firm alliance with any particular power. By the end of 1898, she had gained the Philippines, Guam, and Puerto Rico, and Spain had been defeated resoundingly in the Caribbean. Europe's two strongest powers, Britain and Germany, were increasingly hostile to each other. The population of the United States was over 75 million and rising swiftly. Britain's was 40 million, Germany's 56 million. American steel production was now 10 million tons a year; Britain's was 5 million tons; Germany's not quite 7 million. By 1910 the comparative tonnages were 26 million, 6 million and 14 million. The hard facts of history seemed to favour the United States.

In September 1897 after his talks with Gilman, Seth Low and Charles Eliot in Maine, Bryce made a brief trip to Toronto for a meeting of the British Association. There he talked with Goldwin Smith, growing ever more pessimistic in his declining years. Smith was now a firm proponent of union between the United States and Canada. There was strong sentiment in favour of it in Canada as well as in the United States Senate, he reminded his friend.

Bryce travelled to Washington to seek out Henry Cabot Lodge and Theodore Roosevelt. Bryce knew that both men were under the spell of Mahan's naval doctrines.[3] Lodge later told Roosevelt that he much enjoyed his meeting with Bryce, though it is unlikely that they agreed about imperialism.[4] As for Roosevelt, now Under-Secretary of the Navy, he welcomed Bryce's visit and wrote: 'There are many things about which I wish to talk to you. On questions of foreign policy, both in your country and mine, while I agree with you in the main, I do not agree with you entirely.'[5] Their discussions were forthright yet cordial. Bryce put his case, and argued against the expansionist doctrines which now gripped members of the Senate. Save for a few dissenting voices (among them that of Senator George Hoar of Massachusetts, the New Englander who had shown Bryce around the Congress in 1881 and

1883), the supporters of Henry Cabot Lodge now held the public ear.[6] Roosevelt retained his deep respect for Bryce's opinions, as his published letters make plain. But Roosevelt was more fundamentally convinced by the doctrines of Mahan and the argument that America must secure its spheres of interest before it was too late.

In New York, Bryce talked once more with his other friends – Godkin and Henry Villard. By now he realised that imperialism had taken hold of those controlling American policies. There was little hope of stemming the tide. Bryce visited many more friends on this trip than we have space to record. They included scholars, lawyers, journalists, editors and civil servants. A list of Bryce's American friends would make laborious reading, and no such list could possibly pretend to be complete. His wide circle of American friends included many who had visited or resided in Europe and other parts of the world. From them he gained comprehensive views of the state of American public opinion.

Towards the end of his visit in 1897, Bryce stayed with his old friend Wayne MacVeagh, who had been Attorney General in 1881 and since then American Ambassador in Italy. MacVeagh had just left his Ambassador's post and was about to set up a law practice in Philadelphia. An ardent Civil Service reformer in the 1880s and strong opponent of the old Cameron machine in Pennsylvania politics, MacVeagh was typical of the statesmen with whom Bryce liked to converse when time permitted. With his four years in Italy just ended, MacVeagh was also a valuable informant on events in Europe, as well as the American attitudes towards the European powers. The two friends talked at length.

Bryce could no longer travel anywhere in eastern America without his presence being observed. Fame brought with it some disadvantages. On one occasion in 1894 Bryce wrote urgently to Godkin: 'I have just had two cablegrams from Richmond, Virginia, asking if I have a son in the United States, which makes me fear that a rogue who a year ago was obtaining money from unwary persons as a son of mine must be at his work again.' Godkin promptly printed Bryce's disclaimers in the *Nation*, and other editors followed suit.[7] Although Bryce invariably received friendly treatment in the press during his visits to America, nevertheless newspaper reporters imposed a strain in their constant search for copy and comments. In 1897 Bryce would have preferred to avoid all press reporters, but an enterprising Philadelphia editor despatched a reporter to MacVeagh's home to seek an interview with the famous visitor. Bryce combined courtesy with firm refusal to be drawn. The chief usefulness of the reporter's account is to give us a portrait of Bryce in America as he approached his sixtieth year.

'Great Englishman Observant but Coy', the Philadelphia editor headed the story, and after the usual tributes to Bryce's fame and learning, the reporter's slim gains were recorded:

Mr Bryce is better than of middle height. . . . His face is distinctively that of a man of deep thought and close observation. He wears a full beard, which is now nearly white. His eye is clear and sharp, and his complexion ruddy. When in conversation he looks directly into the eyes of his vis-à-vis, and though he frequently smiles, he gives one the impression of a man accustomed to the serious things of life.

It was evidently not the first opportunity Mr Bryce has had of expressing his opinions through the American newspaper press. He has become accustomed to American reporters and knows how to give the soft answer that turneth away reportorial research. . . .

'No, I should prefer to be excused from speaking on American politics', was his polite response to my request for his opinion.

'But Mr Bryce, I am sure the public would like to know your opinion on the New York mayoralty tangle, for instance. Can't you say a word – ?'

'. . . I must ask to be excused. I made a resolution on coming to America two months ago not to discuss American politics for publication, and as I have adhered to that resolution during the entire summer, I shall not break it on the eve of my departure from your country. . . . It would be equally bad taste for me to discuss my home politics while away from home. . . .'[8]

The reporter gave up the attempt. Bryce returned to his host and their discussions continued privately. In fact Bryce had become increasingly distrustful of sections of the daily press. He deplored the tendency of the new type of newspaper, which men like Joseph Pulitzer and William Randolph Hearst were now promoting, to seek sensational headlines. Undramatic facts were sought with much less zeal. The 'yellow press' was still in its infancy, but it marked a complete departure from the bland newspapers which preceded them. In London, the same phenomenon had appeared. Alfred Harmsworth had brought out the first issue of the *Daily Mail* on 4 May 1896. Its use of headlines, its staccato style and its reliance on sensationalism mirrored the tabloid journalism of New York. When Kennedy Jones, one of the first editors of the *Daily Mail*, was asked, 'What sells newspapers?' he replied, 'The first answer is "War"'.[9] That reply was all of a piece with Randolph Hearst's famous telegram to the illustrator whom he had despatched to Cuba in 1897 to draw pictures of the Spanish atrocities. The artist wired Hearst in New York: 'There is no trouble here. There will be no war.' Hearst replied promptly: 'You furnish the pictures and I'll furnish the war.'[10]

Such remarks did not surprise, though they alarmed and even saddened James Bryce. In his 1896 *North American Review* article on the Venezuela crisis he had remarked of sections of the press on both sides of the Atlantic: 'The newspapers fan every spark of annoyance into a flame and cover violence and misrepresentations with the cloak of patriotism. They are as great a danger to peace in our hemisphere now as the jealousies of kings and queens were in earlier centuries.'[11]

These were strong words, but Bryce was convinced that they fitted the facts. He did not shrink from publicly deploring the sensationalism he observed in many – though happily not all – of the mass circulation newspapers in America and Europe. The connection between sensationalism in the press and jingoism among the electorate seemed to Bryce a direct one. He was convinced that the mass circulation newspapers, acting on a mass electorate near election times, could produce dangerous, even incendiary situations which could have international repercussions.

Yet Bryce also knew that statesmen and leaders gave heed to informed opinion as this was reflected in the more serious journals of opinion. The editors and journalists who produced responsible newspapers such as the *New York Times* or the New York *Evening Post* fully realised that the sensational journalism had its weaknesses: it relied on the ephemeral, the quixotic, the mood of the moment in its daily diet. New headlines and new sensations must replace yesterday's overwritten dramas. In short, there was still a place for thoughtful, measured comment in serious journals, and their influence was much greater than the numerical sum of their readers would suggest. Thus journals such as the *North American Review* and the *Atlantic Monthly* had an even more important role to play in the era of the yellow press. They were read carefully by those in positions of leadership in American society, and indeed the articles were often written by leading statesmen. Soon after he returned from his 1897 trip Bryce was once more engaged in the continuing but now crisis-laden dialogue between the United States and Europe.

Bryce returned from his trip to America in 1897 more than ever convinced that the imperialists and expansionists in the Senate had set the United States on a dangerous course. In December he sent off an article to another influential American journal. This article, on 'The Policy of Annexation for America',[12] flatly opposed expansionism. Bryce declared that such policies were 'a complete departure from the maxims of the founders of the Republic'. The United States could surely have no legitimate interest in territorial expansion – how could she? And how could she hope to administer 'tropical dominions' thousands of miles away, with no historical, religious or even ethnic connection with the American people?

Bryce's New England friends wrote to him praising his article. But they knew as well as he did that with expansionism powerfully installed in the United States Senate, with jingoism in the tabloid press, and thus among large sections of the American electorate, there was little that anti-imperialists could do to stem the tide.

In 1898, the *Atlantic Monthly* published several articles on the subject of America's new place in the world. It was a timely series. By April, the United States was at war with Spain, the American navy was engaged in the first round of naval actions in the Pacific, and troops were mustering for the attack on Cuba.

The series began in May 1898 when the *Atlantic Monthly* published an article by Richard Olney on 'The International Isolation of the United States'.[13] Its tone was a long way removed from the belligerent message of 1895. The retired Secretary of State had progressed considerably in statesmanship since relinquishing the cares of office. Olney first reviewed the extraordinary changes which had come upon the United States since George Washington had counselled the new nation in his farewell address to have as little connection as possible with foreign nations, and no artificial ties with Europe's interests, for 'it is our true policy to steer clear of permanent alliances with any portion of the foreign world . . .'.[14]

Times had changed, observed Olney. The United States was now involved and committed in vital areas well beyond its borders. For good or ill, Washington's counsel was now irrevocably superseded. Yet the world posture of the United States also brought its problems. She could not maintain a policy of protection on the one hand, a colonial and expansionist policy on the other, and at the same time fondly imagine that Washington's advice against 'artificial ties' with other powers, or 'permanent alliances' elsewhere could be followed. 'So far as our foreign relations are concerned', Olney went on, 'the result is that we stand without a friend among the Great Powers of the world, and that we impress them, however unjustly, as a nation of sympathisers and sermonizers and swaggerers . . . not above the sharp practice of accepting the advantages for which we refuse to pay our share of the price. . . .'

The United States must now shake off 'the spell of the Washington legend', for 'isolation that is nothing but a shirking of the responsibilities of high place and great power is simply ignominious'. In these new conditions, the United States must choose an ally or allies. The most sensible, most appropriate ally was undoubtedly England. 'There is a patriotism of race as well as of country', observed Olney in a remarkable phrase. And whereas the 'Anglo-Americans' – in a term he now borrowed – 'have had family quarrels . . . which only the fondest and dearest relations engage in, nevertheless, that they would be found standing together against any alien foe by whom either was menaced with destruction or irreparable calamity, it is not permissible to doubt. . . . In such a community lies the best hope for the future of the human race itself. . . .'[15]

In July 1898 another important article appeared in the *Atlantic Monthly*. The title was 'The essential unity of Britain and America' and the author was James Bryce. It was a subject he had pondered carefully since his long discussions with many Americans on his 1897 trip. The article began:

The editor of The Atlantic Monthly, a magazine which has always sought to treat current questions in a broad and impartial way, asks me to say a few words on a subject which is much in men's minds on both sides of the Atlantic – the underlying unity of the English and American peoples. . . . The sense of unity and sympathy between these two peoples ought in reason and nature always to have existed. It has, in point of fact, existed to a much greater extent than has generally been realised. . . .[16]

Having thus prepared the ground for argument, Bryce plunged into history. He argued that despite some discords and misunderstandings in the past – often inflated by a press given to hyperbole – an affinity of purpose could be detected in the two nations. Each was devoted to the preservation of liberty and freedom of conscience for the individual; in both, the rights of the individual citizen against any arbitrary assumption of power by the State or by its representatives was a prime concern and a central heritage. Bryce drew persuasively on his knowledge of both nations as he developed his argument.

But the article was by no means a pious affirmation of some supposed natural harmony between the two nations. History often makes strange bedfellows among nations. Bryce looked about him and saw a world of big powers – Russia, France, Germany, England and America. It was clear by now that deep suspicions had already developed among these great powers, especially in Europe. France and Russia were formally allied, but merely from self-interest against Germany. Germany and Britain were hostile to each other. 'In this state of facts', Bryce went on, 'England has been forced to look round and consider with which of the four other world powers she has most natural affinity and with which of them there is the least likelihood of any clash of interests. That one is unquestionably the United States.' Bryce set out further arguments carefully and dispassionately. To condense them may be to misrepresent them and certainly fails to do justice to their persuasive force. In sum, however, they amounted to an assertion of the common goals and common aspirations of the United States and Britain. The existence of these common aspirations was demonstrable in the history and thought of the two nations. Bryce supplied the evidence as he moved about the centuries with scholarly competence.

Yet Bryce was also careful to include a hard-headed appeal to national self-interest. 'The alliances of nations are usually based upon interest alone, and last no longer than the cause which has produced them. A coincidence, or at least an absence of any conflict, of interest is the almost indispensable condition of cordial relations.' American and British interests were historically inter-woven and remained fundamentally similar: the defence of liberal and democratic values.

Bryce reminded his readers that Britain herself was now far more of a democracy than in previous decades, and that political control in England, as in the United States, now lay with the common people. Old-fashioned notions of a monarchical society plagued by an entrenched aristocracy simply did not fit a democracy reformed and changed by a spate of reform legislation over many decades.

The article was a model of hard-headed, skilful rhetoric. If its influence cannot be gauged accurately, its subtle persuasiveness is beyond doubt. Bryce was not necessarily creating a change of mind in his American audiences so much as capitalising on a mood of uncertainty in America. It was in a similar spirit that Bryce helped to found the Anglo-American League in London that same year. Bryce felt that America had come to a turning-point. He played his part in striking while the iron was hot.

This special series of articles in the *Atlantic Monthly* had not yet run its course. In October Carl Schurz added his authoritative voice in an article entitled 'The Anglo-American Friendship'.[17] Few first-generation Americans could claim a more distinguished career than Carl Schurz. The reading public knew that his public service reached back to the 1850s, when he took up the anti-slavery cause, campaigned for Lincoln, mercilessly exposed Douglas in a brilliant speech in New York, and then went on to become a chief of staff in the Northern army during the war. Since then, his service as a United States Senator, as a civil service reformer and opponent of the spoils system, as a Republican who excoriated Ulysses Grant, as a Cabinet minister and then as an eminent journalist and commentator – all combined to give his expressed opinions a unique authority. In his article in the *Atlantic Monthly* he exerted all his talents.

The full details of the composition need not detain us. Schurz powerfully reinforced the most telling of Bryce's arguments in his July article and added some of his own. High praise for Bryce as an understanding friend of America was of course a commonplace of American writing at this time: but pointed praise by Carl Schurz had a special distinction. Bryce's realistic mention of the self-interest of nations had clearly had its effect. 'It does not detract from the claim to sincerity of the British friendship, or from its value, that there is this consideration of interest in it', Schurz observed. 'On the contrary, if the interest is a mutual and a well-understood one, so much the better. It will make the friendship all the more natural and durable.' Carl Schurz, like his friend James Bryce, had been in politics long enough to realise that in the affairs of nations charity begins at home. In sum, the October article added one of the most influential voices in the country to that of Olney and that of James Bryce.

The formation of public opinion in a democracy is difficult to trace with exactitude. The articles contributed by Olney, Bryce and Carl Schurz to an esteemed journal possibly did little to alter the thinking of the greater part of the American nation. What can be asserted, however, is that these articles circulated where men of influence, and in most cases men of power, moved and discussed. When ex-Secretary of State Olney – the man who had so delighted the Jingoes in 1896 – joined with Carl Schurz in urging Anglo-American harmony, Bryce allowed himself a little optimism once again.

14

Legacy of Imperialism

Though the Liberal party was out of power in England from 1895 to 1905, Bryce was returned as Liberal member for South Aberdeen during these years. He continued to speak in the Commons for Irish home rule, but with the retirement of Gladstone in 1894 the cause had lost its most illustrious voice in Parliament. The Grand Old Man died in 1898. Bryce was deeply grieved. His friendship with Gladstone and his loyalty to the greatest political figure of the epoch had been unswerving. At dinners at 10 Downing Street and at Bryce's house in Buckingham Gate, the two men had often allowed their minds to roam far beyond the immediate agonies of the Irish troubles. They had often talked of Homer and the Icelandic sagas; of Rome and the medieval world.[1] With other learned men they had formed a small, highly select band of Dante enthusiasts meeting quietly in London to discuss their favourite poet. Now that Gladstone was gone, Bryce was a sadder and, intellectually, a lonelier man.

Bryce was now sixty, yet his physical energies were unflagging. With Marion, he had taken up the new sport of bicycling, and each spring and summer between 1897 and 1900 they could be found pedalling abroad in Normandy, Touraine, or the south of France. In 1898 Bryce bicycled through Weimar and the Black Forest with an old Oxford friend, Edward Bowen. The trip also allowed for a careful look at Bismarck's Germany: Bryce preferred the old Germany of 1863 to Bismarck's creation.

The closing years of the century were also years of literary endeavour. Bryce's journeyings of 1895 resulted in *Travels in South Africa* in 1897. Thereafter he worked hard at his *Studies in History and Jurisprudence*, which was published just before he set off with Marion Bryce on his sixth visit to the new world in 1901. It is worth pausing to consider the intellectual and political perspectives which *Studies in History and Jurisprudence* revealed in the author.

The *Studies* included essays on the American constitution, the new Australian constitution, and those of the two Dutch Republics in South Africa. There was also further analysis of Bryce's distinction between flexible and rigid constitutions and of the action of centripetal and centrifugal forces on political constitutions. Two essays concentrated exclusively on these aspects of politics. The author was preoccupied with the challenges to democratic institutions which Socialist theories had introduced. Bryce could not accept doctrinaire theories of politics but, like other thinkers, he was compelled to recognise the strong challenge of Marxism and international socialism.

The long essay with which the *Studies* began treated the 'Roman Empire and the British Empire in India' and ranged well beyond its title in a discussion of colonialism. The essay plunged immediately into problems posed by 'conquering and ruling powers, acquiring and administering dominions outside the original dwelling-place of their peoples, and impressing upon these dominions their own type of civilisation'.[2] Bryce was also preoccupied with the growing problems of colonialism. The essay on the Roman and British Empires was a vehicle for examining ways of solving – or failing to solve – the problems raised by colonial empire. There was also a remarkable prescience in the author's opening passage on 'the position in which the world finds itself at the beginning of the twentieth century . . .':

Europe – that is to say the five or six races which we call the European branch of mankind – has annexed the rest of the earth. . . . Thus, while the face of the earth is being changed by the application of European science, so it seems likely that within a measurable time European forms of thought and ways of life will come to prevail everywhere, except possibly in China, whose vast population may enable her to resist these solvent influences for several generations. . . .

The disquisition which followed this passage examined at length the problems encountered by the Romans, by other colonial powers and, at a more recent period, by the British in first planting, then administering and maintaining institutions in foreign lands where native religions, native habits and a different structure of society all presented problems for alien rule. The need for a standing army, the need for skilful administrators, the need to raise standards of living and to avoid pressing undue burdens of taxation on the native peoples were lessons which the new colonial powers of the nineteenth century would need to learn, perhaps to their cost. Even so, an experienced colonial power like England might well encounter those problems which spelled the end of the Roman Empire. In India, for example, '. . . when the differences of caste and religion which now separate the peoples of India from one another have begun to disappear, when European civilisation has drawn them together into one people, and European ideas have created a large class of educated and restless natives ill disposed to brook subjection to an alien race, new dangers may threaten the permanence of British power. . . .'[3]

This digression serves to illustrate important aspects of Bryce's thinking at the turn of the century. He was profoundly worried by the tide of events in Europe and Africa, but was equally concerned about imperialism in the United States. In November 1898 (by which time Hawaii, Wake Island and Puerto Rico were annexed) he asked Henry Villard in New York: 'Does the American people see no difficulty in governing tropical regions full of semi-barbarous races by means of its present system of government? Or does it think that that system will be easily changed and adapted to the new conditions? Or is it not thinking much at all about the problem but merely letting itself drift?' In March 1899, Bryce wrote to Godkin: 'The Hawaiian annexation seemed to me to be the turning-point in United States policy. It was the fatal departure which carried all else before it. One can't help blaming Cleveland a little for not having acted more firmly when he came in in 1893. He ought surely to have re-established some sort of native government, as the U.S. authorities had connived at and aided in the revolution which established the utterly illegal government to be found in Hawaii. To leave that government subsisting and clamouring for annexation was almost certainly to bring annexation in the long run.'[4]

Bryce followed the course of American imperialism with the

closest scrutiny, but anti-imperialists could no more arrest the expansionist spirit in the United States than they could turn back the jingoism of the British in 1900. Bryce decided to cross the Atlantic once more and visit another area of colonialism and imperialism. South Africa had shown him some aspects; perhaps Cuba and Jamaica would show others. A visit to Mexico could also be combined, so that he and his wife could examine the archaeological treasures and see the remnants of Spanish culture. Of course, an Atlantic crossing which neglected to include a call on at least some of his American friends was unthinkable to Bryce. More than this, there were further urgent discussions he wanted to take part in, especially with the many intellectuals – most of them his friends – who had gathered at Faneuil Hall in Boston in 1898 to form the Anti-Imperialist League. Bryce had maintained a voluminous correspondence with Eliot, Rhodes, Godkin and Henry Villard on the subject of American imperialism, and he knew that his friends shared his fears.[5]

In September 1901, a few days before the Bryces embarked for Boston, newspapers carried the shocking news of the attempt on President McKinley's life. When the boat reached Boston, the city was in mourning.[6] McKinley had died from the assassin's bullet on 14 September. The Vice-President had succeeded him immediately. Theodore Roosevelt was now in the White House.

Bryce talked at length with Charles Eliot and another Harvard friend, Abbot Lawrence Lowell, a professor of political science who was to be Eliot's successor as President of Harvard. The Bryces also dined in Boston with James Ford Rhodes, the historian, and with other Harvard professors who had gathered at Faneuil Hall to protest at American imperialism in the Far East. But there was little progress to report from the Anti-Imperialist League. The New Englanders were convinced that imperialist policies, even under the guise of the 'Open Door' in the Far East, were a complete denial of America's historic mission and would very likely lead to future wars. But Theodore Roosevelt was now President of the United States. They knew enough of the new President's qualities – he was already dubbed by one of his countrymen as 'that damned cowboy in the White House' – to realise that their hopes had suffered a further setback.

Roosevelt had little time for the Anti-Imperialists. He tended to identify them with the Mugwumps who bolted the Republican ticket in 1884; they were Utopians, living in an ideal world without sin. They cared nothing for martial spirit. Now that he was in the office which he later described as a 'bully pulpit', Roosevelt could afford to ignore them. His friend and intimate Henry Cabot Lodge was on the Senate Foreign Relations Committee and Roosevelt had powerful support in both Houses of Congress.

Although he detested Mugwumps and deplored the Anti-Imperialists in the United States, Roosevelt was still in touch with James Bryce. Learning of their present visit, Roosevelt invited the Bryces to dine with him at the Executive Mansion on their way south to Mexico. The visitors arrived on 1 October to find the youngest President in American history hardly settled into his high office. That evening they dined with the President and his wife.[7] Bryce stated his opinions frankly on the unwisdom of America's recent course of foreign adventures. Roosevelt's views had not changed, but he was a thinking man and he respected intellect. When Bryce was in the United States again three years later, Theodore Roosevelt bade him stay at the White House. By then, the spirit of the age had produced the Russo-Japanese war and Theodore Roosevelt was urgently proposing an international peace conference at the Hague to prevent future wars. Even so, the hero of San Juan Hill had not lost his taste for the just war. This was the essential difference between Theodore Roosevelt and James Bryce. Like his friend Woodrow Wilson, Bryce had a personal horror of bloodshed in any form. For the moment, Roosevelt was in the Presidency: Wilson's turn would come, though not at a propitious time for a man of peace.

From Washington the Bryces travelled south by way of St Louis, where an old friend, Professor Marshall Snow, historian and Latinist, showed them the university of which he was soon to become President. From St Louis, they travelled on through Arkansas to Texas. At the State capital, Austin, the Governor and the President of the University waylaid the train and urged Bryce to give an address at the city. Bryce pleaded the need to conserve his energies on a long, exhausting trip, and they escaped the Texan embrace to complete their journey to Mexico City.[8]

Here they stayed almost a month, visiting the new archaeological excavations in a series of ambitious visits to distant areas. These trips also afforded Bryce a means of judging the social and political order maintained by President Diaz. The President received the famous visitor, and Bryce made a quick estimate of the man and those surrounding him in the short time allotted. In Mexico City he talked with other officials. 'The government is a pure despotism', Bryce confided to Charles Eliot in a letter a few weeks later. Yet it seemed a popular despotism, 'in which everyone contentedly acquiesces, wishing Porfirio Diaz to live for ever.'[9] Diaz had been President since 1877. His 'strong-arm' rule had maintained order, but in 1911 he would be driven into exile: Bryce's judgment erred. Even so, the despotism of the regime and the plight of the peasants had not escaped him.

From Mexico the Bryces crossed to Cuba, where they planned to stay two weeks. Cuba was now a protectorate of the United States: in a fit of idealism, Congress had stopped short of outright annexation after the defeat of Spain. The island was controlled by a military governor, Leonard Wood, Theodore Roosevelt's personal friend and a Rough Rider at San Juan in 1898. The President had provided introductions for the Bryces and the military governor welcomed them personally.

Leonard Wood was a remarkable man. Physically a giant, utterly fearless, in the prime of life, he was a physician as well as a soldier. A graduate of the Harvard Medical School and a trained surgeon, Wood was already modernising the medical and sanitation system of the island, besides introducing schools and laying the groundwork for a judicial system.[10]

In Governor Wood's company Bryce was shown new roads, new houses, drains, the work of medical teams, and the first experiments of agronomists. Marion Bryce was equally interested in the good work and wrote home enthusiastically. Her letters also confirm that James Bryce had recovered his old habits of ceaseless interrogation. Leonard Wood was delighted by the visitors' marked interest.

Bryce wrote to tell Charles Eliot at Harvard how deeply im-

178

pressed he was with the vigorous plans now being prosecuted by Harvard's energetic alumnus in Cuba. Eliot was somewhat surprised himself to find American imperialism introducing positive improvements to the island so soon.[11]

The visit to Cuba had a powerful effect on Bryce's thinking. In Mexico he had observed a backward native population suffering from disease, lack of nourishment, primitive agricultural methods, a general lack of education, and those concomitant fears and superstitions on which the Diaz regime relied for its power. In Cuba, by sharp contrast, these evils were being attacked with the aid of modern science. Thus advanced races could bring new, and more immediately useful gospels to these peoples – medicine, education, economic advance and the rule of law. Already Bryce was piecing together thoughts which would find utterance in his Romanes Lecture at Oxford in the following year.

Leonard Wood and James Bryce were firm friends at the end of this two-week stay. When the time came for them to leave for Jamaica, Wood insisted that the Bryces make the journey in his private yacht. The couple arrived at Kingston in style and stayed with the Governor, Sir Augustus Hemming, at his residence.[12] There was no shortage of comforts and servants. High-ranking British officers were summoned to pay their respects and the Bryces were wined and dined by leading residents on the island. Marion Bryce admitted to some pleasure in the grace and luxury of these homes, the elegance of those who inhabited them, and the patrician ease with which the English residents filled their allotted stations. For her husband, however, the dinners and the conversation were boring affairs. He was reminded of the doleful days and evenings he spent in 1892 at Balmoral Castle as a Liberal Minister in Attendance to the Queen.*

Bryce took what opportunities were offered to inspect the flora of the island and there was an enjoyable excursion to the top of Blue Mountain Peak, 7,400 feet high, where the true beauty of

---

* On that occasion, Bryce had written to Godkin: 'There is a flavour of the servants' hall about living in a place where everything is dominated by a Presence which appears at intervals. She talks intelligently and knows something about a good many things, but has not much penetration (tho' a good deal of shrewdness as regards persons) and no originality nor intellectual distinction. . . .'[13]

the island could be appreciated. The sea, turquoise by the shores, a rich Prussian blue beyond, gave Bryce at least one warm memory of the colony. As for British colonial rule, his eyes had spotted too many shacks and hovels on the outskirts of Kingston, and he had suffered too many stilted conversations on privileged lawns and balconies not to experience some forebodings.

The Bryces sailed at the end of November to arrive at Bristol on 12 December. Parliamentary duties awaited him. On the domestic front in the House of Commons, important legislation was under debate for improving secondary education in England. In 1895 Bryce had served as Chairman of the Royal Commission on Secondary Education in England, and he now took a leading part in the debates. The important 1902 Education Act setting up Local Education Authorities embodied many of the proposals that Bryce had urged for more than a decade.[14]

In the summer of 1902, Bryce gave the Romanes Lecture at Oxford. Some clues to the subject he would select for his address appear in letters to his American friends. In February he asked Eliot: 'Do you know of any ethnologist or physiologist who has scientifically examined the question of the effects of race mixture? One is sometimes told that mixed races are physically inferior to pure races, and apt to die out, i.e. when the races are very different as, e.g. whites and Negroes, or whites and Indians, but I know of no adequate discussion on this point. It is one of great consequence. . . .'[15]

Eliot's wide reading in the sciences was placed at his friend's disposal, though the paucity of literature on these topics was undeniable. Bryce's library contained works on the ethnology of primitive peoples, but no scientific treatise on race mixture. From his shelves Bryce took down Tylor's two volumes on primitive culture, F. L. Hoffman's *Race Traits and Tendencies of the American Negro*, E. F. Thurn's *Among the Indians of Guiana*, and J. T. Short's *North Americans of Antiquity*, the latter inscribed with an affectionate greeting from George Bancroft in 1881. There was also Darwin's *Descent of Man* for a general frame of reference. But these works hardly answered the questions buzzing in Bryce's mind. When he addressed his audience in the Sheldonian on a warm afternoon in June, however, he grasped the nettle. Bryce held forth on 'The Relations of the Advanced and Backward Races of Mankind'.[16]

In the second half of the twentieth century it is difficult to realise that the Victorians honestly believed that racial admixtures could lead to 'inferior' stock. Ethnology and anthropology had still to provide the evidence which was to dispel such views. Since then a good deal of scientific knowledge has come to us from the labours of anthropologists. It is worth noting, however, that despite many professions of ignorance during his lecture, Bryce had something constructive to say in 1902 on the bewildering problem of race relations. This problem would emerge with compelling urgency in the United States of America during the next few decades.

The problem of the contacts between races had been brought 'insistently to the fore' by the marked upsurge in policies of colonial annexation, Bryce declared in his Romanes Lecture. Those policies had resulted in races living side by side, yet quite separately, and with unequal status. Such inequalities must inevitably lead to certain consequences. One might be the destruction of the native people; another might be its absorption in the colonising race; yet another that two peoples might 'continue to dwell together unmixed, each preserving a character of its own. . . .' A fourth possibility was that the two might 'commingle' and produce a common stock.

Bryce argued at some length against the likelihood of the first three possibilities occurring. The spread of knowledge to colonised peoples must continue. The liberal and Christian duty to bring to all mankind the light of learning as well as the blessings of science and human invention could not be evaded. Attempts to do otherwise would lead, through time, to incendiary situations which colonial regimes could not, in the long run, withstand.

Turning to the fourth possibility, the 'commingling' of races, Bryce reminded his audience at some length, and with a wealth of detail, that in fact the whole of human history was one of the mixing of races. Thus any modern aversion to the mixture, for example, of Negro with Teuton, was an unusual exception to a long and continuous human practice. Therefore a prejudice against such mixture had no foundation in reason or experience.

As to arguments about inferior stock, Bryce pointed out that there was no conclusive evidence to support the view. If anything, the evidence was to the contrary. After all, Alexandre Dumas was a mulatto. Again: 'At this moment there is living in the United States the son of a white father and Negro mother, himself born in slavery, who is one of the most remarkable personalities and perhaps the most moving orator in that nation of eighty million. . . .' Booker T. Washington was one of Bryce's American friends. The Negro leader's book *The Future of the American Negro* was despatched to Bryce in 1899 with the author's greeting enclosed.[17] Bryce had not been content merely to read the book: he had thought about the questions it raised.

But Bryce was realistic in his present plea. It was one thing to discuss the irrational basis of racial prejudice: it was quite another to remove it. There was an immediate need for the subject of race mixture to be 'fully investigated by men of science'. In the meantime, however, in any discussions of civil and political rights, 'race and blood should not be made the ground of discrimination'. The Romanes Lecture of 1902 was an eloquent and early contribution to a vital debate of the twentieth century. It was also a courageous denunciation of the vast doctrinal superstructure which Social Darwinism had heaped upon all discussions of race during the previous three decades.[18]

15

1904: Marathon Lecturer

Between 1902 and 1904 Bryce worked quietly with a number of individuals in London to found a sociological society. Bryce dined frequently with the Webbs, where he talked with other visitors, such as Edward Westermarck and L. T. Hobhouse. In April 1904 the first meeting of the British Sociological Society was held in London at the School of Economics and Political Science. Bryce was chairman of the meeting and first President of the Society. In his introductory address he set out the objects of the society and suggested possible avenues of enquiry and research for those who wished to further sociological studies in Britain. Among these, he urged the need for a study of 'the doctrine of heredity in its relations to the various races of mankind'. Sociologists should seek to extend to such studies methods hitherto applied to the physical sciences. There was a need for rigour and sound deductive methods, rather than *a priori* or inductive reasoning.

Bryce was thus developing the plea he had put forward in his Romanes Lecture. The significance of what he now urged is best judged against the long and tortuous discussion pursued in previous decades under the name – or rather the guise – of Social Darwinism. The discussion had proceeded on both sides of the Atlantic, but particularly in the United States it had been mixed with curious, often reactionary racialist doctrines on the survival of the fittest.[1] In the age of imperialism, Darwin's *Origin of Species*, with its notable section on 'The Preservation of Favoured Races in the Struggle for Life', had proved a useful tract for expansionists anxious to bolster their views with a spurious scientism. As Richard Hofstadter reminds us, it did not matter to the expansionists that Darwin was discussing pigeons in the much quoted section, and not human beings. Darwin's *Descent of Man* was also pressed into service by the expansionists. The grosser forms of the doctrine could be found in the utterances of monopolists in the business world. But even Theodore Roosevelt, writing his *Winning of the West* and *The Strenuous Life,* appropriated both Darwinism and Manifest Destiny as pillars to support his brand of Americanism. In the United States Senate, the expansionist Albert Beveridge echoed Roosevelt's writings, whilst John Hay, Secretary of State for McKinley and Roosevelt, added his own speeches to the chorus.[2]

Viewed against this mixed and often muddy intellectual background, Bryce's appeal for genuine scientific enquiry into heredity and ethnology assumes a special importance. At subsequent meetings of the Sociological Society he took a full part in the discussions, though few of its members chose to pursue the difficult lines of enquiry which Bryce suggested in his 1904 address. Then, as now, sociologists and anthropologists had many axes to grind; they had waited for official recognition too long to surrender their special interests in such subjects as primitive magic, myth and religion, and the structures of primitive societies.[3]

Meanwhile, demands for Bryce to lecture in the United States arrived in a steady stream, as they had for many years. Bryce's intimate friends in America knew the demands on his time and energies, and courtesy often made them forbear. Even so, Eliot at Harvard and Low at Columbia looked forward to the occasion when Bryce would take up the discreet requests in their letters.

In 1904 Bryce consented to give three courses of lectures, one at Columbia, one at Harvard, and the third at the Lowell Institute in Boston. The schedule promised to be a taxing one – fifteen lectures in almost as many days – but the opportunity to address the faculty, the graduates and undergraduates of two illustrious universities and informed audiences in Boston was a rare honour.

The invitation from Harvard had a special poignancy, for Bryce was to give the first of the famous annual series of lectures to the memory of E. L. Godkin. In 1902, Godkin died in England whilst convalescing there from a long illness. Bryce had seen much of his old friend in his final days, and witnessed the pessimism which gripped the litterateur towards the end. Only a few years earlier, in 1898, Godkin had expressed his feelings in his book *Unforeseen Tendencies of Democracy,* where the ardent idealism of his youth had ceded to grave doubts about man's ability to govern himself through democratic institutions. In Godkin's memory the annual Godkin Lectures would be devoted to aspects of government and politics.[4]

Bryce sailed with his wife to Boston in September 1904. At their request, the Cunard Company kept the Bryces' name off the passenger list. This was necessary because of the reporters who would crowd for an interview as soon as the passenger list was received in Boston. Even so, Bryce could hardly hope to escape recognition, and American reporters would try many stratagems to get copy. When they arrived, Marion Bryce wrote in a letter home: 'James has been bearded by several reporters, one of whom assured him that six million American citizens were ready to hang upon his words next morning if he would state in five minutes his views on American economic questions.'[5] Bryce declined.

Bryce had also accepted an invitation to attend the World's Fair and international exposition to be held in St Louis that year, and after arranging for the Godkin and Lowell Institute lectures in late October, the Bryces set out for St Louis. They were met at the station by the mayor's son, Erastus Wells, and brought in his private carriage to the mayor's house, where they stayed during their visit to St Louis. Bryce ran the gauntlet of news reporters as usual, and when the visitor proved reticent, the *St Louis Post Dispatch* had to be content with printing large photographs of James Bryce and his wife on the front page.[6]

The exposition covered an area of almost two square miles, and visitors attended from all over the world. With the German background of so many citizens in the region, it was natural that a considerable group of businessmen and industrialists should be invited from the old homeland. There were also numerous Japanese visitors. What they saw undoubtedly impressed them, for the exposition featured a Congress of Arts and Science devoted chiefly to engineering products and the practical arts. Here, the extraordinary accomplishments of American engineering were on view. The endless variety of machine-made products showed the advanced state of American technology in almost every field of engineering. There was also evidence of America's ability to turn her steel industry to more warlike purposes. The bessemer converters could produce howitzers as well as the steel skeletons supporting the tall buildings of St Louis. The message was not lost on Bryce. Doubtless it was not lost on the manufacturers and industrialists from Germany and Japan. The political situation in Europe and the Far East helped to sharpen the faculties.

Bryce's attention was also caught by a bizarre section of the Fair containing a group of Philippine Islanders in a contrived native habitat. The houses of bamboo and grass were faithfully reproduced, and the imported islanders performed native dances for the assembled white people. Bryce found the spectacle pathetic. His mind went back to 1883 and the Crow Indians assembled by the Northern Pacific Railroad for the entertainment of the conquering race.

The Bryces would have departed earlier, but public dinners were to be held on each of four successive evenings. Bryce was called upon to speak at every dinner and was guest of honour at a banquet given by the President of the Exposition, ex-Governor David Francis, who was Cleveland's Secretary of the Interior in 1896. At a dinner given by the Japanese Commission, Bryce was thanked for his speech by the head of the delegation 'in the name of your many pupils in Japan'. 'Everywhere, people seem so pleased to see him', Marion Bryce wrote.[7]

Apart from the foreign visitors, Bryce was delighted to meet many American academic friends. The historian Marshall Snow, who had completed a scholarly work on St Louis city government, was on hand at the nearby Washington University. The two friends discussed their common interests. Other scholars were present from cities and universities in the mid-west. Mayors and civic officials also came forward. 'One was in a constant handshaking all the time', Bryce recorded, 'with many references to *The American Commonwealth*. They are a very effusive people compared to the English and they gave me an extraordinarily warm reception when I rose to speak.'

The making of many new friendships and the renewal of old ones in the heart of the mid-west reaffirmed Bryce's faith in the good nature of the American people. Less welcome were the continued attentions of reporters jostling for interviews. Most sought to draw Bryce on political matters. He steadily refused comment, but noted ruefully: 'Very likely they have invented something for me: one has no time to read the papers to see.'

On the fifth day the Bryces slipped away. They travelled to Biltmore House near Asheville in North Carolina, where their friend George Vanderbilt had invited them to spend a few days. Unlike his brothers Cornelius and William, George Vanderbilt had shunned financial speculation and the making of further family fortunes in the railroad industry. Instead, he had devoted his share of their vast patrimony to scientific farming and stock breeding at the beautiful Biltmore estate in North Carolina. The great conservationist Gifford Pinchot was his first Superintendent of Forests, and Vanderbilt worked tirelessly to improve agricultural methods in the South. Bryce was fascinated by all that he saw on the estate. Though it needed little prompting, Bryce's interest in the conservation movement in the United States owed much to the enthusiasm of George Vanderbilt and the work of Gifford Pinchot at the Biltmore estate.

However delightful the host, the sheer opulence of Biltmore House was not entirely to Bryce's taste. The Vanderbilts had 'not contracted the usual faults of millionaires – they are nice people, he cultured, artistic, she genial and simple, so we have had quite a pleasant visit, tho' luxury is always trying to one who would like at least to live as a philosophical ascetic'.[8]

Marion Bryce probably enjoyed the gracious interiors of the house more than her husband. There was less Calvinism in her veins. In her letters to her mother she dwelt on the luxury of their suite, the balcony giving on to splendid groves of forest and the distant hills, and the perfect calm and restfulness of the place. But she no doubt needed and deserved some rest after the exhaustion of the St Louis Fair. Not least among the demands on the wife of James Bryce was a constant, bewildering array of introductions to scores, indeed hundreds of Americans who knew, or claimed to know her instantly recognised husband. There was also the constant travelling entailed by her husband's insatiable curiosity, his vast circle of friends, and his willingness to go anywhere, whatever the distance involved. They had already travelled almost two thousand miles since leaving the Eliots at Harvard only a week earlier. Now they were leaving for Washington, then on to Toronto to visit Goldwin Smith, and so back to New York by way of Niagara.

At Washington, they visited the White House again. Roosevelt was intensely busy at this time, with the November elections only a few weeks away, but he wanted to talk with Bryce on a number of topics. The Bryces stayed at the White House and at dinner Roosevelt introduced members of his Administration. Gifford Pinchot, now a leading conservationist, was there, eager to discuss what Bryce had observed at Vanderbilt's forestry station on the Biltmore estate. Justice Henry Brown of the Supreme Court was in the party, together with the Italian Ambassador and his wife.[9] Roosevelt's Secretary for War William Howard Taft also dined with the party. Bryce and Taft got on well together and struck up a friendship. Taft had recently been civil governor of the Philippine Islands and Bryce had heard flattering reports of his efforts to harmonise relations between Americans and Filipinos. The problems of race relations were still uppermost in Bryce's mind. The big, genial Ohio lawyer seemed oddly cast as Secretary for War in Roosevelt's Big Stick Administration, though in Bryce's eyes this commended him all the more. Five years later Taft and Bryce met once again in the White House, both of them in new roles.

The short stay in Washington allowed only a quick trip to Mount Vernon for Marion to see George Washington's home, then a visit to the imposing Library of Congress now gracing Capitol Hill, and also to the Smithsonian Institution, where Bryce lingered among the natural history collections. But time was passing. They made their farewells to President Roosevelt, travelled to Baltimore for a brief stay with old friends, and then went north to Toronto to talk with Goldwin Smith.

Smith was now eighty-one, rather deaf, and angry at the American victory in the Alaskan boundary dispute. The dispute had arisen from the gradual intrusion of American settlers in the boundary area, and was exacerbated by the Klondike gold rush of 1897. Sharp exchanges between Canada and the United States had led to the setting up of an arbitration commission, which gave its award in 1903. The award favoured the American claims. In Goldwin Smith's view, there was no need for any boundary dispute between the two great nations of the North American continent. Smith was still for a hemispheric union. 'He is more pessimistic than ever about Canada', Bryce wrote to Eliot, 'and sees her only salvation in Union with the United States – not a popular doctrine in Toronto.'[10] Bryce had no inkling that within three years the intractable problems of Canadian-American relations would be in his own lap.

The Bryces crossed Lake Ontario on 7 October to return to New York and Marion Bryce recorded a typical Bryceian vignette. Customs inspection took place as the steamer crossed Lake Ontario: 'The baggage man made me open my trunk for inspection', Marion Bryce wrote, 'and as James and I stood by the customs officer came up and looked at us. "Is this Mr Bryce?" "Yes." "The author?" "Yes." "Sir, I have read your books with pleasure and profit.";' and practically there was no examination of the baggage and everything was marked at once. . . .'[11]

In New York, where they stayed with Godkin's widow Katherine, Bryce divided his time between his lectures at Columbia and discussing the forthcoming Presidential elections with friends.

Seth Low had retired from the Presidency of Columbia and his place was now taken by Nicholas Murray Butler, a leading educationist and thus, inevitably, another of Bryce's friends. They had corresponded regularly with each other for almost fifteen years. Murray Butler was a close friend of Theodore Roosevelt, but differed with the President on the subjects of war and peace. During the following two decades, Butler worked tirelessly for international peace. Like Bryce, he was to argue later that the Great War could have been avoided if leaders and more men in public life had acted in time.[12]

Another friend in New York was Wendell Phillips Garrison, literary editor of the *Nation* and a long-time Bryce correspondent. When Godkin had begun to fail around 1900, Garrison kept up the flow of letters to Bryce on American domestic politics and the state of opinion on international matters. Throughout the age of imperialism, the *Nation* vigorously opposed the views of the expansionists, and Bryce had written frequently in its pages against the imperialist doctrines.[13]

At Columbia Bryce's lectures were delivered under the auspices of the Carpenter Foundation, and he gave seven addresses on the theme 'Law in its Relations to History'. The lectures attracted capacity audiences of professors, graduates and students, drawn chiefly from the faculties of law, history and political science.

Bryce concerned himself chiefly with the development of Anglo-American law, but he widened the treatment to a comparative view of other systems. His first lecture dealt principally with the relations of law to other cognate branches of thought. He then argued the case for a comparative study of the law. History itself was the key to the comparative method, Bryce observed, and he illustrated his theme with examples showing how nations and systems had acted one upon the other over the ages.

In the lectures following, Bryce developed his plea for comparative studies, drawing his illustrations from French, German and Scottish legal history. The final lectures moved to an examination of the state of international law, the difficulties besetting it, and the urgency of promoting it.[14]

Once more Bryce had chosen his theme with care. The world of thought was related to the world of action. Scholarly exegesis was mixed with an urgent awareness of contemporary problems outside the scholar's den, of a world whose crises might not await scholarly solutions.

It was almost time to depart for Boston for the lecture series at Harvard and at the Lowell Institute. Every mail brought further requests and demands on Bryce's available time. 'It has been raining invitations', Bryce wrote despairingly to Eliot, and asked for his friend's advice on which he should accept, which he could decline without giving offence. '[James] is deluged with requests for lectures, addresses, speeches and talks of every description', Marion Bryce wrote to her mother. Among the deluge were invitations from Yale, from Brown University at Rhode Island, and from Princeton's President Woodrow Wilson. A visit to Princeton allowed a good talk with Woodrow Wilson and a restful overnight stay, though there was no time to meet the President's request for an address. The Bryces returned to New York and departed for Boston.

Bryce had already discussed with Eliot the subject he would treat in his Godkin Lectures. It was one of which his old friend would undoubtedly have approved. Bryce offered five lectures on 'The

Study of Popular Governments'. The Sanders Theatre at Harvard was crowded on each occasion and many of Bryce's friends travelled in from other parts of New England.[15]

Political science was in its infancy when Bryce gave his Godkin Lectures in 1904, but the jurisprudential and historical approaches were already being questioned on both sides of the Atlantic. What would replace them was still a matter of conjecture.[16] As we have noted, Bryce had spent the spring and early summer of 1904 helping to found the Sociological Society in London. In discussions there he had called for greater rigour in the study of society. In the Godkin Lectures at Harvard he embarked on proposals for a more scientific analysis of political institutions.

In his characteristic fashion, Bryce staked out the ground before he developed his arguments. He traced the development of political studies from Plato, through Hobbes, Locke and Machiavelli. The chief characteristics of that tradition were *a priori* reasoning and a concern with philosophical and ethical matters, to the exclusion, in many texts, of the world of observed facts. There was a concentration on what might be or what ought to be, to the neglect of what is. 'Down even to the time of Hobbes and Locke', Bryce observed, 'there was little attempt to base the ideas advanced upon actual observation of phenomena.' The one exception was Machiavelli, whose world abounded with 'things that actually occurred'.[17]

The method now proposed by the lecturer would be that of 'carefully observing phenomena, of recording them with the minutest particularity, of separating the relevant from the irrelevant – when we have arrived at the point where we can be sure that the matter discarded really is irrelevant – of critical analytical study of the materials obtained, of inference and generalisation, and finally of the process of synthesis by which we endeavour to build up a system of generalisation of observed and recorded fact'.

Of course, Bryce continued, there were difficulties in such a programme, and he proceeded at some length to examine the many pitfalls that would be encountered by these proposed methods. For example, the phenomena of leadership, the varieties of men and of societies, the different stages and conditions of development – all presented obstacles to the scientific study of politics. Again, history itself was inextricably involved in every social and political institution, be it a monarchy, a parliament, a civil service or a political party. Yet this did not automatically prohibit the ultimate goal of generalisation in political studies; nor did generalisation entail precise prediction. Bryce illustrated his points in the succeeding lectures, ranging from the governments of England and the United States to those of Switzerland, France, and Australia in the modern period, and to Rome and Greece in the ancient period. The merits and strengths, as well as the failures of each system were carefully compared and contrasted.

The modern study of comparative government owes something to the Godkin Lectures of 1904. Two students of politics in Bryce's audience who soon accepted the challenge were Abbott Lawrence Lowell and William Bennet Munro. Lowell and Munro made outstanding contributions to the study of comparative government. Both scholars freely acknowledged immense debts to James Bryce.[18]

Between the Godkin Lectures Bryce found time to discuss with Lowell his projected two-volume work *The Government of England*. When it finally appeared in 1908, the author's preface gave unstinting praise to James Bryce, 'the master and guide of all students of modern political systems'.

The chief value of the 1904 Godkin Lectures was perhaps to strengthen the move – already incipient in some quarters – for a closer and more scientific scrutiny of political institutions. Bryce had taken care to remind his audience that although the study of politics could be made more scientific, it could never be an exact science. The qualifying utterance was important. When Bryce was asked on another occasion whether the study of politics was a science, he replied: 'One may as well ask whether the sea is blue or green. On some days and from some directions it is one colour: on other days or from other directions it is the other.' And in his valedictory opus in 1921, Bryce repeated a long-held belief: 'Prediction in physics may be certain: in politics it can be at best no more than probable.'[19]

The Bryce lectures at the Lowell Institute in Boston were as crowded as those at the Sanders Theatre in Cambridge. Bryce spoke on changes in thought, literature and political ideas during the past fifty years. The treatment was more descriptive and less analytical than that of the Godkin Lectures, to suit an audience drawn largely from the townspeople of Boston. Bryce was a familiar figure in Boston now, and there were those in his audience who remembered his lectures of 1881. He still retained a slight Scottish accent, with clear vowels and a faintly musical intonation. It was not a loud voice, but it was firm and resonant. On the rostrum, he was an arresting figure – slim, agile in his movements, white-bearded, with bushy eyebrows and bright, blue, piercing eyes.

Invitations had continued to shower upon the Bryces before and after they arrived in Boston. Only a proportion could be accepted. On Eliot's advice, Bryce accepted at the Massachusetts Historical Society, the Tavern, the Beacon and the Saturday Clubs. He declined at the University, the Victorian, and the Massachusetts Reform Clubs. Even without these further invitations, the Godkin and Lowell lectures together with the Carpenter lectures at Columbia added up to a speaking marathon.

The Bryces stayed with President Eliot at Harvard, but the historian James Ford Rhodes claimed them as his guests for a few evenings, and there was good talk with an old friend who was now at work on the sixth volume of his great history. The days at Boston ended once more in a flurry of engagements. Rhodes arranged receptions at his house on Beacon Street. Charles Francis Adams gave a dinner for the Bryces at the Somerset Club. Somehow Bryce managed to make a hurried trip to Rhode Island to give his promised address to Brown University, where he was also entertained by the University Club at a reception for a hundred and fifty notables.[20]

After a final round of farewells at Boston, the Bryces travelled to New Haven, where Bryce spoke once more, met old friends and as usual made new ones. In New York, the City Club gave a reception in his honour. The November Presidential election was now imminent. Bryce had already planned to stay until the returns were in. On 9 November it was confirmed that President Roosevelt was re-elected with huge majorities. Bryce despatched his congratulations to the White House and with his wife sailed from New York on 12 November. He may have wondered what four more years of the President's bustling, sometimes bullying Americanism would produce on the world stage.

16

America Re-appraised

The Bryces now made their home at 'Hindleap', a small country house which Bryce had bought in a rural part of Sussex convenient to London. There an ample study accommodated his large personal library and – more noticeable to the eye – the vast, swelling archive of journals, papers, pamphlets, notes, and intellectual memorabilia which represented the treasure trove of Bryce's world travels and his insatiable curiosity about man and his environment.

In London a flat was also maintained for his frequent visits for Parliamentary duties, speeches and meetings. But he preferred the stillness of Sussex, with the birds outside his study window and the woods nearby where he would walk in thought, puffing on his pipe, now and then pausing to draw from his pocket a piece of paper neatly folded in three, on which he would jot down in pencil an idea or a sudden thought. Refreshed by his walk, he would return to his study, take up paper and pen, and begin another article or review. His essays for the *Nation* continued. He reviewed the volumes of the *Cambridge Modern History* as they appeared, each critical essay revealing an extraordinary breadth of learning. Almost every issue of the *Nation* contained a Bryce essay or review, and one merely needs to glance at their titles to grasp the range of thought. 'A new History of Rome in her Middle Period.' 'The historical sagas of Iceland.' 'The unveiling of Lhasa.' 'The beginnings of the Third French Republic.' 'The life of Lord Randolph Churchill.' 'Hanotaux's History of contemporary France.' 'Ancient Ireland.' 'Lang's History of Scotland.' 'Sicily.' 'The administration of tropical dependencies.'[1]

From New York, Boston and London requests for articles and reviews came to Bryce's desk constantly. Most had to be declined. One which he accepted came from the *Outlook*, the lively New York journal of opinion which Theodore Roosevelt was to join when he left the Presidency in 1909. The *Outlook* asked Bryce to reflect on the changes which he had seen take place in America over twenty-five years. The suggestion appealed to Bryce and a long article in two parts appeared in 1905 under the title 'America Revisited: the Changes of a Quarter Century.'[2]

The most obvious changes were in America's material and industrial development, resulting in a greater stress and pace of life. Bryce went on to deliver some criticisms. The financier and manufacturer had become much more important and influential; the 'business is king' ethic had affected all parts of American society, even the professions. 'Lawyers are now to a greater extent than formerly business men, a part of the great organised system of industrial and financial enterprise.' Bryce regretted these developments. Bryce also regretted that power now seemed to reside in fewer and fewer hands – especially in cases of industrial combinations such as the Trusts. Such combinations tended to bring 'a loss of that individual liberty which the last generation was taught to expect from the progress of civilisation'.

On the credit side, Bryce noticed the immense expansion of education – particularly higher education – in the United States. The level of public and private expenditure on universities was a tribute to the American belief in the virtue of higher education. Harvard now had more students than Oxford; Yale had more than Cambridge. Their standards were fully comparable. 'Five leading universities of the Eastern States – Harvard, Yale, Columbia, Princeton, Pennsylvania – count as many students as do all the universities of England.' It was a timely statistic for Bryce's fellow countrymen. Half a century later they took steps to redress the balance.

There were also noticeable improvements in aesthetic appreciation, the cultivation of the arts and public investment in cultural activity. Literary criticism had improved, though the public taste for *belles-lettres* had apparently not developed likewise. Nor had the growth in population been accompanied by a corresponding increase in the demand for books. This could partly be attributed to the passion for observing sporting activities, Bryce suggested, and perhaps also to increased participation in sports.[3]

The second *Outlook* article examined the political changes that

Bryce had observed over the past twenty-five years. Once more criticism was mixed with praise. Corrupt city government remained a blight. The word 'boodle', Bryce recalled, was not in use in 1870: today it was on everyone's lips. Bryce took note of Lincoln Steffens' current series of articles on corrupt city governments in *McClure's Magazine*.[4] These articles, though strident and polemical, echoed chapters of *The American Commonwealth*. Theodore Roosevelt coined the term 'muckraking' to describe this type of journalism. Bryce remarked that even if only half of what Lincoln Steffens reported were true, 'the reformers have plenty of work before them'.[5]

On the federal government itself, Bryce struck a cautious note. This was delicate ground. Bryce knew that native American pride was quick to resent foreign insults to national institutions. He suggested that the House of Representatives appeared to have lost power and influence compared to 1870, whilst the Presidential office had grown stronger. 'Much depends on the man who happens to fill the chair,' he went on, 'and if Mr Roosevelt seems to count for more than any of his predecessors has done since General Grant in his first term, or any President between Andrew Jackson and Abraham Lincoln, this may be due to the impression of his personality, especially upon the West.'

Bryce had discussed Roosevelt and his predecessors often enough in correspondence with friends across the Atlantic, and at greater length in conversations. In this *Outlook* article, he was issuing a mild corrective to the chapter in *The American Commonwealth* entitled 'Why great men are not chosen President.'*

Concerning the Senate, Bryce was not complimentary. For some

---

* Bryce is sometimes assailed for this chapter. Critics point to the names of Washington, Jefferson, Lincoln, the two Roosevelts, Woodrow Wilson, and in our own time to John F. Kennedy and perhaps Harry S. Truman. This makes eight out of thirty-five Presidents to date. Three came after Bryce's death. Greatness is an elusive quality and some Presidents have greatness thrust upon them. John F. Kennedy's Presidency may not be judged a great one in history, though the man was undoubtedly remarkable. The subject is too big to discuss here, but it is worth speculating how many 'great' Americans were passed over by the American electoral process during many lean years. Were there no greater Americans available than Harding, McKinley, Garfield, Hayes, Andrew Johnson, Fillmore, Pierce, or Polk – to name but a few – in the years when these men held office? Statistically, Bryce's point is supported over the history of the Presidency.

years Bryce had privately deplored the behaviour of the Senate on important issues affecting foreign relations. With its built-in rural bias, and a special fondness for the chauvinistic appeals of the expansionists in its midst, the Senate had repeatedly demonstrated a paradoxical combination of isolationism and imperialism.[6] In Bryce's view, the Senate was isolationist when it suited American pride, and expansionist when America stood to gain. He quoted examples. The Senate had emasculated the Hay-Pauncefote Treaty between Britain and the United States for the construction of an isthmian canal in Central America. The Senators amended the proposed treaty to death mainly because they wanted total control of a fortified canal in peace and war. Britain, with possessions in Central America and the Caribbean, had definite interests in the area and so rejected the amended treaty. In the following year, after further negotiations, Britain accepted the Senate's demands for United States control of the proposed canal whilst stipulating that the canal should be free and open to all nations under equal terms. Bryce had followed these recent developments closely. His point was that as a body, the Senate often treated solemn agreements in a cavalier manner. The issue of the Panama Canal was by no means closed, and Bryce would have much stronger things to say about the Senate in future years.

Bryce argued that there had been a decline in the quality of the legislators in the Senate over the past thirty years although, he was careful to add, it still contained 'some very eminent and able men'. One possible way to improve the quality of the Senate might be to institute the popular election of Senators, instead of the election of Senators by the State legislatures, which was the constitutional practice at this time. The proposal had long appealed to Bryce, and he had discussed it often enough with American students of politics. Eight years later, the Seventeenth Amendment to the Constitution brought the popular election of United States Senators. Bryce did not live long enough to judge whether the new system permanently improved the calibre of Senators.

Bryce also took up the subject of American expansionism. Whilst recognising the absolute right of the United States to formulate and promote foreign policies to suit her own aspirations and ambitions, Bryce nevertheless questioned whether the gaining of colonies

197

overseas had been accompanied by any real appreciation of the administrative and political problems they might eventually produce. He rather doubted that they had, remarking that already most Americans had forgotten about the overseas possessions of the United States. 'The islands are far away, and now that the first excitement of curiosity has died down, little [is] heard of them.' Bryce wanted to remind imperialists that colonies brought responsibilities as well as new markets. His quarrel was not with American imperialism in particular, but with all imperialist doctrines.[7]

In the final section of the article Bryce turned again to the problem of racial mixture and miscegenation, especially between Negroes and whites. Here, he found little cause for optimism in America. Race prejudice on the part of white men still existed and if anything was more deeply held in the South than before. 'The colored problem, which in 1883 seemed to me immeasurably difficult, a problem which it would take at least several generations to solve, does not seem any easier now, nor any nearer its ultimate solution.'[8]

The most notable characteristic of these two articles was their frankness. Bryce came neither to praise nor to blame the America he had observed in seven extensive visits over a period of thirty-six years. He examined trends, made comparisons, offered opinions and drew cautious conclusions. No opinion or judgment was stated dogmatically. The reader could accept or reject the opinions offered. Others could contradict them. That was, after all, the meaning and purpose of free comment in a liberal democracy.

A few months after the articles appeared, Bryce was himself once more involved in the democratic process at home. In the autumn election of 1905 he was again returned for South Aberdeen. The Liberal party routed the Tories, and Bryce was summoned once again to 10 Downing Street by a Liberal Prime Minister. Henry Campbell-Bannerman offered Bryce the post of Chief Secretary for Ireland. Bryce knew it was a bed of nails, but Campbell-Bannerman also knew of Bryce's deep concern for Ireland. Some felt Bryce deserved better, but then Bryce was only half a politician. He would always prefer to seek knowledge than to seek office. Others were striving and exerting their claims in the Liberal party; Asquith,

Lloyd George, young Winston Churchill – those were all men of ambition. Morley claimed India: Bryce claimed nothing. He was a member of no cabal. He accepted the post which Campbell-Bannerman wanted him above all others to accept, even though the Liberal party had played down Irish Home Rule in the election campaign and made no firm promises.

As Secretary for Ireland, Bryce had the task of taking up residence in Dublin but at the same time commuting regularly across the Irish Sea to answer questions in the House of Commons – most of them from Irish members – or working in the dingy Irish Office in Whitehall. For Bryce it was an unhappy interregnum. Fortunately the fates – assisted by Edward Grey at the Foreign Office – plucked him away from a thankless task.

That Bryce should be offered the post of Ambassador to the United States almost before he had time to accustom himself to his responsibilities as Secretary for Ireland requires some explanation. Campbell-Bannerman was keen that Bryce should continue at the Irish Office. No one knew more about the complexities of the Irish problem. The Irish could have no better or more sympathetic friend in the Cabinet at Westminster, and Bryce was willing to serve. Having given his word, he was ready to discharge his duties as well as the dictates of conscience and the policies of the Liberal Government permitted.

When Grey offered him the post of Ambassador to the United States Bryce hesitated. Letters exchanged between Bryce, Grey and Campbell-Bannerman, and more privately between Bryce and his closest American friends, confirm that Bryce was reluctant to accept Grey's offer.[9] He had never served in the diplomatic service. He disliked protocol and too much formality even though he fully comprehended the need for it at the ambassadorial level. Again, his appointment would undoubtedly cause offence to career diplomats who had served long and faithful years in less illustrious stations, some of whom were certainly reckoning their chances of the plum at Washington when Sir Mortimer Durand ended his term there.

On the other hand, Edward Grey had become convinced that Bryce must be the next Washington Ambassador. He also convinced Campbell-Bannerman and other members of the Cabinet of the compelling reasons for the appointment. Bryce was prevailed upon to accept.

Grey's compelling reasons arose partly from President Roosevelt's utter dissatisfaction with Sir Mortimer Durand at Washington. Durand was a faithful servant of the Foreign Office but he never came to understand America nor the ebullient character who was now President of the United States. A product of that honourable mill, the Indian Civil Service, Durand started his career in Bengal, spent some time in the Middle East, took a short spell at Madrid, and was then appointed to Washington in 1903. He was a patient administrator rather than a brilliant diplomat. He was desperately anxious to do well in his Washington post, but his mind could not match Roosevelt's either in agility or in sheer intellectual force. He did not care to join in the President's athletic walks and scrambles in Rock Creek Park.*

Roosevelt had already succeeded in replacing the German Ambassador in Washington with one he found more congenial. This was his old friend Hermann Speck von Sternberg, or 'Speck', as Roosevelt usually hailed him.[10] The new German Ambassador shared the President's penchant for shooting, hunting, and a parade of the manly virtues. Roosevelt's relations with the French Ambassador Jusserand were also cordial. In Washington Jusserand was an honoured fixture as a scholar-diplomat with long diplomatic experience. With Durand it was different, and Roosevelt wanted to get rid of him. From 1904 onwards, Roosevelt began to complain frequently to Joseph Hodges Choate, the American Ambassador in London. Gradually the President severed social contacts with the British Ambassador. Using Joseph Choate, together with an old friend Henry White, Secretary of the London Embassy, as intermediaries, Roosevelt moved from cajoling to bluster and coercion barely within the limits of diplomatic propriety. A Roosevelt letter to Henry White on 27 December 1904 contained an early salvo. 'There is no one in the British Embassy to whom I can talk freely. . . . I do not know whether it is my fault

---

* One of the curious sights of Washington during these years was that of a string of diplomats anxiously following the athletic President as he led the way over boulder and bough at the bottom of the creek. A nation's relations with the United States depended partly on its ambassador's gymnastic ability.

An American cartoonist portrays a possible encounter between Ambassador Bryce and the athletic President Roosevelt

or Sir Mortimer's, but our minds do not meet.' By June 1906, Roosevelt was writing to the new American Ambassador in London, Whitelaw Reid: 'I think you ought to let them [Edward VII and Sir Edward Grey] both know confidentially of the utter worthlessness of Durand.' In the same letter, Roosevelt added: 'I like the Kaiser and the Germans. I wish to keep on good terms with them. I agree with you in thinking it even more important that we should keep on good terms or better terms with the English; but of course when the English are such fools as to keep a man like Durand here while the Germans have a man like Speck [Sternberg], it increases the difficulty of my task.' Roosevelt invited Reid to show 'all of my letter that you deem proper to show to the King and Sir Edward Grey'.[11]

It was an open secret that Roosevelt wanted his old friend Cecil Spring-Rice as a replacement for Durand. Spring-Rice had been a close friend of Roosevelt for more than twenty years: he was a career diplomat and in 1905 was Minister to Persia. Already he had served in a junior post at Washington in the late 1880s and early 1890s. But there were possible dangers in appointing as Ambassador someone who was an intimate of the President. Roosevelt liked to have his own way. He could use charm or bluster as it suited him in order to secure his ends, even with friends. Spring-Rice was certainly willing to be offered the Washington post: in 1913 he gladly accepted it in succession to Bryce, even though by that time Roosevelt was out of office and Woodrow Wilson was in the White House.[12]

Grey and his advisers can be credited with a brilliant stroke of diplomacy in 1906. Bryce was chosen 'after more careful consideration than any cabinet ever gave a diplomatic appointment'.[13] This consideration took note that Bryce was known, respected and admired in almost every part of the United States; that although Roosevelt was perhaps the most brilliant and widely read of all the Presidents for a century past, Bryce was demonstrably superior in intellectual power. Physically he could match men much younger than himself, whether it was on a scramble in Rock Creek Park or a stroll up a snow-covered peak. As for diplomacy, Bryce soon showed that Foreign Office orthodoxy is not always the shortest path to outstanding achievements.

17

1907:
Ambassador in Washington

To assess Bryce's achievements as British Ambassador at Washington during the six years 1907 to 1913, we must first glance at the diplomatic background to his mission.

The description that W. H. Auden gave to the Thirties applies also to the first decade of the twentieth century: it was 'a low, dishonest decade'. The ambitions and strategies of the big powers were clothed in protestations of peaceful intention. Nevertheless, naval programmes continued to expand, armies grew, and the munitions factories of Britain, Germany, France, the United States, Japan and Russia were an ominous counterpoint to the abortive disarmament conferences at The Hague in 1899 and 1907.[1]

In the Far East, the Russo-Japanese war ended when Roosevelt's good offices brought about the Portsmouth Peace Conference in August 1905. The fighting ceased, but not the power politics behind the war. China, Manchuria, Korea – these prizes were still eyed greedily by empire builders in Russia and Japan, but also in Europe and the United States.

In Europe, statesmen still thought in terms of the balance of power, as the alliances and ententes of the period reveal, even though diplomats formally disavowed the doctrine. The rivalry between Germany and Britain in the search for markets and colonies, and then in naval expenditure, gave rise to the greatest fears. Small nations watched anxiously. By early 1907, hopes that the armaments race could be halted were growing dim. The 1898 Hague disarmament conference had failed to produce any binding agreements for disarmament or for the international arbitration of differences. Few expected that the June 1907 conference would produce one. It did not, and efforts to establish a world court for the settlement of disputes were equally unsuccessful. From the British point of view, the nervous shifts of alliances and ententes among the great powers between 1899 and 1906 brought renewed fears of isolation in Europe.

It was against this background that Edward Grey at the Foreign Office sought to fashion his grand design for union between the English-speaking peoples – not necessarily formal or political, though he hoped this might come through time. Britain, the United States and Canada would form the most powerful triumvirate of powers in the world; the adhesion of Australia and other British dependencies would add to its strength. The British and American navies with their string of colonies and islands (whose port facilities had been carefully developed as coaling stations) would police the world.

It is a popular thesis that by 1906, when Edward Grey became Foreign Secretary, Britain and the United States were firm allies; that in any future confrontation between the big powers the United States would align itself on the side of Great Britain. This view is derived mainly from much persuasive evidence that Britain and the United States had developed the habit – sometimes painful to Britain, but developed none the less – of settling their differences peacefully. The settlement of the *Alabama* claims, the Venezuela settlement, and the Alaskan boundary agreement* stand out as examples of conciliatory habits of accommodation between the two nations. Other evidence tends to support the view. Britain declared her neutrality in the Spanish-American war; she did not interfere in the Far East during Roosevelt's mission to end the Russo-Japanese war, even though the Open Door in China was deemed the concern of Britain as well as the United States. Finally, an implicit understanding to divide the oceans of the world between their two great navies may be deduced. Hence the conclusion that a war between Britain and the United States was now inconceivable.[2]

This tidy thesis is blessed by the comfortable hindsight that Britain and the United States were allies in two world wars. Yet it also contains certain assumptions which may be questioned. Power politics makes strange bedfellows among nations. The bitter enemies of yesterday are the sworn allies of today. Prediction is the

* See page 208.

least popular pastime among diplomats. Again, it is rarely the statesmen who take the final, or even important decisions on whether to make war against another nation or nations. Politicians make these decisions, and for a variety of reasons politicians do not always act rationally or reasonably. Most declarations of war are made in the expectation of victory, yet the losers frequently out-number the victors. It was a worldly-wise United States Senator who observed: 'If politicians had as much foresight as historians have hindsight, we'd all be better off by a darned sight.'[3]

The view that a natural harmony existed between Britain and the United States by 1906 suggests a careless reckoning of the facts of American politics. The Congress of the United States is a large, complicated and in its behaviour an unpredictable institution. The membership of both Houses contains many different groupings, alliances, and interests. To suggest that between 1896 and 1914 there was any permanent or natural majority in either the House of Representatives or the Senate in support of an entente between the United States and Britain is largely an Anglo-Saxon illusion.[4] Even though Theodore Roosevelt wished to keep on good terms with Britain, as his published correspondence reveals, it was equally true that he shared with Senators, Congressmen and ordinary Americans a mixture of cautiousness and suspicion concerning British motives, especially where imperialism and colonialism were involved. This current in American thinking runs deep. It was present in the mind of Franklin Roosevelt at Yalta in 1943 as it was in the mind of his cousin in the Presidency forty years earlier. The term 'perfidious Albion' has never quite lost its currency in chancelleries abroad and Americans are particularly prone to recall it for historical reasons, real or imagined. Theodore Roosevelt firmly maintained that the Eleventh Commandment for Anglo-American sentimenta-lists was: 'Thou shalt not slop over.' He always proclaimed his complete ignorance of 'the whereabouts of Anglo-Saxony'.[5]

The thesis that by 1906 Britain and the United States had moved to a state of understanding which made war between them un-thinkable rests largely on the retrospective truth that the United States joined the Allied cause in the war of 1914. Yet Britain was only one of the Allies and the United States joined the war with the utmost reluctance in April 1917.

The Great War was prepared during the previous decade. So were the alliances and ententes which eventually decided the outcome of the war, though in 1907 no one knew where and when the arms race might end. It is against this background that Grey's grand design and Bryce's appointment as Ambassador to the United States is best examined.

Bryce took up his duties as Ambassador in Washington on 21 February 1907. He remained in his post for six years – a much longer period than he originally anticipated or eventually desired. Only the repeated requests of Edward Grey persuaded him to remain long after he sought the leisure to continue his interrupted work on the study of democracy. Before he took up his post, Bryce was offered a peerage. He declined it, convinced that it would be a hindrance rather than an asset in the egalitarian society he knew so intimately.[6]

His record as Ambassador falls into two parts. There was firstly the formal diplomacy of the period, immediately affecting relations between Britain, the United States and Canada (for Canadian interests were represented in Washington by the British Ambassador) but with wider implications, as we suggested earlier, for Grey's grand design. Secondly, there was the prodigious number of speeches, addresses and talks which Bryce gave to audiences throughout the United States, and in many parts of Canada. Speeches are, of course, the common lot of ambassadors everywhere, but the extraordinary volume, the unusual merit and the wide publicity earned by Bryce's speeches during these six years give them uncommon significance.

Bryce gave notice of his intentions as Ambassador in a despatch soon after he assumed his duties:

... I feel that the real use of being here is to address the people and make them feel that Englishmen are interested in what they are doing and are in real sympathy with them. That is why I have accepted so many invitations to Chambers of Commerce and Universities – the places where one gets best into touch with those who form and lead them.[7]

For the sake of clarity, these two parts of Bryce's diplomacy – the formal and the informal – will be treated separately, but it will be clear that the success of the one part was an ingredient of the other.

The major items on the diplomatic calendar at Washington concerned the urgent need to settle many outstanding differences between Canada and the United States. These were numerous, complex and by 1907 at a very delicate stage. They involved boundary disputes, tariff arrangements and fishing rights. Grey's design for a triangle of North Atlantic powers could easily have foundered on the rock of Canadian-American relations. Bryce's task was not lightened by the strong belief among Canadians that their national interests had been poorly served by a succession of British ambassadors in Washington. To establish this point, a brief digression is necessary.

Canadian-American relations were an uncertain mixture of attraction and repulsion; of amity and suspicion, of friendliness and, in the case of Canada, of some legitimate fears. The existence of strong expansionist sentiments in the United States Congress was well known to Canadian officials and political leaders. Some expansionists had talked of annexation. At the same time, there were in the Canadian Parliament powerful groups who sought a commercial union with the United States; some even desired political union.[8] Just as Grey realised that a North Atlantic triangle must appear invincible to Germany or Russia, so many Canadians and Americans – and not simply Anglophobes – sought a less complicated hemispheric union confined to the North American continent. After all, Canada was also part of the new world.

Other Canadians disagreed. Among them was the Prime Minister, Sir Wilfrid Laurier, who had no desire for such a union. His first loyalty lay with Canada and an abiding wish to improve French-English relations there; his second to the British Crown.

Representing the Crown was Albert Henry George Grey, the fourth Earl, who was appointed Governor-General in 1904. He had served as a Liberal in Parliament with Gladstone, and had known James Bryce for many years. His high regard for Bryce continued, despite differing views on imperialism and home rule for Ireland. From every point of view, Earl Grey's loyalties lay first and last with the British Crown.

In the conduct of Canadian affairs, Laurier was the key figure though, unlike the'Governor-General, Sir Wilfred Laurier had to face the uncertainties of electoral politics. Here was another complicating factor. Since the 1890s, the Tariff, protectionism, imperialism and expansionism were prime issues in Canadian election platforms.

Trade between Canada and the United States had expanded considerably over the previous decades. Canada, with a population of six million, could export to a contiguous market of more than 90 million people. Compared with this, the commercial tie with England across a vast ocean was more sentimental than economic. Whenever the United States adopted the Tariff, Canadian manufacturers and food producers were the first to feel its effects; but it also strengthened the arguments of those Canadians favouring outright annexation by the United States.[9]

The Alaskan boundary dispute of 1903 brought a sharp setback to such proposals. The dispute over the exact boundary line between Alaska and Canada had finally erupted in 1903. Roosevelt's behaviour during the arbitration which followed has been fully recorded and documented.[10] The arbitration tribunal of 'six impartial jurists of repute who shall consider judicially the questions submitted to them' consisted, for the American side, of Henry Cabot Lodge, the declared expansionist, and ex-Senator Turner, who hailed from Washington on the Canadian border and whose strong feelings against the Canadian claims were no secret. Neither Cabot Lodge nor Turner could, by any stretch of the imagination, be termed 'jurists of repute'. Roosevelt's explicit instructions to his 'arbitrators' is well known: there was to be 'no compromise' on the American claim. Roosevelt let it be known in London that he would back up the American claim with troops in Alaska if it proved necessary.[11] When the result was announced at the end of 1903, it was clear that the tribunal had favoured the American claims. Henceforth Canada was denied the important ocean inlets of the Alaskan 'panhandle'.

Canadians were convinced that the chief British negotiator, Lord Alverstone, by voting with the Americans in the four to two verdict, had simply sacrificed their interests at the altar of Anglo-American accord.[12] By 1907 they could hardly be blamed for wondering whether the status of a dependency, lacking direct diplomatic representation in Washington, served their best interests.

This was the background to the many delicate tasks confronting Bryce when he arrived in Washington early in March 1907. It was not the easiest of missions.

After presenting his letters of credence to President Roosevelt, the new Ambassador's first official act was to make a visit to Canada. Protocol required that his first visit should be an official Ambassadorial visit, though Bryce would have preferred to omit many of the formalities. He wanted above all to talk at length with Sir Wilfred Laurier and Earl Grey. This would bring him up to date. His knowledge of Canada was not entirely deficient – indeed, he had written a long article on Canada's history, geography and political system following his trans-Canadian trip in 1890.[13] But now he wanted first-hand information on Canadian-American relations, especially from the Canadian point of view.

Just before Bryce set out for Ottawa, he received a pessimistic note from Earl Grey: 'The idea that Canada has been sacrificed again and again by John Bull in his desire to cultivate the friendship of Uncle Sam is rooted so deep in the conviction of Canada, that nothing I can say, nothing you can say, nothing that any Englishman can say, can uproot it.'[14]

Privately, Bryce had not the slightest intention of subscribing to such pessimism. His faith in the essential goodness of ordinary people, and thus in their capacity to give new men and new measures another chance, was perhaps more marked than Earl Grey's.

Bryce talked at length with Sir Wilfred Laurier and heard from the Prime Minister's lips the Canadian view on many matters then affecting Canadian-American relations. They discussed the long dispute over fishing rights in North Atlantic waters; the dispute over sections of the Canadian-American boundary between New Brunswick and Maine; a further dispute on boundary waters in the Great Lakes; the claims to pelagic sealing in the Bering Sea; and the vexed overall problem of tariff and trade arrangements between the two countries. There were also outstanding pecuniary claims going back over many decades, which the American authorities had never settled and which continued to rankle in the minds of

Canadians. The high-handed 'settlement' of the Alaskan boundary dispute had put the Canadians in no mood for compromise.

The situation in Ottawa was complicated by Earl Grey's private conviction that Anglo-American harmony was more important than outright insistence on Canada's claims. Grey was very exercised over what he conceived to be the German menace in Europe.[15] His views were largely shaped by balance of power doctrines: the quarrels and claims of fishermen in Canada must not be allowed to sway the destinies of the globe.

Following his talks with Laurier, with Canadian officials and with Earl Grey, Bryce attended a dinner held in honour of the Ambassador's 'semi-official visit', as he preferred it to be known. This was given by the Canadian Club at Ottawa and was attended by ministers of the Canadian government, members of the legislature, civic officials and leaders of the community drawn from many parts of the Province.

Newspaper reports took note of Sir Wilfrid Laurier's observation that the visit of Ambassador Bryce 'marked a new page in the history of British diplomacy on this continent in so far as it affected Canada. For the first time in history His Majesty's representative was making a semi-official visit to the country, finding out something of the Canadian point of view and of Canada's desires in international relations. . . .'[16] In his speech at the dinner the Prime Minister went on to state frankly that 'the past record of British diplomacy on this continent did not provide the most cheerful page in Canadian history. A glance at the map of Canada emphasised what this country has lost to the United States through various treaties negotiated by the British plenipotentiaries. . . .' Sir Wilfred developed his points. But he concluded in a more friendly vein: 'Mr Bryce . . . has done something new in connection with British diplomacy in America. He has visited Canada.' The audience greeted the final remark with 'laughter and cheers'.[17]

If Ambassador Bryce had any earlier illusions about the delicacy of his mission in Washington they were surely banished by now. But Bryce received warm applause as he rose to speak. The first part of his speech was designed to assure his audience that there was no real basis for feeling that Americans were opposed to Canada's aspirations. Drawing on his own experience, Bryce argued that ordinary Americans together with the 'higher and wiser' minds in the United States – those with whom he would be treating on Canada's behalf – had nothing but respect and friendliness for their neighbour across the border. The more rabid expansionists in the United States had no real basis of power in popular sentiment. The second part of Bryce's speech dealt with Canada's relations with Britain. There was no longer the feeling in Britain that Canada and the other Dominions should be regarded as colonies. 'We have come to look upon them as sister states. Both parties [in Britain] agree that self-government is desirable and proper; but we value the *connection*', Bryce emphasised, 'and want it to continue on a basis of equality and co-partnership. It must be arrived at with the full and gradual assent of every one of the sister states.'[18]

Bryce also praised Canada's economic achievements, the calibre of the Canadian House of Commons debates (which he had taken the trouble to attend during his short visit), and the wisdom and reasonableness he found among the representatives of both the Liberals and Conservatives in the legislature. There was much else in the speech to please, and undoubtedly to flatter the audience. Bryce was quite capable of mixing skills he had learned at the hustings in Britain and at the lectern in America with sincere statements of intent.

The Canadian press gave front-page treatment to the Ottawa banquet and speeches. A large photograph of Ambassador Bryce adorned the front page of the *Toronto Globe*. Editorials struck notes of cautious optimism. In all the reports, it was clear that the personal reputation of the Ambassador largely accounted for the coverage.

On 3 April Bryce spoke to audiences at Toronto, where a luncheon and a dinner were given in his honour by the Canada Club there. More than six hundred attended the luncheon, and though the Lieutenant-Governor of Ontario Province almost caused an incident with a somewhat belligerent anti-American speech, Bryce in his reply expressed his determination to obtain justice for all Canadian claims that could honestly and fairly be termed just. Bryce sat down to cheers.

Goldwin Smith was present to make a speech, and prudently devoted it to a defence of British diplomacy in the recent past. The

Bryces were staying with the Goldwin Smiths at their home in Toronto, and it is likely that the two old friends had put their heads together before the luncheon. Whatever the case, Goldwin Smith muted his belief in the need for a confederation of Canada and the United States and spoke in defence of past British diplomacy with the authority of one who had taken a leading part in many discussions and exchanges on Canada's future during the previous twenty years.[19]

The Bryces departed on 4 April. In an editorial that day the *Toronto Globe* paid a warm and lengthy tribute to Bryce on the occasion of his visit. Thus in a few days Bryce had achieved what the skilful politician often seeks to secure in a far flung territory: he had formed a political base on which he could build. If he had not visited, talked, and spoken to important audiences in Ottawa and Toronto, any efforts on his part in Washington might have foundered on Canadian mistrust or lack of confidence in the Ambassador's good offices in Washington.

The British Embassy was at that time housed in an unbecoming mansion on Connecticut Avenue. Badly planned, with bad plumbing and doleful furnishings, the house presented formidable challenges to the resident hostess. Yet the Bryce receptions soon became notable, not so much for the quality of the decor as for the interesting company which congregated there. At no other embassy was one likely to meet, as personal friends of the Ambassador, two or three justices of the Supreme Court, scholars from the Smithsonian Institution, geologists from the United States Geological Survey, or a variety of scholars visiting Washington from California, Chicago, or New England. With Jusserand, the French Ambassador, Bryce quickly struck up a personal friendship whose basis was a warm mutual regard. Jusserand's scholarly works on the literary history of England and on Shakespeare in France, together with his deep interest in historical studies proper, easily appealed to Bryce. The two men often shared restful hours stolen from the diplomatic round to discuss historical topics or Shakespeare.

'Bryce has started well', President Roosevelt remarked privately to a friend.[20] The Bryces were frequent guests at the White House, and Marion Bryce could often find in her diary for one week two afternoon visits to Mrs Roosevelt and an evening at dinner. Roosevelt's time was of course chiefly taken up with his Cabinet ministers, the broad direction of foreign policy and the incessant burdens of domestic politics in the United States. But Bryce saw a great deal of Roosevelt's Secretary of State, Elihu Root.

Root had come to the State Department from the War Department after a short interval out of politics. He fully merited the special trust that Roosevelt put in him as a wise, judicious administrator and negotiator. It was Root who selected Leonard Wood as military governor of Cuba and who advised on administrative reforms in the Philippines designed to improve the lot of the native population. He had a background of legal practice in New York and retained clear notions on questions of right and wrong, whether they involved parties in lawsuits or relations between great powers and small ones. Above all, he earnestly supported any genuine move designed to maintain world peace and stability.[21]

Root found an immediate accord with James Bryce. The two men saw much of each other in the spring of 1907 and even more in the autumn. Their relationship soon developed to one of personal friendship. After a year they had dropped formal exchanges and wrote to each other informally when they were not tête à tête.

Root listened patiently to Bryce's presentation of the grounds for Canada's sense of grievance. Together, the two men carefully and without rancour reviewed the case for either side. Their legal training helped. Negotiations then began and much hard work ensued. Bryce made another visit to Canada in February 1908, and by the spring of that year, the first fruits of the Bryce–Root diplomacy appeared. These included two treaties and an important Arbitration Convention.

On 10 April 1908 Root was writing almost casually in his own hand to Bryce: 'Let me confirm the arrangements made orally yesterday to meet at half past ten tomorrow morning for the signature of the Boundary Treaty. The Fisheries Treaty will also be ready for signature if you are prepared to sign it at that time....'[22]

The first of these treaties dealt with the long and tortuous dispute over the exact location of the Canadian-American border along the St Croix River between Maine and New Brunswick, across to Ontario and the St Lawrence River beyond Montreal. The ten articles in the treaty traced an agreed line in detail, thus ending further disputes. The agreed line owed much to the fact that Ambassador Bryce had travelled over the disputed portions himself, complete with maps and a rare knowledge of the historical background of the regions, before going on to scrutinise maps and documents in Ottawa and Washington.[23]

The second treaty substantially cleared up the long quarrel over territorial fishing rights off the coasts of New Brunswick and Nova Scotia. The definition of territorial waters (especially the problem of three-mile limits where vast sea inlets were concerned), as well as the Canadian charges of over-fishing by American fleets, were among the many items in the dispute. The treaty now negotiated clarified these points and also instituted the practice of referring further fishing disputes to arbitration at the Hague Court. Thus the bitter feelings of Canadians in the Maritime Provinces whose livelihood depended entirely on the fishing industry were assuaged.[24]

Another important agreement emerging from a year of discussions concerned matters that both Bryce and Elihu Root deemed to be of much greater significance. This was a five-year Arbitration Convention, which provided for the submission to the International Court at the Hague of any dispute between the United States and Britain which did not affect 'the vital interests, the independence or the honour of the two contracting States, nor concern the interests of a third party'.[25]

Bryce would have liked to omit the provisos in order to make the agreement much more comprehensive. He reasoned – and Root partly agreed – that the provisos excepted just those issues on which arbitration was most needed in order to avoid sharp conflicts. But Bryce knew, as Root knew, that one had to build on limited agreements in order to prepare for more ambitious ones. In 897 the United States Senate had stamped on an Anglo-American arbitration treaty. Bryce knew the Senate well enough to realise that it would do so again.

Root could claim chief credit for the present convention; his industry during the same period had produced no less than ten similar, though again limited, conventions with other powers.[26] Although Bryce was content to bide his time for the moment, an effective arbitration treaty with the United States remained the chief object of his diplomacy.

In 1908 the American elections once more thrust American party politics to the fore. Theodore Roosevelt had made a fateful declaration just before the 1904 Presidential election that in no circumstances would he be a candidate for a third term, thus accepting the strong convention of a two-term limit on Presidential office. William Howard Taft emerged as the Republican candidate in 1908, blessed by the support of the retiring President. In the November election, Taft defeated the Democratic nominee William Jennings Bryan by a majority of more than one and a quarter million votes.

The successful Republican platform had declared itself 'unequivocally for a revision of the Tariff by a session of the Congress immediately following the inauguration of the next President'. As an 'unequivocal statement', this worked a charm on the voters, even though it carefully omitted to state whether Tariff revision would be upwards in the direction of protection, or downwards in the direction of free trade. But it did guarantee that the Tariff would once more dominate international discussions in 1909 and thus markedly affect Canadian-American relations.

By March 1909, when Roosevelt bowed himself out of the White House – though not out of Republican politics – Bryce had good reason to reflect on the extreme urgency – from the British point of view – of solving the remaining Canadian-American disputes and promoting Grey's policy of a North Atlantic triangle.

The London Naval Conference of December 1908 to February 1909, attended by the ten main naval powers, failed to stop the armaments race. The 26 February declaration to limit armaments was not subsequently ratified by the major powers. In British eyes, Germany was beyond doubt the chief menace as war clouds began to gather over Europe.[27]

From London, Grey's deputy Sir Charles Hardinge kept Bryce informed of British policy and thinking. As early as 2 December 1907, Hardinge was informing Bryce fully, and confidentially, of the reception given to the Kaiser during his visit to London.

'. . . I should describe his reception by the crowds in the streets as good but not enthusiastic, but in the Guildhall he had a very warm reception. Unfortunately the value of the Emperor's peaceful assurances has been somewhat discounted in the eyes of the public by the almost simultaneous publication of the German naval estimates, which give food for thought.'[28]

Hardinge's confidential notes on these vital topics continued during the next two years. On 26 February 1909 he sent to Bryce a confidential memorandum on his conversations with Prince Bülow in Berlin. 'Please regard it as secret', Hardinge wrote, 'since only a portion of it has been issued to the Cabinet. There is a good deal of leakage from the Cabinet at present, which shows itself in the Manchester Guardian, so we have to take special precautions. . . .'[29]

Hardinge's long memorandum described his attempt to reach an understanding with Bulow on Germany's policies or ambitions in European, Near Eastern and Middle Eastern spheres of influence, and on naval expenditures. On 4 June Hardinge was writing again to Bryce, who had meanwhile reported to London on widespread comment in American newspapers concerning the Anglo-German rift.

. . . I cannot help thinking that the American press depicts our relations with Germany as being very much worse than they really are. There is no great tension between the countries except that of naval armaments. Thus we are unable to relax until we see that Germany is doing the same. From all appearances, and from the secrecy that is maintained as to naval construction there, the Germans seem to be accelerating rather than retarding the completion of their programme. Our Naval Attaché is not allowed to visit any important naval yards in Germany, and consequently we cannot help thinking that, after the declaration which they have made there is something which they are anxious to conceal.[30]

Two weeks later, Hardinge gave Bryce his confidential opinion on the visit of King Edward VII to Germany: 'I do not think that the King's visit to Berlin has been in the slightest degree advantageous to our relations with Germany, nor do we find that Bulow has ever acted up to the smooth words which he used to me on that occasion.'

These confidential briefings from Hardinge served to remind Bryce, if that were necessary, of the importance of his mission in North America. Further notes from Edward Grey continually stressed the extreme importance of preserving Anglo-American accord at all costs.[31]

In March 1909, Roosevelt handed over to the new President, William Howard Taft. Elihu Root had retired from the State Department in order to seek election to the United States Senate. His place was taken by Taft's appointee Philander Knox, whom Bryce described in his report to the Foreign Office thus: '. . . quick, keen, shrewd, inclined to be autocratic, rapid in his decisions, and not easy to move from one which he has made . . . an upright man, not swayed by unworthy motives nor masking schemes or intrigues behind overt acts. . . .'[32]

Bryce never enjoyed with Knox the intimacy he shared with Root, but Knox was well disposed to the policies Root had helped to formulate. Moreover, the new President was an earnest advocate of international arbitration treaties for the settlement of disputes between the great powers. As early as 1897, when he was serving as a Federal judge, William Howard Taft had publicly supported the move inaugurated by Charles Eliot and Carl Schurz for an arbitration treaty between Britain and the United States – the movement which was stopped short by the displeasure of the United States Senate. 'If we do not have arbitration, we shall have war', President Taft observed in a notable speech in 1910.[33] Bryce could therefore count on the support of the President in his further efforts to secure an arbitration treaty. But neither Taft nor Bryce could assume the support of the Senate.

By 1909, therefore, the main objects of Bryce's diplomacy were firstly to achieve an effective arbitration treaty between the United States and Britain, and secondly to settle the vexed question of tariff and trade arrangements between the United States and Canada. Unfortunately, as events would show, success in the first aim was largely contingent on success in the second.

Minor objectives included the settlement of the remaining disputes between Canada and the United States. On these subordinate – though by no means unimportant – matters, Bryce was able to build on the good will he had already established on the part of both sides. As soon as Philander Knox had reviewed the issues with his colleagues, discussions and negotiations proceeded. Once more Bryce travelled several times between Ottawa and Washington to act as a mediator between the parties. At other times he took the unprecedented step of inviting Canadian officials to Washington for face to face discussions with American representatives. In this way, negotiations went ahead speedily.

Between 1909 and 1910 Bryce, Knox, and Canadian and American officials laboured hard. By the middle of 1910, an agreement was concluded for referring to arbitration the many pecuniary claims against individuals and parties in the United States. The various claims had languished without settlement for decades. They mostly arose from American seizure of cargoes in disputed boundary waters. Other claims related to shipwreck retrieval. Agreements concluded between Knox and Bryce provided for reciprocal rights for salvaging shipwrecks in boundary waters. They also settled the acute problem of Canadian-American use of boundary waters in the Great Lakes area. Here, the principal bone of contention was an American proposal to divert the waters of the vast Niagara River between Lake Ontario and Lake Erie for irrigation purposes. There were also disputes over navigation rights in the intricate series of rivers and lakes along the Canadian-American border. These too were settled by the Knox-Bryce conventions. Finally, two treaties were negotiated for the 'Preservation and Protection of Fur Seals'. This old dispute had grown from the quarrels of competing merchant fleets in the area of the Bering Sea. Overfishing had so depleted the herds that there was imminent danger that the species would vanish – and with it the livelihood of many Canadian and American merchant seamen. Appeals for restraint on both sides had gone unheard. Suspicion and mistrust had prevailed and the rising demand for pelts in the 1890s and early 1900s had increased the slaughter. Now, with the proposed treaties, common sense conditions were laid down providing for total prohibition in certain areas of the ocean for a period of fifteen years. When agreement by Russia and Japan was added to the Canadian-American agreement, the old, irrational feuds were brought to an end.[34]

Each of these treaties required arduous work, skill, tact, and an extraordinary attention to detail on the part of the negotiators. The work was spread over many anxious months, but finally it was completed. Bryce's part is adequately summed up in a letter from the Governor-General Earl Grey in August 1911. At the request of Sir Wilfrid Laurier and leaders in the Canadian Parliament, Earl Grey took an unprecedented step. He informed Bryce:

I have this morning approved a Minute of Council giving expression to the gratitude felt by the Dominion Government towards you for the services you have rendered to Canada and the Empire by negotiating no less than ten treaties with the United States during the short term of your Embassy in Washington. That you should have been able to remove so many sources of possible friction between the two countries will be no less gratifying to yourself than it is to the Canadian people whom you have served so well.[35]

Other personal tributes came to Bryce from Edward Grey and Sir Charles Hardinge in London, from Sir Wilfrid Laurier and Lieutenant-Governors of the provinces in Canada, and even from American officials. A tribute from Elihu Root, now in the United States Senate, especially touched Bryce. When the complicated Boundary Waters Treaty was officially accepted by Canada, Elihu Root wrote to his friend:

. . . It furnishes an occasion for me to say something of what I have long felt about the very exceptional service that you have rendered not only to Great Britain but to her American colonies and to the United States. I think there has been a new order of things inaugurated with relations between Canada and the United States, and a new departure of the greatest importance; and it is extraordinary that the author of The American Commonwealth should have been able to step out of his book into the practical affairs of government and bring such a thing about. For you have been three fourths of the whole. All the other elements were here before you came and nothing was done. You knew all the parties too well to be suspicious and you have too genuine an interest in all of them to wish for anything unfair, and you had the confidence of all of them . . . you thought much less of diplomatic formality than of statesmanship, so you reached levels of great and lasting value.

It has been a delight for me dear Mr Bryce to work with you, and to profit by the influence of the spirit in which you work and to feel that I may call myself

Your friend,
Elihu Root.[36]

Bryce was greatly encouraged by the many expressions of thanks and goodwill from so many quarters. Even so, he knew that his task was far from finished. A general arbitration treaty and Canadian-American trade reciprocity were still on his diplomatic calendar. For the moment, Bryce was badly in need of a change of scene. He had been unable to take his leave in 1909 during the long negotiations on Canada's behalf. In September 1910, he sailed with his wife for a journey to South America. They were away for three months, and arrived back on 1 January 1911 after a voyage of almost 18,000 miles.

Although Bryce made many calls on heads of state in the course of the long trip to South America, nevertheless the voyage provided restful days on board when he could regain his energies. This was necessary not only to prepare for the difficult diplomacy that lay ahead on his return to Washington, but also to recoup his strength to meet the continued demands for speeches in all parts of the United States. Bryce's record of speeches, lectures and addresses was already astonishing. When we bear in mind the intricate diplomacy which he also conducted between 1907 and September 1910, the total performance seems almost incredible.

18

Unorthodox Diplomacy

The speeches, lectures and addresses Bryce gave during his six years as Ambassador formed a significant part of the intellectual experience of the Americans between 1907 and 1913. A detailed treatment would occupy a volume in itself. Indeed, when Bryce's publisher urged him to collect some of the main addresses of these years, they filled a large volume.[1] Among the scores of notable speeches to important gatherings which Bryce could not include in his selection, for reasons of space, there are many that deserve notice because of their content, and the special nature of the occasion or the audience.

The marathon began as soon as Bryce left Toronto in April 1907 to return to Washington. The Ambassador and his wife stopped off at Chicago on the way south so that he could give a speech to the Chicago Club. Bryce examined various proposals for improving city government in the United States and welcomed the spirit of reform now infusing many city administrations. The muck-raking articles of Lincoln Steffens in *McClure's Magazine* had alerted American citizens to the political corruption existing – to a greater or lesser degree – in almost every major city in the United States. Steffens was elaborating, although in a much more strident tone, observations and warnings first set out at length in *The American Commonwealth*. In a certain sense the Progressive era began in 1888, not 1901.[2] Bryce urged all support and strength to the municipal reform movements now springing up in the east and mid-west.

One week later, Bryce gave one of the chief addresses at James-town, Virginia, to mark the tercentenary of the first English settlement. President Roosevelt and members of the Cabinet were present. The Bryce address traced historically 'The Beginnings of Virginia' and included a round criticism of the later follies of the English Crown and the King's advisers in the eighteenth century. But Bryce also argued that the spirit which led to the foundation of Jamestown had its source in that assertion of individual rights and freedom which was equally a part of the English heritage. The men who landed at Jamestown in 1607 certainly possessed Bibles and prayer books, Bryce observed, but they also 'carried in their breasts the principles and traditions of the Common Law of England . . . fully pervaded with the spirit of liberty and the most favourable to the development of personal self-reliance and individual responsibility'.[3] The Ambassador illustrated the point with persuasive quotations and historical evidence. This was the first of many major addresses in which this same theme would be adverted to, for it was a fundamental purpose of Bryce's overall mission to stress the unity of the English-speaking peoples. On many occasions, before audiences great and small, the wine of sentiment was carefully diluted with the water of diplomatic utility.

Of course Bryce was too skilful an orator and knew too much of American susceptibilities to allow his message to appear too obviously. Thus his remarks on the spirit of English liberty implanted in Virginia in 1607 were also neatly linked to observations appropriate to a patriotic occasion. After paying high compliments to all that the American people had achieved during the past three centuries, Bryce concluded: 'Cherish alike and cherish together liberty and law. They are always inseparable. Without liberty there is no true law, because where law expresses the will not of the whole community, but merely of an arbitrary ruler or a selfish class, it has neither moral force nor guarantee of permanence.'[4]

Audiences in the United States had long come to expect of Bryce not only eloquence but frankness. He did not shrink from offering advice, occasionally warnings, sometimes admonitions. He mixed praise with his warnings or exhortations where praise was due. For this reason he was regarded as a genuine friend of America; for this reason letters requesting his presence continued to form small mountains on his desk in Washington.

In May 1907, Bryce could be found speaking to a Laymen's Christian Missionary convention at Chattanooga in Tennessee, a visit which he combined with another trip to the deep South to see conditions among the Negro population. What he saw provided little comfort, though he was glad to find some State legislatures now making increased grants towards Negro education.

In June Bryce was booked for a rash of Commencement Addresses at American universities. From the point of view of most university authorities, James Bryce was a 'natural' for Commencement exercises. Eloquence, learning and advice to the young would be skilfully mixed. Of the many which came to his desk in the spring of 1907, Bryce accepted invitations from Chicago, Harvard, and St Louis. Other universities claimed him each succeeding June until his final departure from Washington in 1913.

At Chicago on 11 June Bryce spoke on 'Intellectual Pleasures for Later Life'. The occasion was suitable, both geographically and chronologically, to remind the assembled faculty and students of the claims of humane studies – especially literature and languages. Bryce was fully aware that scientism was now in the ascendant at Chicago, and that a marked enthusiasm for the methods of science was tending to squeeze out less 'scientific' branches of learning. Bryce was not one to dismiss the value of scientific studies, and he paid tribute both to their intrinsic worth and to their contribution to training the mind. But there was a need for balance. History, literature and poetry had equal claims on the mind even though these were not susceptible to scientific rigour. Bryce offered to his Chicago audience some lines of Virgil from the second book of the *Georgics*:

> Me vero primum dulces ante omnia Musae,
> Quarum sacra fero ingenti perculsus amore . . .[5]

Scientific investigation had its part to play, Bryce went on; but as Virgil appreciated, the riddles of the universe may require other forms of explanation.

At Harvard two weeks later Bryce gave the annual *Phi Beta Kappa* address. With his audience composed of scholars young and old, Bryce could afford to speak on a fairly recondite theme. He chose 'What is Progress?' and told his audience he wanted to examine 'the meaning and content of the idea of progress itself, and of the relations of each kind of progress to other kinds'.

A brief summary can hardly do justice to Bryce's address, but the outlines can be sketched. The approach was characteristically

223

Bryceian. He first noted several different kinds of progress at work in the world: material, economic, technical, even political. These could be charted with varying degrees of certainty. Yet there was another kind of progress which was much more difficult to chart or measure: this was moral progress. Bryce examined critically various supposed gauges of moral progress – such as the Benthamite felicific calculus. Happiness provided some sort of measure, but not a dependable one. Mill had exposed the fallacy. The conundrum remained. Bryce ended on a note of honest doubt. '. . . It may be necessary to wait some considerable time before attempting to determine whether the excitement and variety of modern life make for happiness. We are really not much better placed than the ancients for solving these problems . . . the mists that shroud the horizon hang as thick and low as they did when the journey began.'[6]

Bryce rarely over-estimated the intellectual level of his audience, and he was even more careful not to under-estimate it. One of the secrets of Bryce's popularity was that he could judge his different audiences to a nicety. He knew perfectly well that a *Phi Beta Kappa* audience could think for themselves. His task at Harvard was to raise questions in alert minds, not to offer doubtful panaceas. Even so, Bryce showed his audience that he parted company with the optimists of the first half of the nineteenth century and with certain evolutionists of the second half.[7]

Suiting the speech to the occasion had long been one of Bryce's special gifts. A mere glance at the titles of his speeches during these years conveys their wide range. His address to the annual meeting of the American Bar Association in 1907 was devoted to 'Common Law and History'. Once more his theme of the essential unity of the English-speaking peoples appeared fugitively in a speech suited to a large elite audience drawn from all parts of the United States. An address to the American Institute of Architects gathered at Washington in December 1908 was devoted to 'The Art of Augustus Saint-Gaudens'. Bryce showed not only his familiarity with the works of this foremost American sculptor, who had recently died, but a fine aesthetic appreciation of what his art had bequeathed to the American spirit. Next day, at their earnest invitation, Bryce gave a second address to the assembled architects. This time he spoke on 'Architecture and History' and stressed the value of architecture for understanding different historical epochs. He drew his examples from Byzantine Perigueux, medieval Provence, Romanesque Germany, Renaissance Italy, and from other periods and locales. In the same month Bryce was giving an address to the Washington Classical Club. Elsewhere he spoke on 'The Landing of the Pilgrims in 1620', 'The Study of Ancient Literature', 'Thomas Jefferson' and 'The Constitution of the United States'.[8]

If proof were needed of the high regard in which Bryce was held by the academy in the United States it could be found in the joint meeting of the American Historical Association and the American Political Science Association in 1908 where Bryce gave an address on 'The Relations of Political Science to History and to Practice'. Bryce had already received the honour, unique for a non-American, of being elected to the Presidency of the American Political Science Association. His address to an illustrious assembly of historians and political scientists was catholic and humane. Once more he urged that politics should not be regarded as an 'exact' science. Facts were important, but only in their relation to other facts. They were of little use alone. 'The data of politics are the acts of men. The laws of political science are the tendencies of human nature and are embodied in the institutions men have created.' Political science and historical studies were thus inter-dependent. Neither could achieve an exact 'science' with predictive laws. 'So-called historical parallels are usually interesting, often illuminative. But they are often misleading. History never repeats itself. . . .'[9]

The major speeches and addresses came from Bryce's own pen. When he was greatly harassed by diplomatic business and a crowded programme of speeches, he might turn to a secretary at the Embassy to jot down a few suggestions for some minor occasion such as a civic lunch; but even on these occasions, the Ambassador was as likely to turn to his own rough draft sketched on the train. Just before a Boston function a secretary proferred a suitable quotation from Emerson. 'There are three New Englanders before me', Bryce remarked. 'They will get that from one of the others.' In fact the first speaker used the quotation.[10]

Bryce travelled to every state of the Union to make speeches. In November 1908 he was again in the deep South, this time visiting his friend Booker T. Washington and addressing a large gathering at the Tuskegee Institute. Later, in January 1910, Bryce could be found speaking once more at the Hampton Normal Institute on Founder's Day. In this way, he not only made direct contact with his friends among Negro teachers and future leaders of the movement for Negro emancipation, but brought himself up to date on the social and economic conditions of the South and on the Negro cause.

Even as Bryce was making these speeches, he was preparing another completely revised edition of *The American Commonwealth*. Happily the immense load of work was somewhat lightened by assistance from a young assistant professor of history at Columbia University, recommended by Seth Low. His name was Charles Beard.[11] During the same period Bryce was returning to Lowell at Harvard carefully checked proofs of his friend's *Government of England* – a two-volume work replete with statistical detail and close argument. Meanwhile, on the side, Bryce still found time to send essays and reviews of a non-political nature to the *Nation*, including essays on John Stuart Mill and Lord Acton, two essays on the career of Cecil Rhodes, a long review of Professor Frazer's *Golden Bough*, and reviews of the latest volumes of the *Cambridge Mediaeval History* and the *Cambridge Modern History*.[12]

Requests for articles and reviews were insistent: Bryce was forced to decline all but a few. Requests for speeches were unrelenting: Bryce granted more than even his remarkable stamina safely permitted. Yet his energies never seemed to flag. In March 1909 he agreed to visit California to make a number of speeches to university and civic gatherings. As the national press was quick to observe, this was the first time that a British Ambassador had visted the far west.

James and Marion Bryce crossed the continent together, resting quietly where they could. At Los Angeles and San Francisco Bryce addressed crowded banquets given in his honour. The mayors of the two cities acted as hosts and the Bryces met the Governor, members of the State legislature and the State Supreme Court. On each occasion the warmth of the welcome amazed Marion Bryce, as she candidly admitted in her letters to her mother.[13]

The main purpose of the visit was to give the Charter Day Address at the University of California at Berkeley; 1909 being the forty-first anniversary of the Charter. The Greek Theatre nestling in the hillside behind eucalyptus trees was crowded to capacity as Bryce spoke on the subject 'What a university may do for a State.' The title, simple and direct, was appropriate for a state university which had at times felt the intrusion of the State legislature on its functions and curriculum. In the course of a long address, Bryce suggested the many points at which a university could enrich the cultural and intellectual life of the state. A university, he reminded those who would read his address on the front page of the San Francisco newspapers next day, had certain duties and functions in this regard 'which no other organised body in the State is so well fitted to discharge. . . .'[14] Bryce went on to describe those duties and functions boldly and fully. But there were homilies for the University also. The address included mild admonitions against the cult of athletics to the neglect of studies – a tendency which Bryce had begun to observe in some parts of the United States and which he hoped would not spread to California. Athletics had their place – and an important one in any great university – but they should not be honoured above intellectual excellence in the traditions of a growing university. Bryce ended with warm tributes to California and a salute to the future of the young state:

One cannot help but feel that it is destined, more perhaps than any other part of the United States, to develop a new and distinctive type of art, perhaps of landscape painting, perhaps of literature.[15]

The huge audience welcomed the implied compliment and gave Bryce a standing ovation. Next day Bryce's address was printed in full and portraits of the familiar face dominated the San Francisco newspapers.[16]

Two days later, Bryce gave another address at the special invitation of the student body. The Berkeley student newspaper reported that Ambassador Bryce spoke 'before one of the largest gatherings of students that has ever assembled at a University meeting'.[17] In summary Bryce offered to the packed meeting four simple, direct pieces of advice:

(1) Keep in touch with your friends, wherever they are.
(2) Never read a book that will do you no good. Life is too short. Read good books.
(3) Take up a spare time occupation – either outdoors or indoors: one of the natural sciences, for example, or music, or art.
(4) Study the workings of popular government and go into public life.

At the end, the students stood to cheer, just as 'several thousand cheering people' had stood in the Greek theatre two days earlier when Bryce received from President Wheeler the honorary degree of Doctor of Laws.

Other banquets and occasions awaited the Bryces. They visited the Leland Stanford University, where Bryce spoke on 'Problems in American Statesmanship'. His lecture ended with a plea to Stanford men to enter the public service.[18] Returning to the city of Berkeley once more, Bryce gave the Earl Foundation lectures at the Pacific School of Religion on 'Religion and Ethics in Modern Life'. Once again the lecture hall was crowded to capacity. In a few short days, James Bryce had stimulated thousands of Californians both intellectually and morally. This was all of a piece with his contributions elsewhere. His reception at Berkeley was little different from those he received at Chicago, at Harvard, at Milwaukee, at St Louis.

Although university audiences provided a natural forum for the scholar-diplomat, his speeches were equally well received elsewhere. In the big cities of the east Bryce was ready to address a St Patrick's Day dinner and a St Andrew's dinner within a few days of each other. As an Ulster Scot he was welcome at both gatherings. On a visit to Tampa in Florida to receive the freedom of the city, Bryce delighted three separate audiences in one day by addressing each in the language of the assembled group – Spanish, Italian and German. At Yale University Bryce gave a course of lectures on the duties of citizenship, which Yale quickly published for a wider audience.[19] Elsewhere, Bryce addressed state Bar associations; several state classical associations; a farmer's congress in North Carolina – where he went on to give an address to the State Historical Society; a Presbyterian conference at Baltimore; gatherings of civic reformers and administrators in a dozen cities;

and a major address at the Eighth Annual Convention of the American Civic Association in 1912. Other notable occasions included a special address at Springfield in Illinois for the Lincoln Memorial Day; another for the Pilgrim Fathers at Provincetown; and another for the birthday of Thomas Jefferson before the members of the University of Virginia and many eminent Virginians.

Even though Bryce spoke to widely differing audiences in every state in the Union, there was nevertheless a pattern to his selection from the mountain of invitations. He was always ready to address university gatherings. There was method – indeed good politics – in this. The faculties included men and women who influenced the popular mind today; the students would be influencing it tomorrow, perhaps in the teaching, legal and literary professions, or in business life. However busy – and occasionally exhausted – he was, Bryce was willing to make the journey for an important university occasion, whether it was to northern Wisconsin, to Alabama, or to the other side of the continent.

The results of this vast odyssey over a period of six years cannot be gauged with accuracy. That Bryce made an important contribution to the intellectual life of the American people goes without saying. If his main thrust was at the academy, he was at the same time a familiar figure to Americans of all sorts and social conditions. Recalling these years at a later date, when Bryce had been laid to rest, President Lowell of Harvard University remarked that James Bryce had acted as though his mission was to charm a people rather than represent a government. This mission, Lowell observed, he fulfilled completely.[20]

19

The North Atlantic Triangle

On the sea trip around South America in 1910 Bryce rested as much as he could, well removed from speeches, banquets and the minutiae of Chancery work in Washington. But Edward Grey would have been a poor Foreign Secretary if he had not seen diplomatic opportunities in the Ambassador's scheduled calls at the South American republics. Earlier that same year the British minister at Montevideo had warned Grey of British carelessness about trade possibilities with South America and the further need to keep a close watch on political developments in the republics.[1] Grey privately asked Bryce to see 'how much the Germans are doing to push themselves in South America, especially in S. Brazil and by what methods they do it. . . . Anything you pick up as regards our economic interests in the Argentine would be of special interest.'[2]

The 18,000-mile voyage – with its many ports of call and audiences with heads of state – was therefore not entirely one of ease and leisure. The future of South America was of immediate interest to the great powers. Bryce observed, then reported to Grey. Inevitably, perhaps, he also rendered a public account in the form of another work, *South America: Observations and Impressions*, which appeared in 1912. Once more, the reader is staggered that Bryce could find time to collect so much material on social, economic and political matters and then write it up during rare moments of leisure in Washington.

The Bryces were back on 1 January 1911. The immediate item on the diplomatic calendar now concerned Canadian-American trade reciprocity. Things had not stood still during Bryce's leave Indeed, they had moved with unusual speed during his absence, though not in a direction calculated to favour British interests.

In the long and tortuous history of Canadian-American trade

reciprocity Canada's problem amounted to 'a kind of book-keeper's puzzle; that is, computing a balance of how much she gained by any improvement in Anglo-American understanding as against how much she gave up in order to make it possible'.[3] By the turn of the century, however, north-south trade was more vital to the Canadian economy than trade with the mother country, and the American Tariff continued to be the prime concern of Canadian businessmen. The bright hopes of Tariff revision raised by the Republican promises in the American election of 1908 were not subsequently realised. The Payne-Aldrich Tariff passed during Taft's first year in office reduced duties on many Canadian items, especially agricultural commodities, but it provoked bitter opposition in the American mid-west and far west, voiced by prairie Senators and Congressmen. Thus, in the 1910 Congressional mid-term elections, Taft received a galvanic shock. In the House of Representatives a Republican majority of 47 was converted to a Democratic majority of 67. In the Senate, Taft's majority was reduced from 28 to 10. At the same time a rebellious group of Republicans promised further trouble. In other elections that year, Democrats replaced Republicans as governors of the normally Republican states of Ohio, New York, Connecticut, Massachusetts and New Jersey. In November 1910, therefore, Taft was forced to consider what these results foreboded for the Presidential election year of 1912.

Immediately after the 1910 mid-term elections Taft and his advisers cast about for means to restore damaged prestige. The President had received a bad press in the election. Newspaper owners were smarting under the failure to reduce high tariffs on imported Canadian wood pulp and newsprint. Reviewing the situation, Taft reasoned that a reciprocal trade agreement with Canada which safeguarded American interests and which reduced – or better still abolished – the import charge on Canadian wood pulp would have favourable effects. Taft was already under strong pressure from the American Newspaper Publishers' Association to abolish the duty on pulp wood and newsprint. Philander Knox was persistently lobbied by the President of the Association, Herman Ridder, owner and publisher of the New York *Staats-Zeitung*, and also by the Hearst Press.[4]

Taft moved quickly. In his Message to Congress on 6 December 1910 he reported that two representatives from the State Department were already in Ottawa negotiating a reciprocal trade agreement. The meetings with the Canadian representatives were adjourned to Washington in January 1911, by which time the British Ambassador was back from South America. The situation was extremely delicate. Negotiations were already well ahead. Clearly, British interests would be affected by any far-reaching trade agreement between the two countries. At the same time Canada had made it clear that British intervention in the present negotiations would be unwelcome. The meetings continued in Washington, and on 21 January a Reciprocal Trade Agreement was announced. The exact constitutionality of this agreement was questioned by lawyers and by scholars. Although it was signed by Philander Knox for the American side and by the Canadian Minister of Finance, W. S. Fielding, for Canada, it was in no sense a treaty. Ratification was to be carried out in the form of 'concurrent legislation' in both countries.

The terms of the agreement were far-reaching. It practically achieved free trade in most farm products, including livestock, main crops and vegetables. Low rates of duty would apply to agricultural implements, engines, building materials and partly finished lumber. Among the imports to be admitted free to the United States were wood pulp, newsprint and other paper products.

To have legal effect, the agreement still required concurrent legislation in both countries. President Taft was extremely eager to accomplish this, but his eagerness produced some surprising indiscretions. In a special message to Congress on 26 January stressing the identity of Canadian and American interests, Taft suggested that with the measure now coming before their Parliament, Canadians had come 'to the parting of the ways'.[5] The phrase echoed well beyond Washington to Ottawa and Whitehall. In the following weeks Taft repeated this and similar statements to distinguished audiences in eastern and mid-western America. The Hearst Press obligingly chimed in with support. Herman Ridder circulated all newspaper publishers urging support of the agreement and indicating its importance to buyers of Canadian wood pulp.[6] Members of Congress joined the chorus. House Speaker Champ

Clark, a Democrat from Missouri, made his own distinctive contribution in a remark which was destined to enter the history books. 'I hope to see the day', Speaker Clark declared publicly, 'when the American flag will float over every square foot of the British North American possessions clear to the North Pole.'[7] It was a popular remark with many Democrats, most Republicans, and large sections of the American press. But the remark raised eyebrows in Whitehall, to say the least.

As British Ambassador, Bryce was prevented from intruding in the domestic political affairs of the United States. Needless to say, he was actively in touch with London and with Earl Grey in Ottawa. Taft's proposed treaty would clearly affect Britain's trade advantages with her Dominion. By now, the 'book-keeper's puzzle' was not Canada's so much as Britain's. If reciprocity helped to smooth the remaining disputes between Canada and America, and always provided that the Anglo-Canadian connection was firmly maintained, then Edward Grey's grand design would be realised: the 'North Atlantic triangle' would be an accomplished fact.

Election years in the United States had interfered often enough with the strategies of statesmen. In 1911, however, it was Canada's turn to interfere. In the Canadian election that year reciprocity was the key issue. Taft's indiscretions, together with Speaker Clark's wilder utterances, provided the Conservative party and its leader Sir Robert Borden with valuable fuel. The 'annexation' bogy was quickly revived between April and June. The Conservative cry was that reciprocity would make Canada 'the backyard and the lumber camp' of American industrial interests. The phrase caught on quickly. A scare was put about that Sir Wilfred Laurier was about to secede from the British Empire and absorb Canada into the United States. These rumours, spiced with the recent remarks of President Taft and past remarks of expansionists in the United States Congress, finally decided the Canadian election of 1911. Laurier and the Liberals were defeated. Sir Robert Borden became Prime Minister. Reciprocity languished and was not successfully revived until 1934 in the Trade Agreement Act.[8]

The debacle over Canadian-American reciprocity vitally affected the British quest for an effective Anglo-American arbitration treaty, which remained Bryce's major diplomatic objective. Months before the Canadian elections sealed the issue of reciprocity, Bryce was meeting regularly with Philander Knox and State Department representatives in an attempt to produce such a treaty. Although President Taft was a known advocate of peaceful arbitration, his indiscretions over Canadian reciprocity raised the political temperature in the Senate and the House. Congress itself was by no means unanimously in favour of Canadian-American reciprocity. Farm Democrats suspected that once again their interests would be sacrificed in favour of east coast manufacturers in an all round reduction of duties. There was even a rumour that American farm interests were helping to finance Borden's Conservative party in Canada during the autumn election.[9] Whether true or not, the political atmosphere in Washington was both cloudy and charged in 1911. Eyes were fixed on the Congressional and Presidential elections of 1912.

It will be recalled that the Arbitration Convention Bryce negotiated with Elihu Root in 1908 contained important reservations concerning 'national honour', 'vital interests', and the Monroe Doctrine. Not only in America, but elsewhere in the world, men of good will were working to bring about effective arbitration treaties between the great powers. The vital, overriding aim was to prevent the outbreak of world war. Already the armaments race was well advanced and steel navies were alert on the seven seas.

In the United States, several societies and organisations had now been formed to seek peaceful solutions to international disputes. Andrew Carnegie had devoted a major part of his fortune to the Carnegie Endowment for International Peace. In February 1910 at Baltimore, a leading citizen named Theodore Marburg formed the American Society for the Judicial Settlement of International Disputes. Among the sponsors were President Taft and Princeton's President Woodrow Wilson. Elsewhere, at Lake Mohonk in New England, an annual conference of eminent American citizens formed plans to influence and direct public sentiment in favour of international arbitration. Ambassador Bryce delivered an address to the conference in May 1909 urging an 'allegiance to humanity' to replace national and sectional interests.[10]

Another foundation with a huge membership was the World Peace Foundation, numbering among its members more than one hundred and sixty Chambers of Commerce and Boards of Trade all over the United States. The World Peace Foundation strongly endorsed the move for unreserved arbitration treaties between America and other great powers. Undoubtedly, therefore, there was strong public support throughout the United States for arbitration treaties between the nations.[11]

With Taft and Philander Knox devoted to the cause, negotiations for an Anglo-American arbitration treaty went smoothly during the early months of 1911. By early May, a draft agreed on in Washington was despatched to the British government for approval by the Cabinet. This was given readily and Edward Grey was delighted. He was hopeful that 'one or more great European powers would eventually make a similar agreement with us and the United States. The effect of such agreements upon disarmament and the *morale* of international politics should be considerable.'[12]

The proposed treaty was returned to Washington for signature. Bryce sat down with Knox under the beneficent eye of the President to sign for Great Britain. The pleasing picture was recorded by photographers and was widely publicised. One more hurdle remained for the treaty: the 'advice and consent' of the United States Senate.

It was a formidable hurdle: 1911 was a bad year for the supporters of arbitration on Capitol Hill. A group of Senators soon found fault with the all-embracing treaty. The old arguments were aired: national honour, the Monroe Doctrine, America's best interests might still demand that she refuse to refer certain types of dispute to an international court of arbitration. Between the late autumn of 1911 and early spring of 1912 amendments were proposed in the Senate Chamber. Senator Henry Cabot Lodge, Senators Borah of Idaho and Beveridge of Indiana, leaders of a powerful cabal denounced any sacrifice of 'vital interests' covered by the Monroe Doctrine. To complicate matters further, ex-President Theodore Roosevelt now emerged from the wings as the candidate of the Progressive party, thus splitting the Republican party in this Presidential election year. Roosevelt had shed none of his 'America First' doctrines. His supporters included Borah, Beveridge and their followers.

By March 1912, amendments passed in the Senate had made nonsense of the proposed treaty. The Senate agreed by a vote of 76 to 3 that questions involving the 'national honour' and 'vital interests' of the United States would not be subject to international arbitration. It was vain for Taft to point out once again that these were precisley the questions for which arbitration was designed if nations were to avoid war. The Senate had voted and the United States Constitution granted the Senate the right to withhold their consent to treaties proposed by the President. As Secretary of State John Hay had observed a decade earlier: 'A treaty entering the Senate is like a bull entering the arena. No one can say just when or how the blow will fall, but one thing is certain – it will never leave the arena alive.'[13]

For James Bryce the Senate vote was a bitter blow. Clearly nothing further could or would be done until the 1912 November elections had decided the will of the American people and a new President was installed in March 1913. Bryce had now served as Ambassador for more than five years. After the Senate vote on the arbitration treaty, he asked Grey to allow him to relinquish his post. He was anxious to complete the major study on modern democracy which had been forming in his mind for more than ten years.

Grey pleaded with Bryce to remain in Washington until after the American elections in November 1912. In July the Democrats selected Woodrow Wilson as their candidate. Wilson was known to favour arbitration; he was a man of peace, a scholar and, as it happened, he was also an old friend of James Bryce. The split in the Republican party might well secure Wilson's election. There might still be important work for Bryce to do. Bryce agreed to stay until the results of the election were known. Even then Grey did not give up. On 12 September he wrote:

. . . You will leave a great record at Washington and how we are to find anyone who will be able to live up to it I do not know. . . . We must do the best we can, but I am more sorry than I can say that you are retiring. In view of what you have said and written to me I can't urge you to reconsider your decision, though of course if you wish to do so we shall be only too delighted.[14]

Bryce finally agreed to extend his stay beyond the November 1912 elections. 'I must of course do what the public service requires', he wrote.[15] The reason Bryce delayed his departure chiefly concerned the issue of Panama Canal tolls. The canal was at last completed, but it had become a bone of contention.

An Act passed by Congress before the legislature dispersed for the 1912 elections declared that American coastwise shipping using the canal would be exempt from toll charges. As expected, this led to protests from other nations planning to use the canal. Britain, with her big navy and merchant fleets, was particularly concerned. An old treaty between Britain and America – the Clayton–Bulwer Treaty of 1850 – provided that an isthmian canal between North and South America would be a joint venture, and that neither Britain nor the United States should have exclusive control over such a canal. In the early 1900s, however, flushed with success over the 'splendid little war' with Spain in the Caribbean, many Senators and Congressmen wanted to push ahead with plans for the canal without regard to former treaties. Britain objected, and the final result was a compromise: the Hay–Pauncefote Treaty gave the United States the primary right to construct the canal, but included in its provisions a clause that when completed the canal would be operated '. . . on terms of entire equality, so that there shall be no discrimination against any . . . nation . . . in respect of the conditions or charges of traffic, or otherwise. . . .'

This treaty was flouted by the 1912 Act of Congress which exempted American coastwise shipping from all tolls. Although the matter appeared to be one for adjustment between the two governments, 1912 happened to be a Presidential election year in the United States.

The Democratic platform handled the issue gingerly and equivocally. Taft, the candidate of the Republican party, now split by Theodore Roosevelt's Progressive forces, merely mentioned vague support of the American merchant marine. Roosevelt, however, included in his campaign platform the trenchant phrase: 'The

Panama Canal, built and paid for by the American people, must be used primarily for their benefit. We demand that the Canal shall be so operated. . . .' In his campaign Roosevelt reiterated that all other nations should pay tolls, whilst American ships should enjoy free passage.[16]

There was some logic to Roosevelt's case. American capital had financed the enormously expensive undertaking. The volume of American coastwise shipping between the Pacific and the Atlantic seaboards of America would depend on the tolls levied. But if tolls were charged, American shipping would be penalised by comparison with rail and road freight within the United States. Once more, internal politics in the United States bedevilled an international situation. The railroad lobby was roundly accused of supporting canal tolls on American merchant shipping. Charges flew thick and fast in the 1912 campaign. Although the split in the Republican party between Taft and Roosevelt gave victory to Woodrow Wilson and the Democrats, at the same time the considerable vote for Roosevelt ensured that the Panama Canal tolls would be the first headache for the new President.[17]

James Bryce was pleased at Wilson's election. The two men had talked together as friends and fellow scholars at Princeton, and Bryce had received an honorary degree from Wilson's hands only three years earlier. On the tolls question, however, there was strong feeling among leading Democrats – including William Jennings Bryan, the next Secretary of State. Many Senators and Congressmen urged that America should stand firm. Britain would surely climb down, as she did over Venezuela. Grey passed urgent messages to Bryce. In December the Ambassador formally protested to the Secretary of State over the proposed exemption of American coastwise shipping from Panama Canal tolls, declaring that such exemption was contrary to the Hay–Pauncefote Treaty. William Jennings Bryan remained silent. Events then took an unusual turn.

In January 1913 Woodrow Wilson was asked to dine with a small select club in New York calling itself the Round Table. The club was composed of leading citizens from New York and beyond. They included on this occasion Elihu Root, Joseph Choate, ex-Ambassador to Britain, Henry White, Nicholas Murray Butler,

Charles Francis Adams, and Henry Lee Higginson from Boston. As it happened, all were close friends of James Bryce and agreed with the principles he had invoked in his December note.

After dinner, talk in the assembled group turned to the tolls question and the understanding with Britain in the Hay–Pauncefote Treaty. Wilson's biographer records that he listened attentively and asked questions from time to time. At the end he remarked: 'This has been an illuminating discussion. I knew very little about this subject. I think I now understand it, and the principles that are involved. When the time comes for me to act, you may count on me taking the right stand.'[18] On the face of it, this was one of Wilson's typically Delphic utterances, but at a Cabinet meeting on 5 April, he declared his conviction that the 1912 Act of Congress had been morally wrong and unjustified. The President was in favour of repealing the clause giving exemption to American shipping. Furthermore, he stated his resolute determination to bring about repeal.

Bryce was still awaiting a formal answer to his protest. On 16 April he wrote to the Secretary of State Bryan asking whether the Administration was now prepared to make a statement. Bryce now knew that the Cabinet was split on the issue and that Bryan was among those favouring exemption for American shipping. Bryce was invited to the White House and a long private discussion with Wilson ensued. Wilson gave Bryce his word that he would seek a settlement that was just and honourable.[19]

Bryce had no illusions about the problem Wilson faced within his own Cabinet, his party and in the Congress. Bryce again stated the case for his Government fully and frankly. He then wrote to Grey saying that he was convinced that Wilson would honour his pledge, despite the bitter opposition he would encounter in the months ahead. With that, Bryce prepared to depart from Washington. His successor had already been named. Cecil Spring-Rice had chafed at repeated delays of the announcement, but in April 1913 he came into his own at last.[20]

Bryce ended his six years in Washington with an inward sense of disappointment. The failure to achieve a comprehensive arbitration treaty, and the present failure to bring the Canal Tolls question to

239

a conclusion were harsh blows. Bryce hid his disappointment as he made his last round of farewells in Washington and New York. On 25 April in New York the Pilgrims gave a dinner to honour the departing Ambassador and Mrs Bryce. Joseph Choate was in the chair. The company included Elihu Root, the Presidents of several universities, ex-ambassadors, and leaders of thought in the United States. Choate's toast to Bryce was followed by one from the new American Ambassador to London, Walter Hines Page. Both speakers saluted the work Bryce had achieved during the past six years, recalling the ten treaties he had negotiated. When Bryce rose to reply he received a standing ovation, and after his modest speech of thanks, the audience stood again. Suddenly the crowded banquet hall was resounding to 'For he's a jolly good fellow'. Next day, the national press once more showed the white-bearded figure on its front pages. The face was now much older, more lined and even careworn. Editorials combined their warm tributes with genuine regret and even sadness at the departure of a trusted friend of America.[21]

James Bryce was now two weeks from his seventy-fifth birthday. He had earned a rest, but he would not be spending his birthday resting in Sussex, for with his wife he had planned an unusual itinerary for their return. From New York they journeyed west to San Francisco, whence a long sea voyage brought them to Japan. They returned to London by way of Korea, Manchuria and the Trans-Siberian Railway. The journey took several months and Bryce enjoyed it thoroughly.

A mountain of good wishes from Americans waited in the mail on his return to London. Months later, in 1914, Bryce learned that Woodrow Wilson had appeared before the United States Congress and urged repeal of the Canal Tolls Exemption Act. Some of the stormiest debates in the history of the Senate followed. The galleries of the House and the Senate were packed throughout the debates. But Woodrow Wilson used the full weight of his office and his political influence. Eminent Americans spoke in support of Wilson. Their ranks included the members of the Round Table in New York. At one critical stage Wilson threatened to resign if repeal did not pass the Congress. In June, repeal passed the House by 247 to 162 votes, and the Senate by 50 to 35. A week later, Bryce wrote to Wilson thanking him for honouring his pledge. He added:

Such a victory has a moral value reaching far beyond this particular case and is the more valuable because the worst elements in the press seem to have exerted themselves more virulently than ever before. Eighteen months ago I told my government at home that I believed you could carry this because the best sentiment of the nation would respond to an appeal coming from you as its head: it is a satisfaction to one who loves your people to see that this has happened.[22]

Wilson paused from the bitter turmoil which still occupied him and replied to Bryce:

Your letter of June nineteenth gave me deep pleasure. I realised the political risks in undertaking to obtain a repeal of tolls exemptions, but I do not know of anything I ever undertook with more willingness or zest and I think that we have reason to be proud of the way in which public opinion of the United States responded to the challenge. . . .

Thank you with all my heart for your generous words of encouragement. They have done me a lot of good. . . .[23]

Within a matter of weeks the issue of the Panama Canal tolls was overtaken by other events as Europe ignited into war.

20

The Approach of War

In the first half of 1914 Bryce divided his time between his long delayed study of modern democracies and speaking in the House of Lords. He had finally accepted the peerage which Grey first offered to him before he took up his appointment in Washington. Even in 1914 he was persuaded less by the attraction of a title than by the desire to speak in the upper chamber when the occasion demanded. As he remarked apologetically in a letter to Seth Low in New York: 'In this country one can't keep in any useful relationship except as a member of one or the other House: . . . I have accepted a place in the Second Chamber which unluckily we Britishers can't enter except with the burden of a title.'[1] He took his seat in the Lords on 10 February 1914 as Viscount Bryce of Dechmont – the place in Lanarkshire to which the Bryce ancestry could be traced. He spoke in the Lords in support of the latest Government of Ireland Bill. But even the long agony of Ireland paled before the carnage in Europe when in August the old world was swept into war. From now on, Bryce devoted all his energies to securing peace in Europe and then to the attempt to guarantee lasting world peace.

Bryce was genuinely and deeply horrified by the bloodshed, especially as it affected innocent people among the smaller nations. With Belgium already overrun and France threatened; with Britain, Russia, Germany, Austria and Serbia engaged in hostilities, events presaged even greater bloodshed in the months and years ahead.

Across the Atlantic, the United States government declared its neutrality in the first week of August. Far-sighted Europeans, Bryce among them, realised that the United States might have a decisive role to play if the war continued for some time. Of course, Bryce had no executive office or direct power to influence the policies of the belligerents or of the United States of America. Yet in the democracies, and especially in the United States, leaders had their advisers – both formal and informal. In England and in America some advisers were more influential than their lack of office suggested. Heads of governments often receive conflicting advice at moments of great crisis – especially from their own cabinets. At such moments, they frequently turn to the counsels of those without political careers to nurse or defend. Edward House was such a counsellor for Woodrow Wilson. Bryce became an unofficial counsellor to both, as well as to Edward Grey and the Foreign Office.

In August 1914 President Woodrow Wilson faithfully reflected the mood of the vast majority of the American people when he declared the United States neutral. This was a war between European states. It had all the aspects of those dynastic quarrels among the nation states of the old world which George Washington and Hamilton had inveighed against and from which they warned the American people to steer clear. In August 1914, the American people could find a battery of good reasons – some noble and principled, others mixed with a heavy dash of self-interest – for keeping out of the European war. They were led by a President who not only had a horror of war and shrank from any thought of involving his countrymen in the carnage which was now developing, but who also believed that the European nations had brought the catastrophe on themselves.[2]

Yet somehow, somewhere, between August 1914 and April 1917, the American people and its President turned away from their deeply entrenched desire for neutrality and entered the war on the side of the Allies. Clearly, the causes of this volte-face were many and diverse; it is easy to argue that they were innumerable. Among the potent causes of the abandonment of American neutrality was a slow, often hesitant process of opinion formation, acting on the American President and the American people alike, which gradually crystallised into a declaration of war against Germany in April 1917, thus effectively determining the result of the conflict. There were many catalysts in this process and not the least of them, as the evidence shows, was the ex-Ambassador Lord Bryce.

As soon as war broke out, Bryce was in touch with many of his American friends to learn from them the state of American opinion. Among his correspondents were Oliver Wendell Holmes at the Supreme Court, Seth Low in New York, President Lowell at Harvard, Charles Eliot, James Ford Rhodes, and numerous other scholars and lawyers elsewhere in the United States. Closest in spirit and longest in the exchanges which followed was Charles Eliot.[3]

Eliot had retired from the Presidency of Harvard in 1909 to be succeeded by Lawrence Lowell. As a professor emeritus Eliot devoted himself to the cause of peace, and for many years worked unremittingly to advance the ideas of the Society for the Judicial Settlement of International Disputes. But after war broke out in Europe, Eliot was the most outstanding private citizen in the United States to turn from early support of American neutrality to a growing advocacy of American intervention on behalf of the Allies.

Eliot and Bryce had often enough discussed the legacy of Bismarck in a country which each had known and loved and where both had studied happily and profitably in the early 1860s. Like Eliot, Bryce had retained his special affection for the German people – the friendly, gay and talented people he had known in the old Germany.

Bryce had watched the changes which came over Germany between 1870 and the 1890s with the closest attention. His interest stemmed from a genuine concern for a people whose learning and talents he knew full well had contributed enormously to the cultural inheritance of Europe. On several visits to Germany in the 1880s and 1890s Bryce had seen for himself the changes taking place in a formerly peaceful, relaxed people. In addition, friends such as Andrew White or Henry Villard had written privately to Bryce from Berlin on the changes they noticed in the new Germany. Andrew White was Ambassador to Germany from 1897 to 1902, and he shared the views of Bryce, Eliot and Villard on the effects of the Prussian spirit in German society. In December 1897, in fact, Bryce had asked White to arrange an appointment for him with Bismarck and also with 'the wisest men' in Berlin in order to discuss frankly Germany's aspirations and intentions. But the ageing Bismarck was ill and White was unable to make an appointment for Bryce.[4] Bryce was himself forced to cancel his trip to Germany owing to the grave illness of his eighty-year old father-in-law. The opportunity never came again. Thereafter Bryce watched with growing dismay what he felt was a fearful change thrust upon the German people by a military caste.

On all these developments in German history Bryce and Eliot were in complete agreement. Nevertheless in 1914 Eliot viewed British economic imperialism as a contributory cause of the war, and stated this frankly in his letters to Bryce. Between 1914 and 1916 Eliot sent to the *New York Times* several long letters which were published in full, and whose contents the *New York Times* strongly endorsed in editorials on the same page. An Eliot letter of 4 September 1914 was headed 'Probable causes of the European War' and occupied two whole columns.[5] At this stage, Eliot levelled blame at neither one side nor the other. He argued that the selfish dynastic quarrels of Europe and rivalry between the great powers were clearly the chief causes. His letter was by no means pro-British. Americans would take exception, Eliot wrote, to that self-righteous air with which the British monarch summoned a nation to war. Such terms as 'My loyal subjects' or 'My people' implied 'dynastic or personal ownership of peoples' which would shock the average American, Eliot declared. Americans preferred President Wilson's phrase 'My fellow countrymen'. Eliot meant what he said, and his point was not irrelevant. He was expressing a thoroughly American attitude. However, Eliot's letter also dwelt on another element in the European quarrel – that Caesarism whose chief spokesman had made the observation already printed in many American textbooks: 'Might is Right'. Eliot warned: 'Should Germany and Austria-Hungary succeed in their present undertakings the whole civilised world would be obliged to bear continuously and in ever increasing amount the burdens of great armaments and would live in constant fear of invasion. . . .' An accompanying editorial in the newspaper praised the long and carefully argued letter.[6]

Eliot had also written to President Wilson privately and at some length urging American neutrality in the war. But his letter included the remark: 'I remain of the opinion that in the interests of civilisation and peace, neither Germany nor Austria-Hungary should be allowed to succeed in its present undertakings. . . .'[7] There were few men in the United States whose opinions Wilson was more likely to respect for their wisdom, dispassion, and goodwill than the elderly scholar who, like Wilson himself, had been President of a famous university. At this stage, however, a deep hatred of war, and some suspicion of the motives of the Allies prompted Wilson to concentrate on the need to preserve American neutrality rather than any need to prevent a victory for Prussian militarism, by diplomatic or military means.

Meanwhile, Eliot and Bryce were exchanging further letters on what was fundamentally at stake in the European conflict. Often enough Bryce illustrated his points both with the utterances of German statesmen and with the writings of the Treitschke school of historians. 'The real curse of Europe is that Militarism which has reached its highest development in the German military caste', Bryce remarked in his letter of 9 September 1914. He had made the observation before and repeated it in subsequent letters.[8]

On 22 September the *New York Times* published another two-column letter from Charles Eliot headed 'Imperialistic and Democratic Ideals – a Contrast'. In it, Eliot contrasted the American view that the chief object of government should be the promotion of the public welfare by legislative and administrative means, with another view that the will to power and domination should occupy the energies of governments. Once more the *New York Times* strongly endorsed Eliot's views in an editorial on the same day.[9]

Clearly, a newspaper which had identified itself with liberal ideals and the cause of peace for decades could be expected to subscribe to such views. At the same time, the *New York Times*, like other journals and newspapers in the United States, could choose between two broad alternatives in editorial policy. One was to defend the neutralist position favoured by the overwhelming majority of Americans, and to condemn those quarrels and jealousies of European nations which had produced the present slaughter. Another was to take sides (without departing from the American policy of neutrality) – to make a moral choice, in fact, and to see distinctions between the belligerents. As the war continued, opinion in the leading American newspapers came to reflect the view that the war concerned something much deeper than dynastic quarrels; that it involved nothing less than a threat to the most basic assumptions of American liberalism and thus to the foundations of American liberty.[10] This view and these convictions were distilled slowly; in 1914 most Americans believed that Britain's commercial rivalry with Germany was one of the causes of the war and thus one of Britain's reasons for declaring war on Germany. Eventually, however, the issues at stake were deemed more important than the *casus belli*.

In another long letter to the *New York Times* in November 1914, Eliot was still stressing the economic motives of the belligerents. Eliot sent a copy of the letter to Bryce when he next wrote. Bryce held that on the point of commercial rivalry Eliot had somewhat misjudged the British position, and in a confidential reply to Eliot took pains to analyse the situation in Britain at the outset of the war:

Thank you for your letter to the N.Y. Times of Nov. 17, which I have read with much profit and agreement, except as to one small point. You seem to give some countenance to the idea that British jealousy of Germany, i.e. commercial jealousy, was one cause of our joining in the war. Now there certainly was a certain annoyance in our commercial class – a most unreasonable annoyance – at the way in which German merchants were cutting them in some markets, and this had something to do with the want of cordiality in recent years. But I do not think it really contributed to the breach of this summer. Between ourselves, there were three currents of feeling in England: a large section of the Tories, as well as the army and the navy, and the Jingoes generally, believed that Germany had made up her mind to attack us and was only waiting for her opportunity. Another section, including all non-Jingo Liberals, while disliking her militarism and her rather brutal attitude in international relations, believed the Emperor, and the German nation as a whole, to be pacific, and were resolved to resist being drawn into war on behalf of France. The rest of the British people did not quite know what to think, but neither desired nor expected war. When it was plain that there would be a fight between France and Germany, the first named section wished us to join France on the ground that if we didn't, we should be the next victim. The second section resisted this view, thinking the evidence insufficient. The Cabinet was divided, and was on the point of breaking up over the question when suddenly the German Govt. declared it must invade Belgium. That changed the situation in a moment, and united all sections.

Thus the fact was that England might *possibly* have been led into war had Belgium not been invaded, but if so, half the country would have been against the war, not convinced of its necessity, and we should now be disunited. Those were, I think, the only real factors, and I must regretfully admit that what we have since seen and learnt makes one feel that we of the pacific section thought better of the German Govt. than perhaps we ought to have thought.[11]

In another letter to Eliot, Bryce remarked: 'If you have time, you ought to look at a book called "Germany and the Next War" by General von Bernhardi, which has had an immense circulation in Germany, though one hopes and trusts that its detestable doctrines will not commend themselves to the German people. It is the most cynical avowal of a contempt for all moral principles in the international field I have ever seen, and buttressed by more false philosophy, false history and even false biology than has ever been brought together in one volume. . . .'[12]

Bernhardi's book had first appeared in 1911. An English translation appeared in 1914.[13] Reading it, Bryce was appalled at its contents, especially when he measured its proposals against scenes which were now unfolding in Belgium and France. Bryce wrote a blistering attack on Bernhardi which was soon circulating widely. The article appeared first in the London *Daily Chronicle*, and was promptly repeated in substance in the widely read *Review of Reviews* in the United States.[14] Bryce's old friend Albert Shaw, who edited the *Review of Reviews* throughout the war years, gave three pages of the journal to extensive quotation from Bryce's article. Thereafter demand for the full text was so intense that it was printed as a pamphlet for circulation in Britain and the United States. The pamphlet bore the significant title 'Neutral Nations and the War'.[15] It was the nearest Bryce ever came to writing a polemic unsweetened by scholarly detachment, and expressly designed to destroy a thesis completely.

Bryce began with the round assertion that the doctrine in

Bernhardi's book struck 'at the root of all international morality as well as of all international law':

The doctrines set forth by General von Bernhardi and apparently accepted by the military caste to which he belongs are startling propositions, though propounded as practically axiomatic. They are not new, for twenty-two centuries ago the Sophist Thrasymachus in Plato's *Republic* argued . . . that Justice is nothing more than the advantage of the stronger, i.e. Might is Right.

The most startling among them are (1) the denial that there are any duties owed by the State to Humanity, except that of imposing its own superior civilisation upon as large a part of humanity as possible and (2) the denial of the duty of observing treaties. Treaties are only so much paper. . . .

To modern German writers the State is a much more tremendous entity than it is to Englishmen or Americans. It is a supreme power with a sort of mystic sanctity, a power conceived of, as it were, self-created, a force altogether distinct from, and superior to, the persons who compose it. . . .[16]

From this point onwards, Bryce scythed into Bernhardi and the Treitschke school to which Bernhardi attributed his gospel:

If it is right for persons united as citizens into a State to rob and murder for their collective advantage by their collective power, why should it be wicked for the citizens as individuals to do so? Does their moral responsibility cease when and because they act together . . .? Has the State then no morality, no responsibility? Is there no such thing as common humanity? Are there no duties owed to *it*? Is there none of that 'decent respect to the opinion of mankind' which the framers of the Declaration of Independence recognised; no sense that even the greatest States are amenable to the sentiment of the civilised world?

The rhetoric continued for another seventeen pages. Bryce furnished evidence of what such doctrines had produced in the past. Bernhardi was not spared: 'General Bernhardi invokes history, the ultimate court of appeal. He appeals to Caesar. To Caesar let him go. *Die Weltgeschichte ist das Weltgericht.* . . . What are the teachings of history? – History to which General Bernhardi is fond of appealing? That war has been the constant handmaid of tyranny and the source of more than half the miseries of man. . . . That the mark of an advancing civilisation has been the substitution of friendship for hatred and of peaceful for warlike ideals. That small peoples have done and can do as much for the common good of humanity as large peoples. . . .'[17]

In 1915 Bernhardi's work was freely available in translation in the United States. So was Bryce's pamphlet. In the meantime, Bryce had served as Chairman of the Commission set up by Asquith 'To enquire into Alleged German Outrages in Belgium'. The Commission contained distinguished jurists and barristers, including four K.C.s. Bryce attempted through his American friends to have a similar commission of investigation set up by American authorities, but without success. As Bryce remarked to Seth Low, an investigation by neutrals would surely inspire confidence.[18] In the winter of 1914–15 the Bryce Commission examined thousands of pieces of evidence, ranging from the diaries of captured German soldiers to on the spot reports in Belgium. By 1915, the report of the Commission was widely available and received extensive comment in the American press. The outrages on the Belgian civilian population were fully documented, and though some of the evidence was hearsay, nevertheless the report of the Bryce Commission was shocking evidence of military brutality against the defenceless civilians of Belgium.[19]

The war continued on the battlefields and on the high seas. In May 1915 the *Lusitania* was sunk by a German submarine and at the end of July the United States Secret Service obtained proof of German sabotage activities in the United States. These occurrences angered Wilson as they angered large sections of the American public, but anger did not necessarily mean an end to neutrality or a definite move in favour of the Allies. Wilson's Secretary of State Bryan refused to sign Wilson's note of protest to Germany on the loss of American lives on the *Lusitania* and resigned on 7 June. After all, the *Lusitania* was a British ship and Germany and Britain were at war.

Wilson now faced serious opposition in his own party. German Americans and Irish Americans already suspected him of pro-Allied sympathies. They also recalled that Wilson had been elected by a minority in 1912.[20] In 1916 the Presidential elections would come round once more with their iron regularity, and after Bryan's resignation in June 1915 Wilson's hold on his party in the west and among sections of the urban immigrant Democrats in the eastern cities was tenuous. At the same time, having committed himself to keeping America out of the war, he could hardly risk a volte-face unless, that is, he sought political extinction. Quite apart from a genuine wish to keep America out of the war, Wilson was angry with the British government over the issue of the neutrals' trade: repeated representations and, later, formal notes would not shift the British from their interference with neutral shipping in the attempt to blockade Germany.[21]

Despite his growing irritation with the belligerents, Wilson maintained close contact with the Allied and the German governments in the search for a negotiated peace. Here, Colonel Edward House was his chief intermediary. In January 1915, House began a series of visits to the governments on both sides of the conflict. In London, House conferred chiefly with Grey, Balfour, and the American Ambassador Walter Hines Page; but he also talked privately with Bryce, sometimes at considerable length. From these meetings, House learned of the determination of the British government to press on with the war until the German government was completely discredited in the eyes of the world and also of its own people. This was the chief message House brought back from his visits to London and his talks with the French ministers. These visits had other results, however; and if they seem to lack any immediate or observable influence on Woodrow Wilson, they are nevertheless worth bearing in mind for what was eventually to happen to Wilson's neutralist policy.

Bryce and House first met in Washington and New York during Bryce's Ambassadorship, and House had attended the farewell dinner for Bryce in April 1913. Entries in House's private diary testify abundantly to the respect and confidence he gave to Bryce's views and counsel.[22] Their first long discussion on the war was in London in February 1915. The two men were entirely alone and, among other things, they discussed the problem of bringing the war to an end. At this stage they agreed on the need for a cessation of the manufacture of armaments and the calling of a convention for peace such as President Wilson had in mind. House and Bryce also agreed with each other that the tragedy could have been prevented if statesmen had kept in touch at certain crucial moments; however, that was water under the bridge. . . .

Before he departed, House conveyed Wilson's good wishes to Bryce and mentioned that the President had recently read to him a sketch of Bryce in Gardiner's *Pillars of Society*. The opening passage of the sketch, House told Bryce, went thus: 'If one were asked to name the greatest living Englishman I think it would be necessary to admit, regretfully, that he is a Scotsman born in Ireland.' Bryce smiled, House noted in his diary, and said he had not read it, but was afraid to do so 'for fear his head might be turned'.[23] The incident was a small one, though House took the trouble to record it fully in his diary. Bryce returned personal good wishes to the President.

In May and in June 1915 Bryce and House again talked privately in London. On 3 June their talk ranged from Germany and her people, her philosophy, habits and tendencies, to a discussion of Mexico and even the Confederate General Robert E. Lee and his place in history. House noted in his diary: 'We are to keep in touch with one another and to write when we consider the other should be informed about current happenings . . . [for] I agree with A. G. Gardiner in believing James Bryce to be one of the foremost living Englishmen.'[24]

Thereafter, Bryce and House met for private discussions whenever House visited London. Between these talks, they wrote to each other, now and then referring to the subject of their talks. These references were usually cryptic, owing to the constant danger of interference with sea mails; nevertheless, the extensive correspondence between Bryce and House clearly establishes their rapport. Bryce was always at pains to make clear that he sympathised with the President's very difficult position. A Bryce letter of August 1915 was characteristic: 'Those who understand your history and the genuinely pacific mind of your people know how strong is the tradition against intermixture in European complications, and how many facts and sentiments those who guide your policy have to consider.'[25] Among these facts, Bryce knew only too well, were the problems of a divided Democratic party, divided loyalties within the American nation, and the exigencies of

Presidential and mid-term elections. Bryce realised clearly, though perhaps not with the same immediate agony as President Wilson, that patience, skill and electoral strategy must accompany whatever policies the President decided to adopt as the war continued and extended to the high seas.

House and Wilson were hoping for a 'peace without victory' at this stage, without armed American intervention, though with American mediation if necessary. Wilson stuck doggedly to this hope long after Colonel House and Secretary of State Robert Lansing had come to feel privately that American involvement was unavoidable. In the meantime, there is little doubt that Woodrow Wilson and Colonel House studied very carefully and continuously the counsels that Bryce offered. On 12 August 1915, after a further conference with Bryce, House completed a long letter thus: 'I am writing you these things, dear Lord Bryce, because of all men in Great Britain you know our difficulties. You know our sympathies and ideas, and it is through you that I hope some measure of our troubles and perplexities may reach your people.'[26]

Bryce was, however, equally determined to impress on House and thus on President Wilson the full implications of America's neutralist policy. On 26 August 1915 Bryce wrote:

. . . As you desire my own view, I will give it. In the early days of the war your interests seemed to me only slightly affected. Now, however, it is plain that a victorious Germany would threaten America and every maritime nation. If she dominated the seas as she desires she would be a formidable neighbour in the West Indies and probably in South America.

Furthermore, the methods by which she carries on war against non-combatants on land and sea are a step back towards savagery and a challenge to civilized mankind. For her to emerge triumphant after the free use of such methods would be a grave misfortune for human progress to which America, the most humane of nations, could not be indifferent.

These two features of the war have changed its aspect for neutral nations. They go far beyond the original causes and merits of the war. Far more than the fortunes of Britain is now involved.

For the last two months the German Government seems to have been playing with you and we might almost say, – trying how far your patience will go. She is posing before her own people as the strong Power which can defy the whole world.

The conduct of her Embassy in directing disgraceful intrigues within the United States is, if the stories in your press are even half true, without precedent in the annals of diplomacy for two centuries. . . .

Bryce concluded his letter: 'I shall value most highly any expressions of your views and, whenever good can be done, convey them to quarters in which they would be useful.'[27]

Edward Grey and Bryce conferred together regularly. Grey's regard for Bryce's opinions on any aspect of American affairs need hardly be emphasised: the Bryce Ambassadorship to the United States was already legendary in Whitehall. Again, it was recognised that when Bryce discussed or assessed the policies of the American President he was interpreting the views and beliefs of a personal friend of many years' standing, whose mind he was especially able to understand. For Woodrow Wilson and James Bryce were very much alike. Wilson was primarily a scholar who had stumbled into politics, an austere Scotch Presbyterian whose intellectual interests were centred on the problems of politics and jurisprudence. He had a horror of war and bloodshed but also a passionate devotion to liberal causes – especially to individual liberty, to freedom of conscience and to the rule of law for individuals and for nations. These commitments Wilson shared with the older scholar-diplomat, whose lectures and seminar had so much affected him as a graduate in 1883 at Johns Hopkins University.[28]

Both men were lovers of peace, yet at a certain point both Wilson and Bryce were prepared to countenance total war in defence of their ideals. Bryce reached the point of decision when he discovered the nature of German atrocities on the civilian population of Belgium. Woodrow Wilson's point of decision came later.

2 1

The Diplomacy of Friends

Between 1914 and 1917, Bryce was communicating regularly with other eminent Americans on the subject of the war in all its frightful aspects – its causes, its conduct, the issues involved, and the steps which must be taken to avoid future wars. In letters to Lawrence Lowell, Seth Low, Nicholas Murray Butler, Henry White, Joseph Choate, Henry Bayard, Elihu Root, William Howard Taft, Theodore Roosevelt, Henry Cabot Lodge and James Ford Rhodes, Bryce stressed the determination of the British to defeat not the German people, but the German government and the military caste which had taken control of Germany's affairs.[1] Each of these men accepted that, whatever the present motives of the belligerents, the Prussian ethic presented a grave threat to American ideals.

Elsewhere, of course, other voices were raised to persuade the American people that the war had been thrust on Germany by policies of encirclement and then economic pressure by other powers. The German philosopher and psychologist Professor Hugo Münsterberg directed from his Harvard chair a stream of articles, letters and books defending Germany, until his death in 1916. In New York and in the west, the German American press naturally defended Germany's motives and actions in the war. Herman Ridder died in 1915, but the *Staats-Zeitung* had no lack of skilled writers who genuinely believed in Germany's innocence.[2] When Bryce's pamphlet on 'Neutral Nations and the War' was fully reported in the *Review of Reviews*, a rejoinder promptly appeared from Dr Bernhard Dernburg, former Colonial Minister of Germany.[3]

Dernburg argued that neither Bernhardi nor the followers of Treitschke were the guiding spirits of those in charge of German policies. So far as the mass of German voters was concerned, he continued, fully one-third of the population could be considered

255

Socialist 'and had never voted the budget on account of the war expenditure contained therein'. Many Americans must have considered this a curious argument. Moreover an American administration would be cheered to learn that its annual budget had the support of fully two-thirds of the American electorate.

Dernburg then argued that Bernhardi's book was directed against certain effeminate tendencies he had observed in Germany, as well as a growing trend towards materialism. But Dernburg's defence was not assisted by Bernhardi's further writings glorifying war, especially his work *Britain as Germany's Vassal*.[4]

Between 1915 and early 1916 President Wilson continued to press for a negotiated peace and the acceptance by the belligerents of American mediation. The failure of that policy has been fully recorded by the historians of the period.[5] In his letters to House in 1916, Bryce continued to stress that 'there is not the slightest change in British sentiment regarding the duty and necessity to prosecute the war with the utmost vigour and listening to no suggestions for negotiations with the German government.'[6] The reason for this, Bryce insisted, was that the Allies could put no trust in any declarations of intent by the German government. The first task remained to get rid of the present German leaders and then consider arrangements for ending the war and preserving the peace. Bryce reiterated these points in letters to Theodore Roosevelt, William Howard Taft and Henry Cabot Lodge, who was now Chairman of the Senate Foreign Relations Committee.[7]

Naturally Wilson and House were receiving similar messages through official channels from Edward Grey and the Ambassadors in London and Washington. Unfortunately, relations between Woodrow Wilson and Cecil Spring-Rice in Washington were very unsatisfactory. Spring-Rice was proving an irritating presence to Wilson and also to members of his Cabinet.[8] Observing this unhappy situation, House urged Bryce several times to come to America on a speaking tour. At the first attempt in December 1915 House wrote: 'I believe if you could come now you could do your country no greater service. Some reasonable excuse should be given for your visit and I could make this up for you, if you will consider coming. I would not want anyone to know I was advising this and for reasons which I can only give verbally. . . .'[9]

The British Embassy, Washington, D.C., in 1910

Theodore Roosevelt,
President of the United States
1901–1908

Woodrow Wilson,
President of the United States
1912–1920

Ambassador James Bryce and Secretary of State Philander C. Knox signing the Arbitration Treaty between Great Britain and

By now Bryce realised that House was firmly on the side of the Allies and opposed American neutrality, though Wilson's precise attitude was still obscure. Bryce was willing to make such a trip but, after conferring with Grey, he declined. The explanation to House was that 'the wounding of Ambassadorial dignity' in Washington would be too grave.[10] A more likely explanation is that Grey reasoned – probably correctly – that a visit by Bryce would be judged as propaganda to enlist American support and as such would particularly offend German-Americans and Irish-Americans. Irish Home Rule was now at a stage of crisis in British politics and anti-British demonstrations were frequent in New York. Beyond this, a Bryce visit might also offend, on a much wider scale, pacifist and neutralist sentiment in many parts of the United States.

Anglo-American understanding was still a very fragile affair. Although Wilson and Grey, House and Bryce undoubtedly shared certain fundamental beliefs about politics, about the role of the State in a democratic society, or about militarism, nevertheless in the exchanges between Washington and London old enmities often peeped out. Before Bryan's resignation at the State Department, American notes were drafted in a style designed to cause profound irritation in London, where Ambassador Page habitually toned down the language of some State Department missives before presenting them to Grey. One note which he showed directly to Grey brought the remark: 'This reads as though they thought that they are still talking to George the Third.'[11] On that occasion Grey burst into laughter, but on another occasion Page sought to justify an American protest at British interference with American shipping by remarking to Lord Robert Cecil, the Minister in charge of the blockade: 'You must not forget the Boston Tea Party.' According to Page, Cecil looked puzzled. 'But I have never been to Boston', he countered: 'I have never attended a tea party there.'[12] There were still gaps in Anglo-American understanding.

On his visit to London in January 1916 Colonel House brought Wilson's proposal for American mediation of the war. He conferred first with Grey and Balfour, and saw others during the following two weeks. House talked at length with Bryce on 11 January.

Another private talk, lasting two hours, followed two days later.
House noted in his diary: 'I wish the benefit of his advice before I
take up the discussion again with Grey and Balfour. . . . I feel
that he knows America so well that he can understand and advise
in the many perplexing questions confronting us.'[13]

House left London for Paris, then Berlin and after that Brussels
to discuss President Wilson's proposals with the other powers.
Returning to London in February, House found Grey and Balfour
in a more receptive mood to the idea of a peace conference and
mediation under the auspices of the United States. From the
February meetings, the famous House–Grey memorandum of 22
February 1916 came forth. This provided on President Wilson's
behalf that, on hearing from England and France that the moment
was opportune, the President would summon a peace conference.
Should Allied acceptance of this be followed by German refusal,
then the United States 'would probably enter the war against the
Germans.'[14]

In fact House exceeded his mandate by issuing the memorandum
in this form, but it was of no practical consequence: neither the
Allied powers nor the Central powers subsequently made any
definite moves for obtaining a peace conference. Back in Washington, Colonel House heard from Bryce that Britain and France
were determined to push ahead with the war, whatever reverses
were suffered in the near or distant future.[15]

In the United States the debate on American neutralist policies
continued. In February 1916 Charles Eliot brought Bryce up to
date on American opinion, and gave his own views:

. . . . I think we ought to get ready for an offensive and defensive
alliance with Great Britain and France . . . but few agree with me,
some saying 'no entangling alliance for us', and others maintaining
that militarism cannot be overcome by more militarism — as if
German violence could be overcome by anything except superior
fighting force.

There are some faint signs that our people are beginning to see
that the triumph of Germany would be unsafe for all the freedom-
loving peoples. . . .[16]

Bryce readily agreed with Eliot's proposal for an alliance between
France, Britain and the United States, but pointed out that in the

present state of American public opinion it was far better this suggestion should come from Americans than from Englishmen. Then Bryce discussed the views of those who held to the 'no entangling alliances' doctrine. His letter continued:

Washington's advice about 'entangling alliances' was given under conditions totally different from those we see now. America was four times as far from Europe. Europe was dynastic and her wars and alliances mainly governed by dynastic considerations; no moral issues had arisen, it was impossible for any nation after the failure of England to reduce the American colonies, to threaten the United States; the world was not, as it is today, one community, no part of which can escape the influences which become dominant in other parts. There are still European complications which Americans should avoid, but on the other hand there are duties common to Europe and America in which she ought to bear her part. . . .[17]

Yet Bryce could appreciate that in a situation where so many Americans felt honestly divided in their sentiments about the European war, they would naturally fall back on the spirit of George Washington's Farewell Address. Eliot's latest letter suggested that more and more Americans were beginning to lean to the Allied side, but most were unconvinced.

At this point Bryce wrote an article which appeared in the *New Republic* in May 1916. It was headed 'America's Traditional Isolation'. In the article Bryce elaborated the points he had already made privately in his letter to Eliot. The opening passage put forward the proposition that the United States could no longer be guided by the counsels which Washington gave to the nation in his Farewell Address. In the following two pages Bryce carefully traced the historical, geographical and economic arguments which supported this proposition. Whatever the outcome of the present war, Bryce insisted, America could not stand aloof from the frightful problems of making and then preserving the peace. In a shrinking world, now totally different from the world George Washington knew, the United States was inescapably involved in the affairs of the old world.[18]

Although it was known that the *New Republic* leaned to the side of the Allies, nevertheless the young journal had made a name for itself as an independent organ of opinion, and brilliant young writers like Walter Lippman already had a large following among the informed public. The Bryce article was of sufficient interest for the *New York Times* to print it entire in its issue of 19 May.[19] At least one reader felt the *New Republic* article important enough to preserve it among his papers. This was Woodrow Wilson, who kept it in a confidential file which at the time not even his secretary was allowed to see.[20]

One week later, Wilson delivered what was, in his own words, one of the most important speeches of his career. The speech was given before the League to Enforce Peace on 27 May 1916. Founded at Philadelphia in June 1915, the League was a forum where the activities of many existing American peace societies could be combined. Among its sponsors were ex-President Taft, Lawrence Lowell, Theodore Marburg, and many eminent scholars and professional men. The League was thus a valuable platform for airing proposals designed to end the European war and to prevent the outbreak of future wars.*

Wilson decided to make his 27 May address an important policy-making speech. He enlisted the aid of Colonel House in planning the speech and the two men sat down together – in House's words, 'to see how far he should go'.[21] House supplied his chief with the most recent speeches by Asquith, Grey and Balfour. The President also had before him Bryce's article from the *New Republic*.[22] House in fact wrote his draft on the day after Bryce's article appeared. Wilson's final draft, almost identical to House's, ended with the phrase: 'The nations of the world have become each other's neighbours.' This was a capsule summary of the Bryce article.[23]

Wilson's main intention in his speech of 27 May was to call for a universal alliance to maintain freedom of the seas and to prevent future wars; but the most significant statement in the address was that the United States must henceforth be ready and willing to join in such a universal alliance. In short, Wilson's speech spelled the end of American isolation. His biographers have observed that this speech, containing the historic words 'We are participants, whether

---

* As we shall see, James Bryce had been closely involved in the formation of the American League to Enforce Peace.

we would or not, in the life of the world', was a turning-point in Wilson's foreign policy and indeed a turning-point in American history. As Brand Whitlock, American Minister to Belgium, wrote to House: 'It is the most important announcement concerning our foreign policy since the announcement of the Monroe Doctrine, although it will take many years before this fact is brought into relief and fully understood.'[24]

Wilson's reasons for this important policy statement were, of course, many and subtle. Although his speech announced the end of American isolation, at the same time the belligerents could take little comfort from another phrase the President introduced. Regarding the war, Wilson observed: 'With its causes and objects we are not concerned. The obscure fountains from which its stupendous flood has burst forth we are not interested to search for or explore.'

Wilson may have had good political reasons for his little flourish on the complexities of historical causation, but the remark brought anger in London and Paris, just as it nonplussed Colonel House. No one could quite fathom the exact reason for another of Wilson's Delphic utterances. This remark was soon to be placed alongside other obscure phrases he had used and would use about the war: 'Too proud to fight'; 'Peace without Victory'; 'The objects . . . of both sides . . . are virtually the same as stated in general terms to their own peoples and to the world.' Even trained diplomats might marvel at such ambiguities. Yet there was no real mystery. America was divided, and Woodrow Wilson needed votes to get re-elected in November 1916.

Many members of the British Cabinet were exasperated by Wilson's apparent attempt to equate Germany with France and Britain in the present conflict. Bryce was less exasperated, for he knew that there were many explanations for Wilson's combination of commitment and non-involvement. Several months before Wilson's League speech Lawrence Godkin of the *Nation* had mentioned to Bryce:

It does seem to me quite a tenable hypothesis that the President . . . is simply cautious in endeavouring not to go any faster or further than he thinks the bulk of the country will follow, lest, perchance, having taken a line which would involve war with Germany it turned out that the country was not prepared to give him the support which would be absolutely essential. . . . I agree with you in thinking that if the United States had gone to war immediately after the Lusitania affair the war would have been over by now. But in excuse for Wilson it is to be said that he might not have carried the west with him, and war with a divided country is a pretty tough proposition.[25]

Bryce did not have all the facts to explain Wilson's policy in 1916, but from his own knowledge he found Godkin's hypothesis perfectly tenable. Indeed, in a letter to his old and intimate friend Albert Dicey, Bryce observed that he had privately held to this hypothesis 'from the start'.[26]

In June 1916, Woodrow Wilson again received the nomination of the Democratic party for the Presidential elections to be held in November. At the national party convention in St Louis the party platform which finally emerged after protracted discussion contained an important section endorsing President Wilson's stand in his speech to the League to Enforce Peace. The significant passage in the platform read:

The circumstances of the last two years have revealed necessities of international action which no former generation [of Americans] can have foreseen. . . . We believe that every people has the right to choose the sovereignty under which it shall live; that the small states of the world have a right to enjoy from other nations the same respect for their sovereignty and for their territorial integrity that great and powerful nations expect and insist upon; and that the world has a right to be free from every disturbance of its peace that has its origin in aggression or disregard of the rights of people and nations; and we believe that the time has come when it is the duty of the United States to join in any feasible association that will effectively service those principles. . . .[27]

There is no doubting that the incumbent President had insisted on the inclusion of this passage. The Democratic platform of 1916 thus formally renounced isolationist doctrines and conceded that the problems of the old world – including those of small powers such as Belgium – were the concern of the new world. This was a vital shift from the American posture of August 1914.

In London, Bryce rejoiced at the news. When Woodrow Wilson reaffirmed the end of isolation in his acceptance speech at the Democratic convention, Bryce sent his congratulations to the President. Bryce and House continued to correspond with each other. House was left in no doubt that the Allies were determined to prosecute the war and not to trust overtures for peace now emanating from Germany. Bryce firmly insisted that these overtures were merely a device to prolong the war and thus, through time, win concessions from the Allies, for Germany knew that by now the war was thoroughly unpopular on the Allied home fronts. House assured Bryce that the President was keenly interested in his letters, intimating that he and his chief often read Bryce's letters together.[28] The sympathy of House for the Allied cause was self-evident by this time, but President Wilson apparently still wished to keep his powder dry.

In the 1916 Presidential election campaign Woodrow Wilson's strongest appeal was the slogan 'He kept us out of the war'. In November he was returned to the White House, though not with the majorities he had hoped for. Nevertheless as Chief Executive Wilson was newly invested with the power to conduct foreign relations and to command the armed forces of the United States. In the months which followed, events moved swiftly and fatefully. In January 1917 Germany announced the continuation of unrestricted submarine warfare. On 3 February Wilson ordered the severance of diplomatic relations with Germany. Despite this, he still seemed to cling to American neutrality. In his speech before Congress announcing the severance with Germany, Wilson observed:

We do not desire any hostile conflict with the Imperial German Government. We are the sincere friends of the German people and earnestly desire to remain at peace with the Government which speaks for them. We shall not believe that they are hostile to us unless and until we are obliged to believe it; we seek merely to stand true alike in thought and action to the immemorial principles of our people. . . . These are the bases of peace, not war.

God grant we may not be challenged to defend them by acts of wilful injustice on the part of the Government of Germany.[29]

On 1 March the text of the Zimmermann telegram was published. Undoubtedly it gave a galvanic shock to the American President, as it did to the American people. Even so, it should be noted, the Zimmermann telegram was not in itself a *casus belli*. If Wilson had so chosen he could easily have invoked his recent campaign cry 'He kept us out of the war' and coupled this with a skilful speech showing that it was in the best interests of the American people to stay out of the conflict.

On 4 March, after that long interval which the American electoral system then maintained between the elections and Presidential inauguration, Wilson took the oath and was thus constitutionally installed in the Executive Office once more. Less than four weeks later he asked to appear before the two Houses of Congress in joint session. In his speech President Wilson called for a declaration of war against Germany. The speech was long, eloquent, carefully argued, occasionally ambiguous, but it convinced the great majority of his huge audience that the United States had been thrust unwillingly into the war. At the end, Senators, Congressmen and members of the Supreme Court rose to cheer their President. The war resolution passed the Senate on 4 April by 82 to 6 votes and the House on 6 April by 373 to 50. The United States thus entered the European war and placed its vast arsenals behind the cause of the Allies. The final result could no longer be in doubt.

The precise reasons for Woodrow Wilson's decision for war against Germany remain something of a mystery.[30] There is little doubt that even in March 1917 he was desperately anxious to avoid bringing the United States into the war. Yet equally he wished to bring the war to an end as soon as possible, and to establish machinery to guarantee the peace as soon as hostilities ceased. It may be that he became convinced that American entry into the war was the only way to secure a just peace.

There is abundant evidence that between August 1914 and late 1916 Woodrow Wilson was increasingly impressed by the *ultimately* pacific intentions of Grey, Balfour, and their colleagues in

London, because of their declared commitment to the idea of a League of Nations to guarantee a lasting peace at the end of hostilities.[31] Woodrow Wilson came to feel that a League of Nations to enforce peace was his personal mission. This venture, noble in essence, proved to be his final, tragic quest. It was a venture partly inspired by the unobtrusive work of Wilson's friend James Bryce.

2 2

The League Idea

The development of the League of Nations idea* has been carefully traced in two volumes of published documents and numerous monographs.[1] Although the American League to Enforce Peace was formally organised in June 1915, it had its roots in other institutions dedicated to peace, and more immediately in private correspondence across the Atlantic during the preceding five months.

The principal architect of the American League to Enforce Peace was Theodore Marburg, who served as United States Minister to Belgium before the outbreak of war and was deeply moved by Belgium's plight in 1914. Marburg and Bryce were old friends who had met frequently during Bryce's Ambassadorship. Marburg was in touch with Bryce soon after war broke out, and whilst the substance of their early correspondence dealt mostly with the plight of Belgium, Bryce undoubtedly planted some seeds in a letter to Marburg on 15 January 1915. 'One of the saddest things in this war is the total disregard by the German Government of the Hague Convention. What can be done to place its provisions for mitigating the terrors of war upon a more stable foundation?'[2]

In fact Bryce was already energetically seeking for the answer to his question. He formed a small group in London which met privately to discuss a post-war League for Peace. Early in 1915

* All discussions on the League of Nations idea encounter difficulties of terminology. Several organisations existed on both sides of the Atlantic, each bearing a similar name, each devoted to the same broad aims, yet differing in precise proposals for reaching those aims. Each of the several schemes put forward envisaged a number of member states comprising a League of Nations which could and would act together to maintain the peace. In the discussion here, the term 'League idea' refers to that general body of sentiment existing on both sides of the Atlantic between 1914 and 1918 for the creation of some effective international machinery for preserving world peace at the end of hostilities.

Bryce, together with G. Lowes Dickinson, a member of the London group, issued a memorandum setting out their ideas for a 'League of Peace'. The League would be composed of all powers agreeing to refer to the existing Permanent Court of Arbitration at the Hague 'all disputes between them (including those affecting honour and vital interests) which are of a justiciable character and which the Powers concerned have failed to settle by diplomatic methods'. The memorandum was circulated privately so as not to prejudice the British government's call to the people for vigorous efforts to prosecute the present war effort. The call to arms cannot go hand in hand with a summons to peacemaking.

Marburg showed Bryce's letter of 15 January to ex-President Taft and other Americans interested in the cause of peace. On 25 January, a group met at the Century Association in New York to discuss the need for an international League of Peace. The meeting reviewed in turn the failure of the old Concert of Europe, the Holy Alliance and, more recently, the Hague Conferences on disarmament.[3] The exact composition of a League of Peace was not agreed upon at this meeting: proposals ranged from one suggesting that all nations should be included, to another restricting membership at the outset to the 'great powers'. There was, however, complete agreement that the United States should take the lead in forming such a League.

Theodore Marburg sent his notes on this first meeting to Bryce in London and also drew President Wilson's attention to the New York meeting, asking for support from the White House. Wilson was interested, though his reply of 3 February 1915 suggested that it would be 'unwise for a member of the administration to appear at a public meeting called for the advocacy of some particular measure on international organisation just at this juncture'. Wilson concluded his brief note with the observation: 'I feel that we might be in danger of irritating the very persons whom we now wish to serve if we proposed a harness for them which they are not yet in a humor to wear.'[4]

Marburg arranged further meetings in New York on 31 January and 30 March. At the March meeting, proceedings began with a careful scrutiny of the Bryce-Dickinson memorandum on a League of Peace. Out of this meeting and another on 9 April came the formal proposal for setting up an American League of Peace at Philadelphia in June 1915. It was also agreed that a Committee of One Hundred should issue invitations to the June meeting. This distinguished Committee was headed by such figures as William Howard Taft, A. Lawrence Lowell, Albert Shaw, Frank Goodnow and scores of eminent professors. At a later meeting Taft accepted the Presidency of the proposed League.

The meetings of 30 March and 9 April also produced proposals for a constitution and a programme for the International League to Enforce Peace (as it was now decided to call it). These proposals closely resembled those produced by the London group. At the April meeting President Lowell moved, and it was unanimously agreed by those present:

(1) That it is desirable for the United States to join a League of all the great nations in which all justiciable questions between them would be submitted to a judicial tribunal.

(2) That members of the League shall jointly use their military force to prevent any one of their number from going to war or committing acts of hostility against any other member before the question at issue has been submitted to the tribunal.

The second proposal departed from the Bryce–Dickinson proposals, and was eventually to cause much disagreement in the League movement in the United States. At this stage, Bryce was opposed to the use of military force in the application of sanctions against any member of the proposed League of Nations. The New York meeting ended by voting that the steering committee should formulate the results of the conference and send them 'to Mr Bryce, for his concurrence'.

Throughout these early months of 1915 Bryce and Marburg exchanged details of meetings of the two groups at London and New York and of their results. There was concern in both groups for the safeguarding of treaty obligations, especially in the interest of small nations. Discussion on these issues was served by an article Bryce wrote in the *New York Times* on 'The rights of small nations'.[5] Marburg informed Bryce: 'Your article in the N.Y. Times showing how indispensable to progress is a proper regard for treaty obligations was widely read at the time and is still constantly referred to. . . .' At the same time, Marburg regularly circulated Bryce's letters and communications to his colleagues in the American movement.[6]

In April 1915 Theodore Marburg and his steering committee laid before Bryce their proposals for the constitution of an international League. Various problems had arisen concerning the proposal for an international court of arbitration to which disputes between nations could be referred. Another problem was disagreement over the degree to which military force would be employed as a means of supplying strength to the proposed League.

By now, it was known on both sides of the Atlantic that the British and American governments privately hoped that the League idea would prosper, though both governments wished to avoid giving public endorsement to it. In London the Asquith government, in the interests of wartime morale, wished to avoid public discussion of any peace proposals. But on 19 April 1915, Hamilton Holt (one of the original sponsors of the American League of Peace) informed Marburg that he had lunched at Columbia University with C. R. Ashbee, a member of the Bryce group in London; 'Mr Ashbee told me in confidence, which I repeat to you in the same way, of a conversation he had with Sir Edward Grey, who seems to be very anxious to have the United States come out strong for such a League, tho he does not want in any sense to have the English government officially inaugurate such a movement. . . .'[7] Hamilton Holt and Theodore Marburg were greatly encouraged by these informal assurances.

In late April 1915, Bryce despatched a confidential plan 'for a constructive peace' to Marburg and invited comments from the American committee. The plan took up the difficult problem of obligatory arbitration of disputes and enforcement by the League of decisions of the International Court. With Bryce's permission, Marburg showed the communications to William Phillips, an Assistant Secretary of State in Washington, who took copies of Bryce's letters and assured Marburg on 26 April: 'We are naturally interested in keeping touch with these matters, and fully appreciate your cooperation.'[8]

On 17 June 1915 the League to Enforce Peace was officially

inaugurated at Independence Hall in Philadelphia. About four hundred people attended the meeting at the invitation of the Committee of One Hundred. From the discussions several resolutions emerged, advocating that the United States should join a league of nations binding its signatories to the following proposals:

(1) That all justiciable questions not settled should go to a judicial tribunal.
(2) That all other questions not settled by negotiation should be submitted to a council of conciliation for hearing, consideration and recommendation.
(3) That the signatory powers jointly employ diplomatic and economic pressure against any of their number that threatens war against a fellow signatory without first proceeding under (1) and (2).
(4) That conferences among signatories should codify international law.

The four proposals were, in fact, closely akin to those Bryce had forwarded to Marburg in April and which he then discussed with Marburg and Lawrence Lowell in correspondence.[9] A further result of the Philadelphia meeting in June was adoption of the idea of a league of *all* nations, rather than a league of *great* nations, as proposed earlier. From now on, the idea of a League of Nations took firm root in the United States.

In London, meanwhile, some members of the Bryce group had founded a League of Nations Society headed by G. Lowes Dickinson. The aims and programme of the London society were similar to those of the American League to Enforce Peace. However, a point of difference between the American League and the British groups concerned their respective attitudes to Woodrow Wilson's policy in 1915 and 1916. The American League was sympathetic to President Wilson's repeated attempts at mediation for 'peace without victory' to either side in the European war, if only because peace was the first requirement for the successful promotion of a League of Nations and the war showed no signs of coming to an end. The London group, on the other hand, was opposed to 'Stop the War' movements, convinced that these could only be advantageous to Germany. Bryce was further convinced that any League of Nations which included the present German government would eventually founder. No one realised at this time that the first serious blow to the League of Nations would be dealt not in the Reichstag but in the United States Senate.

When President Wilson gave his historic speech before the important annual assembly of the League to Enforce Peace on 27 May 1916, he gave a tremendous boost to the League idea. Not only did the President announce the end of isolationism, but in a passage setting out the ideals for which the United States stood, he added: 'I am sure that I speak the mind and wish of the people of America when I say that the United States is willing to become a partner in any feasible association of nations formed to realise these objects and make them secure against violation.' From that moment on, all those supporting the League of Nations idea felt that they had the sympathy and support of the President. At the same time, however, President Wilson was still ready to use personal and secret diplomacy to end the European war. Whether the idea of a League of Nations would effectively promote or secure his policy was not yet clear.

In the summer of 1916 Theodore Marburg visited England and talked at length with Bryce, with representatives of the League of Nations Society and with a Fabian group also examining the League idea. Marburg learned that support for the League idea in England was hampered by a widespread feeling that it was an American-inspired 'Stop the War' movement designed to deny victory to the Allies by producing a 'dictated' peace under American auspices. Marburg's visit therefore had considerable value in acquainting the American group with British thinking. Marburg also learned the attitude of France and the other Allied powers towards a League of Nations. Already there were severe complications. Differences between British and French thinking on the League proved to be acute and difficult to reconcile. The problems were manifold. Where and when should the preliminary conference of nations take place in order to launch the League? How should the arbitral court be constituted? Should the proposed League make use of the existing institutions at the Hague, despite their history of partial successes and remembered failures? Should a 'Council of Conciliation' be set up, as Bryce was urging, to deal with 'non-justiciable' disputes? Above all, should military force be used against a member nation which refused to accept the arbitration procedures of the League? These complicated questions passed to and fro across the Atlantic in the months that followed. They reappeared at Versailles in 1919.

In the United States, the League began to encounter fresh difficulties in the winter of 1916. Pacifist groups were naturally opposed to the proposal that a League should use force against one of its members. William Jennings Bryan emerged as one of the foremost opponents of the League idea. His following in the Senate promised new difficulties not only for the League but also for President Wilson's political position in the nation. In a written 'debate' with ex-President Taft, now the President of the League to Enforce Peace, Bryan used both pacifist and isolationist arguments to attack its proposals. 'For this nation', declared Bryan, 'to exchange its moral prestige for the expensive privilege of putting its army and navy at the command of European monarchs, to be used in settling European quarrels, would be retrogression, not progress.'[10]

Taft argued skilfully against Bryan, but the fiery Democrat made telling points which struck home in the heartland of America as deeply as his 'Cross of Gold' speech struck home with the delegates to the 1896 Democratic Convention.

Taft and Marburg were in constant touch with Bryce in London. At Taft's request, Bryce wrote a letter urging support for the League idea which was read to a League meeting in New York on 24 November 1916. In London also, however, the League idea suffered a setback when Asquith and Grey resigned and Lloyd George became Prime Minister of the new Coalition government. Lloyd George was no enthusiast for the League, even though events were to propel him into a vital role at the end of the war.[11] In the winter of 1916 the League of Nations idea languished in high places.

Bryce's work to further the League of Nations idea did not end with his discussions in London and his voluminous transatlantic correspondence. During the same period he was using what occasions were offered to speak on the subject which now dominated his thoughts almost to the exclusion of all others.

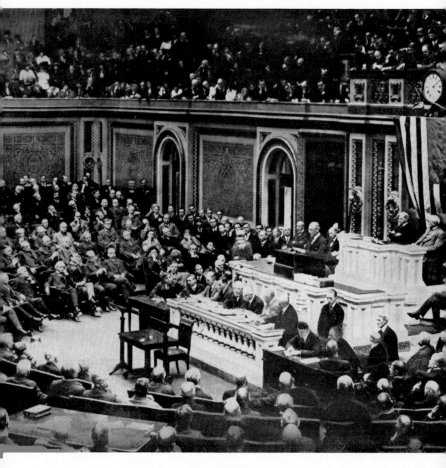

*President Woodrow Wilson before the Congress of the United States in a call
for war against Germany, 2 April 1917*

James, Viscount Bryce, circa 1920

As President of the British Academy, Bryce devoted two Presidential Addresses, in June 1915 and July 1916, to 'Some Historical Reflections on War, Past and Present'.[12] Modern wars had raised grave moral issues much more sharply than before, Bryce observed in his 1915 address. For instance, he asked, 'Is the State above morality?' Once again he took up cudgels against Bernhardi and the disciples of Treitschke.

These would not have been Bryce addresses, however, if they had not also contained constructive suggestions. A considerable part of the 1916 lecture was devoted to answering the question: 'Can any international machinery be contrived to reduce the strength of forces causing war and strengthen the forces that make for peace?' In answering the question, Bryce made a sustained plea for support of the British and American Leagues for Peace, and also for the idea of a post-war League of Nations which these organisations proposed.

Bryce again took up the subject of war and peace at Birmingham University in 1916. In his Huxley Lecture there he chose the topic 'War and Human Progress'. He examined the argument that war brings progress by a Darwinian survival of the fittest and he drew on his long historical memory to attack the suggestion. For instance, he pointed out, between 1490 and 1560 Italy was the prey of foreign invaders and rarely able to match their fighting skill; yet in the same period Italy did more for human progress in art and letters than all the other European nations put together. Among other invaders and fighters in history, Bryce questioned whether the Spartans, the Huns and the Turks had done more for civilisation than the peoples they conquered. In sum, Bryce concluded, Darwinian 'arguments' about the value of war were worthless biological analogies – he denied that they were really arguments – which completely failed to justify the intellectual and moral casualties of war, quite apart from the material destruction and the loss of life among the strong as well as the supposedly weak.[13]

The 1916 Huxley Lecture was possibly the most profoundly humane and liberal of the many hundreds of addresses that Bryce gave during his life. In developing his argument, Bryce drew on the book of Genesis, on Hesiod and Virgil, on Plato, on Pope Gregory VII, on Kant, and on Darwin himself for supporting testimony.

In short, the Huxley Lecture defended the whole history of Judaic and Graeco-Roman ideals as these were nurtured and refined in the European liberal tradition. The lecture was reprinted for a wider audience in the United States by the *Atlantic Monthly* in September 1916, and again as a pamphlet by the American Association for International Conciliation. Bryce's readers could have little doubt that Bryce was once more doing battle with the gods of Nietzsche and Bernhardi. But whether readers were followers of Nietzsche, or of the more opaque prophets of Social Darwinism, or merely uncommitted, they were presented with an eloquent restatement of American ideals.

In the autumn of 1916, the American League to Enforce Peace began to run foul of party politics. From the outset the founders of the League had aimed to keep it free of any party label. But many of its leading members were drawn from the professional middle class of the north-east – professors, lawyers, doctors and men of letters – and to this extent the League had an appearance of being dominated by north-eastern Republicans. When President Wilson showed his sympathy for the aspirations of the League, however, many Democrats turned with fresh interest to its activities and there was increasing support from the rank and file of the President's party. But this in turn led to some defections by Republicans, occasionally on no better grounds than personal dislike of Woodrow Wilson.

Bryce learned of this sorry situation from Lawrence Lowell, who was now chairman of the executive committee of the League. In a long letter on 13 March 1917, Lowell described the latest situation. One notable defector was Henry Cabot Lodge, who had earlier appeared on the same platform with Wilson urging support of the League to Enforce Peace. Now he had moved away, Lowell observed, 'partly, I cannot help thinking, because the President has made it a part of his policy and Lodge distrusts him. A year ago, we were a little afraid that our programme would appear to rest too exclusively upon Republican support; now the danger is that the support will be too largely Democratic. . . .'[14]

Like Colonel House, Lowell had already urged Bryce to come to the United States to speak on behalf of the League, not least because he was known to be one of the founders of the League idea and many ordinary Americans were showing a ready sympathy for its aims. Lowell reminded his friend: 'Our programme, based upon yours, was formulated at a dinner two years ago last February and we have now the ear of the whole public. . . .' A visit by Bryce, Lowell was convinced, would assist the American League enormously: 'I have asked opinions of people from widely separated places. . . . There is no British subject who has the influence over the people of the United States that you have. This is stated as emphatically in the South and in California as it is here. . . .'[15]

Bryce was sure that his visit would not be opportune. By January 1917 he was privately convinced that Woodrow Wilson was edging towards a declaration of war on Germany. Nothing must be done which might in any way affect the willingness of the American people to go to war. Wilson's personal friendship with Bryce was well known. A Bryce visit would undoubtedly be interpreted by some vociferous politicians as propaganda on behalf of Britain and the Allies. Bryce's decision was vindicated by events.

Following the American entry into the war in April 1917, the League idea once more gathered strength. Among the ordinary people of Britain, and in France and all Europe, a deep war weariness was now spreading. Soldiers and civilians alike, among the Allied and among the Central Powers, were interested in one question alone: 'When will it end?' The senseless slaughter on the barbed wire, the horrors of gas warfare, the stalemate of trench warfare – all these, and continued shortages on the home front, with populations sometimes close to starvation, helped to swell the demand for peace. Beyond this a further demand – slow yet insistent – could be detected. It stated simply: 'Never again.' Premiers and Field-Marshals alike were forced to recognise that ordinary people demanded a post-war League of Nations to ensure that the hideous calamity never occurred again. At a crowded public meeting in Central Hall, Westminster, on 14 May 1917 the Archbishop of Canterbury and Jan Smuts urged public support for the League of Nations movement. Bryce was in the chair.

Bryce and his friends also published an important statement, 'Proposals for the Prevention of Future Wars', setting out a positive programme for establishing a League of Nations.[16] In the

Lloyd George government, Balfour the Foreign Secretary, Jan Smuts and Lord Robert Cecil were keenly interested in the proposals, and the chief supporter of the League idea, Edward Grey, was also back in office, as an Under-Secretary. Their fiery and unpredictable chief, however, still showed little enthusiasm for the idea.

On 8 August 1917 Bryce sent to the British Cabinet a memorandum urging the appointment of a committee to consider proposals and plans for a League of Nations. In a covering letter to the Prime Minister, Bryce also urged 'a declaration by His Majesty's Government that it looked hopefully forward to the creation after the war of some machinery for the preservation of a permanent peace – a combination of free peace-loving nations'. Such a declaration, Bryce suggested, would have an excellent effect not only in Britain, but in Europe and the United States, on the Russian people, and 'might also do something to lead better sections of the German people to understand that we are carrying on this war in no selfish or vindictive spirit but for the sake of preventing aggression and strife in the future'.[17]

The Prime Minister, of course, had little time for planning a lasting peace in the midst of a brutal war, but Balfour, Cecil, Grey and Jan Smuts were instrumental in setting up a committee under Lord Phillimore to study the proposals and schemes of several British groups studying the League idea. When the committee was appointed, Jan Smuts wrote to Bryce: 'I need not say how strongly I personally approve your idea. The League of Nations may well prove the most beneficent and far-reaching result of this war; and the foundations of the idea and its practical application should be carefully explored in advance.'[18]

Another committee was appointed with the same purpose in France at this time, though the British and French committees maintained little contact with each other. Bryce was deeply anxious that the United States should act in concert with the Allies to prepare thoroughly for a post-war settlement. He wrote to Marburg in this connection early in 1918, and on 3 May Marburg sent Bryce's letter to Wilson. In the letter, Bryce urged that a committee of diplomats and jurists drawn from the Allies should be meeting now to prepare a plan for the League of Nations. 'The best action is that which is prepared in advance', he stressed. If a German surrender should come suddenly, the League idea might founder in the rush of events which would follow. Bryce was never more prophetic.

Wilson replied to Marburg on 6 May 1918 saying that it was not yet practicable to take up Bryce's suggestions. The meetings could not be kept secret and 'jealousies' would be aroused as soon as it became public. The President did not elaborate, but added that he regretted differing with Bryce's views: 'I have learned to respect his judgement and to suspect that I may be wrong when I disagree with him.'[19]

With the end of the war now in sight, Bryce spoke urgently and frequently for the League idea, and on 26 June 1918 spoke gravely in the House of Lords on the need for action now rather than later. Meanwhile, the Phillimore Committee, now at work in London, was examining the Bryce memorandum 'Proposals for the Prevention of Future Wars', together with the schemes put forward by the Fabian and other groups.

The Bryce Group suggested that the post-war League of Nations would require four principal institutions or organs for effectively maintaining the peace. These were: a tribunal to arbitrate on justiciable matters; a Council of Conciliation to enquire into and mediate other controversies; an Executive authority to determine the time and method of applying sanctions against states refusing to accept arbitration (and also to supervise the application of sanctions); and finally, a representative Conference or Congress to codify International Law. Lord Phillimore was impressed by the relative simplicity, but also by the comprehensiveness of the Bryce scheme. The recommendations in the Phillimore Committee's report gave the Bryce proposals a prominent place.[20]

In the summer of 1918 President Wilson asked for a copy of the Phillimore report, at the same time urging the British government not to make it public as yet. With the British and French committees' reports in hand, Wilson studied proposals for the League, then sat down to write his own draft for its Covenant. He also instructed House to prepare a draft. The Phillimore report was used extensively by Wilson, but the French committee's report was neglected, chiefly because so far it had been ignored by Clemenceau and by the French government. When Wilson had finished his draft he kept it to himself, not even showing it to his own Secretary of State.[21]

Peace came on 11 November that year. The Allies had no common plan for a Covenant. Wilson's draft remained a mystery known only to himself and in part to Colonel House. The French committee's report was finally taken out and scrutinised by Clemenceau's advisers. In Italy, nothing was done to prepare a plan, either officially or among private citizens, until after the armistice was signed.

What Bryce had most feared – a lack of adequate preparation or concerted plans for the Peace conference – soon materialised. On 3 October 1918 Bryce was already writing to Lowell at Harvard: 'Don't you think the President will find that he must before long get a proper Committee to work out a proper [League of Peace] scheme? Could you induce Col. House to do this, as it seems W.W. has left the matter to him? One fears that if the end of the war comes suddenly, it may find neither your nor our Administration prepared with a scheme well thought out. . . .' On 25 November Bryce again wrote to Lowell: 'The Peace Conference and Congress are now almost upon us, and no full scheme has yet been prepared by the Society here. I hope yours has one ready to be submitted to the Conference, and hope also that Woodrow Wilson or his advisers have got one ready. These are not things to be extemporised. . . .'[22]

No one could know what precisely were Wilson's plans. He was now keeping his cards close to his chest, chiefly because he had stirred up the fiercest political storm of his career in the 1918 mid-term Congressional elections. In the campaign, Wilson had made a partisan appeal to the electorate to show support for his wartime policies, and made it clear that he regarded the election as a vote of confidence in his conduct of affairs. This aroused the fury of Republicans, who felt that Wilson had thus violated the wartime truce on party politics. Bitter denunciations were hurled at the President as the campaign mounted in October. In November, far from increasing Democratic majorities in Congress as Wilson had hoped, the President's party lost control of both the House and the Senate. In the House, the Republicans emerged with a majority of 21 seats; in the Senate, with a majority of two seats. Senator Henry Cabot Lodge had now become the leader of a powerful group resolutely opposed to any plans for American membership of a League of Nations. Lodge was also Chairman of the Senate Foreign Relations Committee. In the ensuing months, the Monroe Doctrine was once more paraded through the halls of the United States Senate. Worse, the personal enmity between Cabot Lodge and Woodrow Wilson had turned to hatred.[23]

It was against this political background that Woodrow Wilson sailed for Paris in December 1918. Wilson now felt that the League and the Covenant were his personal mission. He was soon face to face with Lloyd George, Clemenceau and Orlando.

What happened at Versailles has been described in close detail by historians, by brilliant publicists like Maynard Keynes, and by popularisers. The intensive series of meetings for planning the Covenant were chaired by President Wilson. Britain, France, Italy, and Japan provided the chief spokesmen. Ranged about them were the spokesmen for Belgium, Brazil, China, Portugal and Serbia. The small powers were soon complaining at the over-representation of the big powers. Quarrels now developed. Gloomy tidings reached London and the United States. When the first draft of the Covenant appeared, Lowell and Bryce agreed as political scientists and constitutional experts that it was poorly drawn, obscure in parts, and obviously represented an untidy compromise.[24]

On 27 March Bryce reported to Lowell: 'The conference seems to be dominated by Wilson. It has not worked well. No general plan had been laid out; no proper Scheme for the League of Nations had been proposed, and some friends in Paris write me that France, Italy, and Greece are running their own selfish claims with an unprincipled disregard for the principle of nationality. None of the principal factions, including Wilson and the British P.M. seems to have realised what a gigantic piece of work the re-settlement is.'[25]

Although there was truth in his observation, Bryce was perhaps ungenerous. Neither Wilson nor Lloyd George, Clemenceau nor

Orlando could possibly have found the time to study the vast problems which now confronted them. They were politicians and leaders, not scholars in retirement. Wilson, exhausted by a cruel election campaign in October 1918, never had time to think through the enormous complexities which the November armistice thrust upon European statesmen and upon the shoulders of the American President. At Versailles, the old world leaders looked hopefully to the new world to mediate the quarrels which had plunged Europe into war. Wilson was ready to shoulder the burden if others would show the magnanimity required to build a durable peace.

At the moment of victory in November 1918, Bryce received a letter from an American citizen suggesting that Allied armies should march through Berlin 'to impress on the German people the futility of trying to conquer the world'. Bryce replied:

If the German Emperor and his pernicious generals had still been in power a march of allied troops through Berlin would have been an effective punishment. But as now there is a new set of people in authority who seem to be disclaiming the wicked ways of their predecessors perhaps we had better give them and the German people a chance. . . . If they abjure the crimes of the Junkers and heartily embrace democratic principles it may be better not to inflict such a humiliation as they inflicted upon France in 1871. My hope is that when the truth which has been kept from them has come to their knowledge they will share our horror at the crimes of their detestable rulers. We shall see. . . .[26]

In May 1919 the Paris conference communicated the terms of the peace settlement to Germany. The terms brought an immediate outburst of resentment there. A spirit of revenge and greed could be detected in the imposed settlement. Bryce deplored its terms; he felt that the Weimar Republic should at least be given a chance and not strangled at birth by harsh reparations and territorial losses. In Bryce's view, the settlement of May 1919 gave little chance for the Weimar Republic to succeed economically or politically. His opinions were shared by Jan Smuts, who almost refused to sign the document, and Maynard Keynes, who was soon to write a brilliant polemic on the consequences of the Versailles treaty.[27]

Meanwhile, the League of Nations Covenant had run into real

difficulties in the United States. Senator Henry Cabot Lodge had set himself resolutely to oppose it and during the summer of 1919 consolidated his opposition. Lodge was sufficiently experienced a politician not to oppose outright measures which he knew had the support of the great majority of the American people. Instead he introduced the famous Lodge Reservations in the Senate. Ostensibly the Lodge Reservations were designed to protect the independence of the United States by insisting that any punitive actions taken under Article Ten of the Covenant be decided on their individual merits in the United States Congress. President Wilson insisted against Lodge that such a stipulation was bound to undermine the whole structure of the League of Nations. If the United States claimed the right to decide individually under what circumstances and against whom the League's sanctions would be applied, then other nations were bound to insist on the same rights: the Covenant would be stillborn.

In the summer of 1919 Wilson made his historic decision to carry his case to the people of the United States. Already exhausted by the Paris discussions, and ignoring his doctor's advice, he set out on a speaking tour in the west. Wherever he went he found popular enthusiasm for the League and the Covenant. But dogging his footsteps, speaking where he spoke, two Senators from the 'irreconcilable' group denounced the Covenant of the League and the Treaty of Versailles. On 25 September Wilson broke down in Colorado and was rushed back to Washington, where he suffered a stroke on 2 October.

In the Senate, Lodge pressed on with his reservations and amendments. The haste with which the Covenant had been drawn provided legitimate grounds for proposing amendments to some sections, whilst the Treaty of Versailles, to which the Covenant was attached for ratification in the Senate, had provoked genuine indignation there. The two elements – haste in drawing up the Covenant and the vengeful spirit of the settlement – jointly contributed to the ultimate rejection of both Covenant and Treaty in the Congress.

From London, Bryce watched events with growing despair. He corresponded at length with Cabot Lodge between 1919 and 1920, seeking to answer Lodge's objections by appealing to the overriding importance of the League, despite the shortcomings of the Covenant. But Bryce admitted in a confidential letter to Lowell on 4 November 1919:

There is, I need hardly tell you, a general sense here that the Paris Conference has been a failure, having sanctioned arrangements which provide causes for future war, and are in the meantime working injustices. Tyrol, Albania, Macedonia, Transylvania have all been unfairly dealt with and I hear privately that the United States delegation in Paris is heartily disgusted and would like to be quit of the whole matter. . . . It is a thousand pities that Wilson did not take the advice that you and we pressed upon him to prepare . . . a proper scheme before he went to Paris. Many of the grounds on which the Senators have been now attacking the League might have been removed or reduced if this had been done.[28]

Even as Bryce was writing this letter, the Senators were voting to reject the Covenant and the Treaty of Versailles. Thereafter, the United States made its own peace treaties with Germany, Austria and Hungary. Supporters of the League of Nations went on hoping that somehow the Covenant might pass the Senate in some amended form. But the stricken man in the White House remained obdurate and would not accept the Senate's reservations. The quarrels and antagonisms between Woodrow Wilson and the extremists in the Senate had become, in truth, irreconcilable, and contributed to the final rejection.[29]

With the refusal of the United States to sanction the Covenant the League of Nations was dealt a death blow at its very outset. During the next two decades the true dimensions of the calamity were amply revealed.

23

Struggle for Peace

As the 1920s began, Bryce passed his eighty-second year. He had outlived most of his contemporaries, many of whom had died in the previous century. Since then, many younger friends and colleagues had gone to their graves. Bryce had earned a rest from politics and affairs, yet his ceaseless energies would not permit this. Despite his many activities between 1917 and 1918 for the cause of the League of Nations, Bryce somehow found the time to act as chairman of a Parliamentary Commission studying reform of the House of Lords. The thirty-one members of the Bryce Commission included the Archbishop of Canterbury, eminent peers, and sixteen Members of Parliament. Among those invited to appear before the Commission were French scholars intimate with the workings of the French Senate, as well as André Lebon, Minister of Commerce. In its report the Bryce Commission recommended the abolition of the hereditary principle and a democratisation of the Upper House by an elective system based on regional groupings. The models were clearly the French and American Senates. These recommendations were not subsequently adopted, and the Mother of Parliaments continued to institutionalise the assumption that male heirs of British peers are endowed with a special wisdom by birth.[1]

Even as he took the chair at the meetings of this august commission, Bryce was also engaged on the final stages of his two-volume *Modern Democracies*. The work was published early in 1921. In it, Bryce reviewed the workings of democracy in France, Switzerland, Canada, Australia, New Zealand and the United States: twelve hundred pages of detailed analysis. In his own words, Bryce sought to trace the working out of the democratic spirit in the political systems he had selected for study, and he chose the comparative method – the approach which John Stuart Mill had described in his *Logic* as 'the joint method of agreement and difference'. In this way, the successes and failures of the different systems could be thrown into relief, one against the other, with due allowance for diverse historical and social conditions. Comparison and contrast brought out the residuum of common experience.

Bryce deliberately refrained from treating the British political system in his work, partly because he was aware of the besetting sins of unconscious ethnocentricity in any work which attempted to be objective, and partly because he felt that his friend Lawrence Lowell had produced a more than adequate commentary in his two volumes on the government of England. Perhaps the most interesting sections of *Modern Democracies* appeared in Part I of the first volume, where the author discussed various definitions of democracy then current, appending to this thoughtful disquisitions on liberty and equality which modern political theorists may still study with profit.[2]

The work was welcomed on both sides of the Atlantic, and Bryce's American readers were pleased to find the author fully conversant with the most recent constitutional and political changes of the complex system he had first examined in 1888. There was no diminution in the author's powers. As the historian Oman remarked in his review: 'This is a marvellous book to have been written by a man of 83.'[3] Bryce dedicated the work to his 'friend and fellow worker A. Lawrence Lowell', just as Lowell had dedicated his own to Bryce. The President of Harvard further acknowledged Bryce's influence when in 1920 he sent Bryce a photograph of the portrait of himself by Sargent. On it, Lowell inscribed the greeting: 'To Lord Bryce, my guide and friend, from his disciple, A. Lawrence Lowell.'[4]

In June 1921 Bryce saw another of his cherished projects realised, the institution in London of the George Watson Chair of American History, Literature and Institutions. He was invited to inaugurate the chair in a lecture before a distinguished audience of scholars and diplomats in the Mansion House on 27 June. Bryce chose 'The Study of American History' as the subject of his lecture. Here again, there seemed to be no failing of memory or vigour. He reminded his listeners that American history did not begin with the landings at Virginia, nor with Raleigh's enterprise, nor even with Lief, the son of Eric. As Montesquieu had remarked of the English constitution, 'Ce beau système a été trouvé dans les bois'. The history of those who settled North America, observed Bryce, began in the forests and shores of Holstein and East Frisia, far back in the days of which we have no record, save in the worship of Thunor and Freya and in the ancient lay of Beowulf. The history of a nation is the history of the men who compose the nation, and not of their dwelling place.[5] The George Watson Chair thus inaugurated studies in American history on a wide historical canvas and with no parochial confinements of period and place. Serious students of American history could select their period and their specialisations in the years ahead: Bryce reminded them of the richness of the heritage.

It was now eight years since Bryce was last in America. With the great labour on *Modern Democracies* now completed, he was eager to visit his friends again, and in the summer of 1921 agreed to give a course of lectures on international relations at Williams College in Massachusetts. The Bryces sailed for New York aboard the *Celtic* early in July. Bryce had already promised to call on the new President inaugurated earlier that year. He had no very high opinion of Warren Gamaliel Harding, not least because as a Presidential candidate Harding had simply straddled the League issue in the 1920 campaign. However, the President had invited him to call and Bryce was ready to pay his respects. Some of Harding's appointments had drawn praise, and none more than the appointment of Charles Evans Hughes to the State Department.

A man of stature – both physically and intellectually – Hughes had been a successful Governor of New York from 1906 to 1910, and was the Republican candidate for President in the stormy 1916 campaign.[6] In fact it was principally the wish to talk with Hughes that brought Bryce to Washington for his last visit to the nation's capital. Hughes and Bryce were old friends. As Governor of New York Hughes had made the principal speech at the dinner welcoming Bryce as Ambassador in 1907. In June 1921 the Secretary of State had written to Bryce asking him to dine in order to discuss foreign affairs.[7]

After their call at the White House, the Bryces went to the Secretary of State's house and the two men were soon closeted

together. Hughes was already engaged in the preliminary organisation of the Washington Conference on the Limitation of Naval
Armaments, which was to open that November. Precisely what was
discussed between Hughes and Bryce as they talked in Washington
in July 1921 is not known. A few months later, as chairman of the
conference, Hughes was to startle the other great powers by giving
an undertaking on the part of the United States to scrap ships
amounting to 845,000 tons and also to agree to a moratorium on
further building for ten years if other powers would do the same.
Statesmen deemed it one of the noblest gestures by a great power in
modern history.

From Washington the Bryces travelled to Williamstown in
Massachusetts, where Bryce was to give eight lectures on 'International Relations'. It might be thought that the summer school of
a small New England college would not provide a conspicuous
forum for the wide theme Bryce had selected. Yet certain circumstances made the occasion notable. In the first place, the Institute
of Politics at Williams College had already earned a high reputation
for its scholarship. Secondly, no subject was more in the forefront
of the American mind than the problem of international relations
in an unsettled world not yet willing to disarm. Thirdly, there was
the fame of the lecturer. These auguries of a special occasion
brought an unusual audience to Williamstown in August 1921.
From the east and the mid-west, jurists, lawyers, scholars and men
of affairs together with diplomats and officials of the State Department all arrived in the little town nestling among the Berkshire
Hills. Men who attended the lectures said that Bryce never spoke
so earnestly or urgently, or with such eloquence and conviction.

In the first lecture Bryce rapidly sketched the history of the
relations between tribes and nations from the Golden Age to the
Congress of Vienna and the nineteenth century. He placed his
account against Plato's thesis that war 'is the natural relation of
every community to every other'.[8] There was abundant evidence
in history to support Plato. Having cleared the ground in this
characteristic manner, Bryce devoted the next lecture to the
economic and territorial results of the Great War. Here an
astonishingly detailed knowledge of the Paris discussions and of the

286

Versailles Treaty was revealed. From Hungary and Rumania to Azerbaijan and even to Western Mongolia, Bryce traced and commented critically on many of the settlements arranged or imposed.

What factors, human and political, had produced these settlements? In the following lectures Bryce dealt with the intricate problems of diplomacy and international law and man's attempts to resolve them; of the methods of controlling foreign policy in different states and systems. The treatment was dispassionate: Bryce avoided invidious comparisons. When he turned to examine the causes of the war which had so recently convulsed the world, it was to remark: 'The causes which produced the Great War are deep seated. They are part of human nature, arising from faults in political human nature as it exists in all countries. . . . The faults exist everywhere, rooted in the same human propensities, and all nations must bear their share of the blame. A glance back over the last sixty years will show this. "There is not one that doeth righteousness, no, not one."'[9]

Bryce went on to make a solemn appeal to those who listened and to the much wider audience who would read his words in the national press. He had already examined the chequered history of conferences summoned to settle international disputes, and to preserve permanent peace. He had shown that peaceful arbitration, conciliation and mediation for the settlement of disputes had never been properly institutionalised. Yet this was more than ever vitally needed. Bryce now put forward a possible scheme which, though it resembled the League of Nations Covenant, differed in certain essentials. The scheme was not Utopian. It recognised that in the family of man there were great and powerful nations and very small nations; some were advanced in their industries and economies, others were primitive and backward. World government was not likely to be realised in the foreseeable future – least of all a system based on one nation, one vote. The world must proceed from the limitations of the possible – and among the chief limitations were those dictated by human nature and by fear itself. Nevertheless it should be possible to admit representatives of all the nations to an organisation meeting regularly in conference, with a smaller council or executive authority answerable to the larger assembly. Bryce sketched in the central elements of his proposed organisation, with its governing covenant or charter, its Council, its special voting arrangements and its worldwide membership. It is not difficult to find the germ of the United Nations Charter in Bryce's constructive appeal of 1921.[10]

Finally, Bryce entreated Americans to act promptly. It was vitally necessary that the United States, with its unique combination of power and moral authority in the face of an exhausted, dispirited and barely united old world, should provide the necessary leadership. Old enmities must be put aside: the past belonged to the past. The call of duty should make this a time of hope and idealism and not of despair:

When I speak of Idealism, I mean not that blind faith in the certainty of human progress which was engendered fifty years ago by the triumphs of applied science and the prosperity they brought, but rather that aspiration for a world more enlightened and more happy than that which we see today, a world in which the co-operation of men and nations rather than their rivalry . . . shall be the guiding aims. Good-will sweetens life; nobody is so happy as he who rejoices in the happiness of others. Hatred has never brought anything but evil. The sensible idealist – and he is not the less an idealist, and a far more useful one, if he is sensible, and sees the world as it is – is not a visionary, but a man who feels that the forces making for good may and probably will tend to prevail against those making for evil, but will prevail only if the idealists join in a constant effort to make them prevail. . . .

You in America are well fitted to set an example in this effort to the European peoples smitten down by war, and painfully struggling to regain their feet. . . . Your help, your powerful and disinterested help, will be of incomparable service to rescue your brother peoples from the oldest and deadliest of all the evils that have afflicted mankind.[11]

Bryce's lectures ended there. The audience rose to applaud, then to cheer. These were the last lectures Bryce delivered in the United States.

The Bryces returned to the coast to visit the Eliots at Mount Desert Island in Maine. Eliot later recalled the visit in all its

288

details. Bryce observed an island beyond the coast which he had never visited, and organised an excursion. When the boat landed with its small party, the Eliots talked with Lady Bryce on the shore whilst Bryce scouted the rocks and flora nearby. He returned with the botany and geology of the island lodged securely in his memory, and with the knowledge that the three families on the island had long maintained a feud and had no contact with each other.

After farewells at Eliot's house, the Bryces went south to Boston and Harvard. Bryce talked with James Ford Rhodes and his friends at the Historical Society in Boston. At Harvard, the Bryces were once more guests at the President's Lodgings. The Fall semester had just begun as Bryce strolled with Lowell in Harvard Yard. On the evening of 27 September Bryce spoke in the Union to the Harvard students. Next day the *Harvard Crimson* reported: 'A large and enthusiastic audience attended the address made by Viscount Bryce. . . . All the available floor space was taken up; the balconies and windows were packed and lines extended from each doorway far into the hall and up the staircase.' Bryce spoke for forty-five minutes. Harvard men were urged to accept the challenge with which the troubled era confronted them. Theirs was a special mission: to give service not only to the American people, but also, in accordance with an honourable tradition of distinguished alumni, as citizens of the world.[12]

Next day Bryce walked in Harvard Yard for the last time. The Fall was resplendent and the sheltering trees filtered pale sunlight through leaves of scarlet and yellow on to the paths where the crisp carpet of russet and brown scattered before the young men hurrying across to morning classes. Farewells came at mid-morning, when the car – symbol of the new age – arrived at the President's Lodgings to take Bryce and his wife to Boston station. Bryce looked forward to Lowell's planned visit to Europe in the following year. Lowell waved farewell to his old friend and never saw him again.

In New York, two banquets were given in Bryce's honour. On 30 September Bryce was surrounded by many of his old friends at a dinner given by the Sulgrave Institution – yet another of the societies devoted to Anglo-American accord that had come into being in recent years. On Bryce's left were Governor Miller and Judge Parker, Chief Justice of the State of New York; on his right was Elihu Root, who had travelled up from Washington, where with Secretary of State Hughes he was engaged in preparations for the Washington Conference on the Limitation of Naval Armaments. Beyond the official representatives of the state and city which did him honour were Bryce's personal friends, lawyers, scholars and editors predominating.

At the dinner, Bryce was presented with an illuminated booklet which contained personal greetings from many distinguished Americans, including the President of the United States, two future Presidents, and an ailing ex-President. In his tribute from the White House, President Harding observed: 'I know of no man who, to my mind, has performed so great a service as his own, in behalf of those intimate and understanding relations between the two great branches of the English speaking peoples. . . .' Calvin Coolidge wrote: 'No one has done more to secure an understanding of the aims and ideals of the American Republic than he has done. . . .' Herbert Hoover remarked: 'No one man has contributed so much to America's own understanding of America nor so much to the understanding of America abroad as Lord Bryce – and it has been the interpretation of a friend solicitous of our welfare and our future. . . .' Woodrow Wilson sent greetings from his invalid's bed, and other tributes arrived from the Supreme Court, from State Houses and from institutions of learning across the United States.[13]

On 9 October, at the final dinner in his honour, the guest list once more included scores of Bryce's friends and acquaintances of many years past. In his reply to a toast in his honour, Bryce reaffirmed his belief in the underlying unity of the English-speaking peoples, despite occasional and sometimes serious misunderstandings between the United States and Britain. Then he addressed himself to the future. The hideous tragedy of the Great War had at the least demonstrated reserves of courage, self-sacrifice and devotion to certain ideals among peace-loving nations. This was the only virtue to be found in the events of 1914 to 1918. Now men must apply themselves resolutely to making the peace so that the calamity should never occur again. Bryce saluted the Conference on the

Limitation of Naval Armaments which was soon to assemble at Washington. He called for some special gesture of faith from the nations, and especially from that great nation which, he argued, had least to fear from potential adversaries because of its vast and ever increasing resources. Concerning those expressions of uneasiness among some American statesmen in the face of possible conflicts, Bryce reviewed the international situation, then weighed his words carefully: 'I can see at this moment no danger threatening the United States that has come within the range of probability.'[14]

In the final section of his speech Bryce repeated his plea for the new world to identify itself with the old, to share a concern for Europe's acute problems and not to retreat to any fortress of isolation. In the task of rebuilding and making good the havoc of war – both material and moral – he hoped that Britain and America would always be partners and friends, exercising together a beneficent and liberal influence to check tyranny wherever it might arise, to maintain freedom and to extend the light of learning to the poor, the oppressed, and the underprivileged.[15]

At the end, the audience rose and cheered the old man as he stood, a lean and slightly stooped figure, his face lined and showing the years of toil, but dignified as he silently acknowledged the ovation which was also a farewell.

By mid-October the Bryces were back at Hindleap. Bryce was busy at his ceaseless correspondence, writing to two American friends on the condition of the Negroes in the South and the possibilities for their further advancement; to James Ford Rhodes on the character of Theodore Roosevelt, and to his English friends George Otto Trevelyan and A. V. Dicey on historical and political affairs.[16]

On 15 December, in the House of Lords, Bryce welcomed the progress now reported on negotiations between the government and the Sinn Fein representatives for the establishment of the Irish Free State. He rejoiced that a settlement was near at long, long last. He was also cheered by news from Washington of a successful start to the international conference on disarmament. The supremely generous offer which Hughes had made on behalf of the United States on the first day of the conference heartened Bryce as nothing had done for many years. When Bryce's Williams College lectures on international relations were published in December 1921 he dedicated the little volume to Charles Evans Hughes, with a warm personal greeting to his friend. On Christmas Day Bryce sent a message of good wishes to the delegates at the conference. By now the representatives of Britain, France and Japan had largely accepted the terms suggested by Hughes and on 13 December 1921 had agreed to sign a Four Power Pact. The treaty in effect introduced a ten-year 'holiday' in the arms race and substituted a four-power agreement to talk or negotiate first, rather than resort to rearmament first and to discussions second. At the Washington conference, Britain surrendered her traditional naval superiority. There were admirals in Whitehall who rued the day. There were many more statesmen around the world who found renewed hopes of peace. Unhappily, the settlements and the legacies of Versailles had still to do their worst in Europe.

The New Year of 1922 arrived and with his wife Bryce went down to Sidmouth in Devon for a couple of weeks' rest and relaxation by the sea. In the quiet hours of the evening he went ahead with his plans for a long delayed Life of Justinian, the great Byzantine emperor who retrieved Africa from the Vandals and Italy from the Ostrogoths, and whose codification of Roman Law had excited Bryce's mind for sixty years. The book would be a labour of love. On 21 January Bryce was also making notes for an article on Troy and Ithaca, a task which may have brought back those joys of Homer's verse which he had first learned to love as a boy in the 1840s.

In the afternoon Bryce walked with his wife by the sea, enjoying the crisp air, the fresh salt spray and the sights and sounds of the shore. He was also looking forward to completing his catalogue of the flora of Ashdown Forest near their home in Sussex and planned to do this when they returned to Hindleap. After supper Bryce went out by himself to gaze up at the stars as he often did on a clear, bright night, noting the constellations and the stars in their courses as his father had taught him. Then he went to bed, and on Sunday, 22 January, at some hour of the early morning, James Bryce died quietly in his sleep.

A few weeks later Marion, Lady Bryce, replied to James Ford Rhodes, one of the hundreds of friends who had written to condole with the widow: 'It came with absolute suddenness: no illness and no warning . . . he had been in his usual good health and very happy. . . . We went for our walk in the afternoon. No sign of anything amiss. . . . When I awoke next morning he was gone. He appeared to have passed away peacefully in his sleep, from heart failure. I have never seen him more eager and vital and more like himself than he was on that last day of his life, and the end was as he would have wished'.[17]

Memorial services were held in Westminster Abbey, in Lincoln's Inn, in Trinity College and in Oriel College. King George V sent a personal note to Lady Bryce: 'I regarded Viscount Bryce as an old friend and trusted counsellor to whom I could always turn, confident in the strength and wisdom of his advice. . . .'[18]

In the House of Lords peers from both sides of the chamber paid tributes. Lord Cecil of Chelwood said of the dead statesman:

He occupied a unique position in the esteem of his fellow country-men. He was, as it were, their moral referee, and his judgment on any question of public morality was accepted without question. His position was due not only to his wide experience, his extra-ordinary knowledge and natural impartiality. It was [due to] the deep moral purpose which directed every thought and action of his life.[19]

In Washington the delegates at the international conference on disarmament paused in their work on Monday, 23 January to hear tributes from the French delegate, Bryce's old friend Jusserand, from Balfour and from Elihu Root. Root spoke of his late friend's extraordinary ability to understand the thoughts and emotions, the concerns and fears of nations foreign to his own, chiefly because of his wide learning, his command of languages, his insatiable travelling and his deep human sympathy. The chairman of the conference, Charles Evans Hughes, said in his speech: 'His passing away is not only a serious loss to statesmanship, but it deprives the world of one of its great benefactors, because of his vision of democratic possi-bilities, his liberal spirit, and the constant example of his character and attainments. . . .'[20]

James Bryce was buried next to his father and his mother at the Grange Cemetery in Edinburgh, in accordance with his wishes.

Later that year, on 12 October at eleven o'clock in the morning, a small ceremony was performed beneath the dome of the Capitol in the United States Congress. Following an invocation by the Chaplain of the House of Representatives, the Chief Justice of the United States accepted on behalf of the American people a bust of James Bryce. In his speech Chief Justice William Howard Taft said of Bryce: 'He knew us better than we know ourselves, and he went about and among us and gave us the boon of his illuminating wisdom derived from the lessons of the past.'[21]

The bronze bust stands today on its plinth of Knoxville marble in the Senate Wing of the Congress, a few steps away from the entrance to the Senate gallery. The inscription reads:

JAMES, VISCOUNT BRYCE

FRIEND AND AMBASSADOR TO THE AMERICAN PEOPLE

AND

INTERPRETER OF THEIR INSTITUTIONS.

BORN 1838. DIED 1922.

Epilogue

'To be an American is a complex fate', Henry James remarked. To understand Americans is also complex, and there are many reasons why Europeans should find it particularly difficult. The United States was founded by those who had turned their backs on Europe, both physically and philosophically. Whether we speak of the Puritans and the Founding Fathers or of those 'huddled masses yearning to breathe free' who arrived in wave upon wave during the nineteenth and the twentieth centuries, it remains true that the new world is in a vital sense a denial of the old. For Americans to admit that their aspirations, their national interests and thus their policies ought to be identified with those of Europe – or any part of it – is to deny their own history. There must always be at least a tendency for Americans to revert to 'splendid isolation' in thought, word, or deed.

The search for mutual understanding between the new world and the old goes on, not primarily because they have any particular wish to learn more and to understand more about each other, but because in a shrinking world the process is unavoidable. Whether Europeans are confronted with the legitimate interests of the United States at the conference table, or whether they encounter the latest scholarly monograph or pulp novel to cross the Atlantic, they must acknowledge the existence of a self-sufficient culture. At the same time, Europeans have the right to question the assumptions and attitudes of the United States just as Americans have claimed the right to question – and to reject – many of the bases of European society.

This dialogue between the old world and the new – which today gains a new relevance from the thrust of emergent cultures elsewhere in the world – is always complicated by the heterogeneity of American society and institutions. Almost every generalisation about American society seems true, and so does the opposite generalisation. To say this is merely to refer to an aspect of American liberty – the right to differ, to explore, to experiment and to think without let or hindrance. Beneath the surface characteristics of American society in all their diversity and even inconsistency lies a certain permanence, a harmony of assumptions deeper than the superficial discords tend to suggest.

It was with these deeper assumptions that James Bryce concerned himself during the fifty years that he sought first to understand, and then to explain and interpret, the new world. The author of *The Holy Roman Empire*, a chronicle of almost a thousand years of European history, was not likely to confuse the ephemeral with the permanent in America, or the superficial with the essential. His inquisitive and patient explorations led him to certain fundamental conclusions about American society and institutions. He became convinced that despite many distasteful, even deplorable characteristics of its polity and society – some of them the results of unbridled democracy – nevertheless the basic ideas on which the American Republic was founded were honourable, felicitous and just. Bryce fundamentally believed that all men are created equal and that governments derive their just powers from the consent of the governed. It was not always easy to sustain these beliefs in the age of imperialism and Social Darwinism. Bryce was equally convinced that these principles owed much – and more than Americans in the second half of the nineteenth century cared to admit – to that spirit of liberty which, though not created in England, had found fertile soil there, and had been nurtured there for centuries before the birth of the American Republic.

These deep convictions at times led James Bryce into wishful thinking and, more rarely, into sentimentality about Anglo-American harmony. But he was rescued by Scottish common sense and on occasion by the action of the United States Senate. He travelled too much, read too much, and met too many people for the easy optimism of the nineteenth century to take too firm a hold of him. It needed neither the teachings of theology nor the inner promptings of his own austere faith to convince him that man is essentially self-seeking and thus, in both the Christian and the Greek sense, sinful. Yet he also had an ardent belief in the ability of men and of nations occasionally to transcend their baser instincts. For Bryce the fundamental struggle was between man's aspirations and the limitations imposed by human nature; and the history and civilisation of the United States, in all its contradictions and complexities, its combination of idealism and opportunism, of principle and expediency, presented him with the ideal canvas on which to trace the deepest and most catholic assumptions of the liberal idea.

As a nineteenth-century English-Scots Liberal, Bryce of course had failures of perception. He never understood the new science of economics which emerged during his lifetime. Like Gladstone, whom he admired so much, he clung hopefully to Free Trade and – though with diminishing hope – to *laissez faire*. His deep opposition to all doctrinaire theories in politics made him incapable of understanding, far less sympathising with, the socialist movements which spread across Europe as he reached his middle age. These developments, together with the vicissitudes of party politics, the ambitions and strategies of statesmen, the problem of democracy itself, often severely tested his beliefs and his resolution. There were moments of deep disappointment in his life and occasionally he was despondent as the old order of the nineteenth century was replaced by the harsh insecurities of the twentieth. Yet because he was a man of ardent faith and rare compassion, he continued to believe that in the tangled and often tragic human story a fine thread of reason and morality could be discerned, always tenuous, at times losing itself beneath tides of unreason, but always emerging again as man picks his way painfully towards the light.

Appendix I

Structure of *The American Commonwealth*
(1st edition, 1888)

Part 1. *The National Government*

35 chapters on the offices and institutions of the federal government, examined historically and also in the contemporary setting.

Part 2. *The State Governments*

17 chapters. Bryce here follows the logic of the federal system and takes up the second tier of government and administration. No state is neglected in his survey. Constitutional powers are analysed in great detail.

Part 3. *The Party System*

23 chapters. This section contains the celebrated chapters on political machines, bosses, the spoils system, and corruption in municipal government.

Part 4. *Public Opinion*

12 chapters. This section is more theoretical and philosophical. Many of the prime assumptions of American democracy are examined critically, especially the action of public opinion and the 'tyranny of the majority'.

Part 5. *Illustrations and Reflections*

10 chapters. Bryce pauses to take up several of the previous themes for more discussion of the strengths and weaknesses of American democracy.

Part 6. *Social Institutions*

19 chapters. In many respects, these are the most interesting chapters, and reveal much sociological investigation. Bryce examines in close detail, and with his own minute observations everywhere in evidence, many institutions. The Bar, Wall Street, the Universities, Railroads, American Oratory, the Temper of the West, and the Position of American Women are discussed and analysed. There are also further chapters discussing Equality, the Influence of Democracy on Thought, and the Future of Political Institutions.

Appendix II

Assistance to James Bryce in gathering material for
The American Commonwealth

Name	Profession and Location	Information or data supplied
A. J. Anderson	Lecturer: University of Washington, Seattle.	Education at Seattle.
James B. Angell	Scholar and diplomatist: President, University of Michigan.	Michigan State politics.
Edward Atkinson	Economist, author: Boston.	Banking, Savings Banks.
Theodore Bacon	Lawyer: Rochester, New York.	State Constitutions.
James H. Canfield	Professor of History: University of Kansas.	Civil Service in Kansas, etc.
Thomas M. Cooley	Jurist: Professor of Law, University of Michigan.	State and Federal law.
Theodore Dwight	Librarian, State Dept., Washington, D.C.	Compilations of State Constitutions.
George P. Fisher	Professor of Divinity and Ecclesiastical History: Yale University, New Haven.	New England life and religion in U.S.A.
Washington Gladden	Clergyman, writer: Columbus, Ohio.	Ohio gerrymandering.
Henry C. Lea	Historian: Philadelphia.	Pennsylvania politics.
Bernard Moses	Professor of History: University of California.	California politics, bossism, immigration.
Theodore Roosevelt	Rising politician, amateur historian: New York.	Machine politics.
Albert Shaw	Editor, historian, expert on municipal affairs: Minneapolis.	Local government in Minnesota, Milwaukee and Illinois.

300

Name	Profession and Location	Information or data supplied
Marshall S. Snow	Historian: Dean of Washington University, St Louis, Missouri.	Politics in western cities.

More generally, Bryce received a great deal of assistance in the course of voluminous correspondence with his closest friends in America – Oliver Wendell Holmes, Jr., E. L. Godkin, Seth Low, Goldwin Smith and Charles W. Eliot. Again, Bryce derived immense benefit from a vast number of conversations in all parts of the United States, many with friends or acquaintances, many more with strangers as he travelled. Although his memory was prodigious, he did not care to rely on this alone, and would raise specific questions in the course of correspondence. He also collected all manner of publications as he travelled, from government publications to copies of State constitutions, city charters, pamphlets, journals and local newspapers.

It was this scrupulous regard for accuracy, allied to a wide-ranging – and enjoyable – exploration of the American polity which gave *The American Commonwealth* its special character.

Note on Sources

The chief manuscript sources for this study are the Bryce Papers in the Bodleian Library, Oxford. A considerable portion of the papers dealing with Bryce's American connections have now been catalogued (33 volumes to date) and these have been invaluable for the present study. Of the English papers, 19 volumes are now catalogued and these have also been valuable, especially the Bryce correspondence with A. V. Dicey, Edward Freeman, Lord Acton and Henry Sidgwick. Many of Bryce's letters to Americans have been returned to the Bryce collection. The greater part of the Bryce Papers has not yet been catalogued (122 boxes). Some of these boxes were found to contain correspondence and primary material touching on Bryce's American travels and connections.

A fresh Bryce archive came to light in May 1965, when the executrix of the Bryce estate, Miss Margery Bryce, passed to the writer an extensive collection of Bryce manuscripts, correspondence and papers. These were found to include the long lost American travel journal for 1870 in Bryce's hand, and another diary covering travel in the United States. The new collection also contained many letters from Bryce to his parents and sisters, written during his American travels, and a mass of American newspaper clippings, chiefly dealing with Bryce as Ambassador in Washington from 1907 to 1913. The most exciting find in the new collection was the complete manuscript of *The American Commonwealth* (hitherto thought lost), with copious notes, corrections and marginalia in the author's hand. The new archive is now to be added to the Bryce Papers in the Bodleian Library.

The other manuscript collections used in this study are located chiefly in the eastern United States. The following proved most useful:

Charles William Eliot Papers: Harvard University Archives.

Edwin Lawrence Godkin Papers: Houghton Library, Harvard University.

Oliver Wendell Holmes Junior Papers: Harvard Law School.

Diaries of Colonel Edward M. House: Yale University Library.

A. Lawrence Lowell Papers: Harvard University Archives.

Theodore Roosevelt Papers: Library of Congress.

Theodore Roosevelt collection of books, pamphlets and clippings: Widener Library, Harvard.

Elihu Root Papers: Library of Congress.

Albert Shaw Papers: New York Public Library.

Goldwin Smith Papers: Cornell University Library.

Henry Villard Papers: Houghton Library, Harvard University.

Andrew White Papers: Cornell University.

Woodrow Wilson Papers: Princeton University and Library of Congress.

The following collections contained smaller quantities of relevant material:

Herbert Baxter Adams Papers: Johns Hopkins University.

Nicholas Murray Butler Papers: Columbia University.

Thomas M. Cooley Collection: University of Michigan.

Ralph Waldo Emerson Diaries: Harvard University.

Daniel Coit Gilman Papers: Johns Hopkins University.

Frank J. Goodnow Papers: Johns Hopkins University.

Thomas Wentworth Higginson Papers: Harvard University.

Henry Cabot Lodge Papers: Massachusetts Historical Society.

Henry Wadsworth Longfellow Diaries and Papers: Harvard University.

Seth Low Papers: Columbia University.

Bernard Moses Papers: University of California, Berkeley.

Charles Eliot Norton Papers: Harvard University.

Walter Hines Page Diaries and Papers: Harvard University.

James Ford Rhodes Papers: Massachusetts Historical Society.

William Howard Taft Papers: Library of Congress.

References

INTRODUCTION

1. Louis Hacker, Introduction to James Bryce, *The American Commonwealth* abridged edition, 2 vols., New York, 1959), I: vii.

2. Quoted in W. T. Stead, 'James Bryce, Britain's Envoy to the American People', *Review of Reviews*, XXXV (1907), pp. 166–72. Also quoted by G. P. Gooch, 'Lord Bryce', *Contemporary Review*, CXXI (1922), pp. 304–13.

3. A. G. Gardiner, *The Pillars of Society* (London, 1913), p. 308.

4. Diary of Edward M. House, Yale University Library (entries for 25 February 1915 and 3 June 1915). Also cited in Charles Seymour (ed.), *The Intimate Papers of Colonel House* (4 vols., London, 1924–8), I: 390.

5. Sir Arthur Salter, *Personality in Politics: Studies of Contemporary Statesmen* (London, 1947), p. 109. (Salter gives a vivid description of a brisk walk with Bryce in the winter of 1921 when Bryce was 83.)

6. British Museum, Gladstone Papers, Add. Mss. 44780, 44786; Bryce to Gladstone, 24 March 1874 and Gladstone to Bryce, 25 March 1874, Bryce Papers, Oxford. (Hereafter cited as Bryce Papers.)

CHAPTER ONE

1. The genealogy of the Bryce family is contained in two boxes marked 'Family Papers' (uncatalogued) in the Bryce Papers. On the Reverend James Bryce, see *Dictionary of National Biography*, III: 158–9. There are sundry anecdotes on the Reverend James Bryce in Eleanor Alexander, *Primate Alexander, Archbishop of Armagh* (London, 1913), pp. 36–7. See also James B. Woodburn, *The Ulster Scot: His History and Religion* (London, 1915), pp. 318, 394–5.

2. On James Bryce Senior (1806–1877), see *Dictionary of National Biography*, III: 159 and a printed memoir in the Bryce Papers – authorship not stated, but a note on the flyleaf and internal evidence suggest that James, Lord Bryce, was the author. On the Bryce family background, see also *New England Historical and Genealogical Register*, LXXVIII (January 1924), pp. 75–84.

3. H. A. L. Fisher, *James Bryce* (2 vols., London, 1927), I: 10. The biography by Fisher remains the only full-length study of James Bryce. The work gains greatly from Fisher's wide learning and his personal friendship with Bryce. A possible criticism is that by attempting a 'Life and Letters' in

the genre more popular at the turn of the century Fisher does not do justice either to the life, in all its various pursuits, or to the letters, in their range and volume. On the American travels and experiences, Fisher is brief (except for the Ambassadorship in Washington, D.C.) and wrong on some points of fact; e.g. Bryce's itinerary on the 1870 visit to America. It should be added that Fisher had no opportunity to research the widely scattered Bryce correspondence and associations across the Atlantic. Fisher's work remains a faithful attempt at a monumental task.

4. James Bryce, autobiographical fragment cited by Fisher, *Bryce*, I: 25. Unfortunately this fragment cannot be found in the Bryce Papers and a search of the H. A. L. Fisher papers (Bodleian Library) failed to disclose it. It seems not to have survived.

5. Cited by Fisher, *Bryce*, I: 23. For further details of the student life at Glasgow at the mid-century, see a memoir by a Bryce contemporary, James Main Dixon in *Methodist Review* (New York), CV, No. 5 (1922), pp. 707–8.

6. Cited by Fisher, *Bryce*, I: 26.

CHAPTER TWO

1. See Charles E. Mallet, *A History of the University of Oxford* (3 vols., London, 1924–7), III: 298–9 and 331–4. See also V. H. H. Green, *Religion at Oxford and Cambridge* (London, 1964), pp. 297–316.

2. James Bryce to his father, James Bryce, 1 June 1857, Bryce Papers.

3. James Bryce to his father, 5 June 1857, Bryce Papers.

4. Dixon in *Methodist Review*, CV, No. 5 (1922), p. 705. See also *D.N.B.*, III: 159.

5. James Bryce, Journal for 1859. I must thank Miss Margery Bryce for lending this new source, which was invaluable for reconstructing the details of Bryce's second and third year interests at Oxford.

6. Bryce, Journal, 1859, p. 18.

7. Extract from Dicey's diary, quoted in R. S. Rait, *Memorials of Albert Venn Dicey* (London, 1925), pp. 39–40.

8. James Bryce to his mother, Mrs Margaret Bryce, 10 April 1861, quoted in Fisher, *Bryce*, I: 51–4.

9. The minute book of the Old Mortality Club is in the Bodleian Library (Ms. Top Oxon. d 252) and contains lists of members up to 1860, with fairly spasmodic summaries of papers read and the ensuing discussions. The minute book also contains an excellent group photograph of members in Trinity Term 1860.

10. For a further discussion of the intellectual activities of the Old Mortality Club see Melvin Richter. *The Politics of Conscience: T. H. Green and His Age* (London, 1964), pp. 80–4 and Fisher, *Bryce*, I: 48–9.

11. W. Knight, *Memoir of John Nichol* (London, 1896), p. 152.

12. The Bryce–Goldwin Smith correspondence in the Bodleian Library

extends from 1866 to 1910, the year of Smith's death. The Bryce–Freeman correspondence extends from 1866 to 1892, the year of Freeman's death.

13. Elizabeth Wallace, *Goldwin Smith, Victorian Liberal* (Toronto, 1957), pp. 1–16; see also Arnold Haultain, *Goldwin Smith, His Life and Opinions* (New York, 1914), *passim*.

14. Goldwin Smith, *Lectures on the Study of Modern History* (London, 1865), pp. 1–44.

15. *Ibid.*, pp. 62–3.

16. Elizabeth Wallace, *Goldwin Smith*, pp. 17, 137, 148.

17. Haultain, *Goldwin Smith*, pp. 253–92.

18. See R. W. Stephens, *Life and Letters of Edward A. Freeman* (2 vols., London, 1895); see also G. P. Gooch, *History and Historians in the Nineteenth Century* (new ed., London, 1954), pp. 323–9. Bryce gave his personal tribute to Freeman in his *Studies in Contemporary Biography* (London, 1903), pp. 262–92.

19. Freeman included his review (*North British Review*, March 1865) in his *Historical Essays* (London, 1871), pp. 126–60. Freeman's muse is best captured in his *The Methods of Historical Study* (London, 1886).

20. James Bryce, *The Holy Roman Empire* (Oxford, 1864), pp. 168–9. The actual wording is altered in subsequent editions, but not substantially. Between 1864 and 1920 the work received thirty-eight printings in five editions. It was translated into German, Italian, French and Hungarian.

CHAPTER THREE

1. Quoted by Fisher, *Bryce*, I: 63. This memoir is no longer extant.

2. Leslie Stephen proposing James Bryce as President of the Alpine Club in 1898. See Fisher, *Bryce*, I: 119.

3. *Taunton Report and Reports of the Commissioners* (London, 1868). See also *Parliamentary Papers*, XXVIII (1867–8), pp. 78–88, 546–661. Copies of the Reports are in the Bryce Papers. Bryce's recommendations are contained chiefly in Vols. IX, XVII and XX of the evidence, and in the final report of the Commission. See also H. C. Barnard, *A History of English Education from 1760* (London, 1961), pp. 128–34, *et passim*.

4. *Essays on Reform* (London, 1867). Contributors other than those mentioned were G. C. Brodrick, Bernard Cracroft, Lord Houghton, R. H. Hutton, J. B. Kinnear, A. O. Rutson and Sir George Young.

5. See Asa Briggs, *Victorian People* (London, 1954), pp. 243–75. See also *Essays on Reform*, pp. 20–5; and Benjamin E. Lippincott, *Victorian Critics of Democracy* (Minneapolis, 1938), pp. 244–64.

CHAPTER FOUR

1. Bryce to his mother, Mrs Margaret Bryce, 15 August 1870, Bryce Papers.

2. *Ibid.*

3. R. S. Rait, *A. V. Dicey*, p. 55. Rait's book (pp. 55–69) is useful for filling in minor gaps in the Bryce diary of the 1870 Bryce–Dicey travels.

4. On Bishop McQuaid, see F. J. Zweierlein, *Life and Letters of Bishop McQuaid* (3 vols., New York, 1925–7), esp. II: 57–68.

5. Data from *New York Times*, 24 August 1870; also James Bryce to Mrs Margaret Bryce, 24 August 1870, Bryce Papers.

6. Bryce, *loc. cit.*

7. Rollo Ogden, *Life and Letters of E. L. Godkin* (2 vols., New York, 1907); Gustav Pollak, *Fifty Years of American Idealism: the New York Nation, 1865–1915* (Boston, 1915); Alan P. Grimes, *The Political Liberalism of the New York Nation, 1865–1932* (Chapel Hill, 1953), *passim.*

8. The great majority of the articles and reviews in the *Nation* were unsigned during the nineteenth century. However an invaluable *Index of Contributors* is available, compiled by Daniel C. Haskell (2 vols., New York Public Library, 1953). This index (II: 65–9) lists 290 contributions by Bryce in the form of reviews, essays, review-essays, and biographical sketches of eminent men.

9. *Note:* References to Bryce's travels and experiences on the 1870 visit are taken from his 1870 Journal unless otherwise indicated.

10. *New York Times*, 22 August 1870, and Bryce Journal, 1870. New York City in 1870 can also be recaptured through the vast illustrations archive in the New York Public Library (Pictures Collection). See also A. Kouwenhoven (ed.), *The Columbia Historical Portrait of New York* (New York, 1953), pp. 342–5, 349–50.

11. Mary T. Higginson, *Letters and Journals of Thomas Wentworth Higginson, 1846–1906* (Boston, 1921). On the 1870 Bryce–Dicey visit, see p. 229. More details are contained in Higginson's diaries in the Houghton Library, Harvard University.

12. Newport Historical Society possesses a 'Town and Country Club' file which lists the members and describes the activities of the club in the 1870s. See also Mary T. Higginson, *Thomas Wentworth Higginson, the Story of His Life* (Boston, 1914), p. 258. An interesting aspect of the New England Brahmin tradition is the amount of time they spent writing about each other.

13. Bryce Journal, 1870; Thomas Wentworth Higginson, Diary entries for 29–30 August 1870; Higginson Diaries, Houghton Library, Harvard.

14. The Emerson–Carlyle correspondence, maintained for almost forty years, is probably the most important of these connections, but the combined exchanges over many decades deserve the attention of literary and intellectual historians. Cf. the correspondence between Charles Eliot Norton and John Stuart Mill, 1865 to 1870, printed in *Proceedings, Massachusetts Historical Society*, L (1916–17), pp. 11–25.

15. The comments of Mrs Trollope and Charles Dickens are reprinted in part in Allan Nevins (ed.), *America Through British Eyes* (New York, 1948). See also Henry Steele Commager (ed.), *America in Perspective: the United*

States through Foreign Eyes (New York, 1947) and Max Berger, *The British Traveller in America*, 1836–60 (New York, 1943).

16. Cf. A. Whitridge, 'British Liberals and the American Civil War', *History Today*, XII, No. 10 (1962), pp. 688–95. Gladstone's Newcastle speech supporting Jefferson Davis caused bitter resentment in New England. Leslie Stephen in '*The Times' on the American War* (London, 1865) excoriated *The Times* for its support of the Confederacy. See especially pp. 105–7.

17. Bryce Journal, 1870, p. 14. Bryce carried a letter of introduction to Longfellow from John Nichol, now professor of English literature at Glasgow and a friend of Longfellow's. See Bryce to Longfellow, 28 August 1870, Longfellow Papers, Houghton Library, Harvard.

18. See 'Thomas Gold Appleton', *Dictionary of American Biography*, I: 333–4.

19. Bryce Journal, 1870, p. 18.

20. Mark DeWolfe Howe, *Justice Oliver Wendell Holmes*, Vol. I: *The Shaping Years, 1841–70* (Cambridge, Mass., 1957), pp. 226–32.

21. I am indebted to the late Mark DeWolfe Howe for this information and for valuable portions of the Holmes–Bryce correspondence not present in the Bryce collection at the Bodleian Library.

22. Bryce Journal, 1870, p. 19.

23. *Ibid.*, p. 21.

24. *Ibid.*, p. 25.

25. *Ibid.*, pp. 26–7. On John Woods Brooks, see Thomas C. Cochran, *Railroad Leaders, 1845–1890* (Cambridge, Mass., 1953), pp. 166–82. Of course the railroads were simply another sphere in which old New England wealth was being invaded by the new financiers like Jay Gould and Jim Fisk. Gould's stock manipulation of the Erie Railroad and his other business enterprises brought a social as well as an economic challenge to Bostonians like Brooks and Charles Francis Adams. Adams and his brother Henry Adams attempted a counter-attack in their essays of 1869 and 1870 in the *North American Review* and the *Westminster Review* (later reprinted in their chapters of *Erie and other Essays* (New York, 1886). On Jay Gould, see Julius Grodinsky, *Jay Gould: His Business Career, 1867–1892* (Philadelphia, 1957), pp. 38–55, 595–604. See also Edward C. Kirkland, *Charles Francis Adams, Jr., The Patrician at Bay* (Cambridge, Mass., 1965).

26. Bryce Journal, 1870, p. 31.

27. *Ibid.*, p. 34.

28. *Ibid.*, p. 36. Dicey also recorded this meeting. See Rait, *Dicey*, pp. 63–4.

CHAPTER FIVE

1. See Chapters 17 and 21 below.

2. James Bryce to his father, James Bryce, 14 September 1870, Bryce Papers.

3. *Ibid.*

4. Bryce Journal, 1870, p. 51.

5. *Ibid.*, p. 53.

6. *Ibid.*, p. 51.

7. *Ibid.*, pp. 54–5.

8. An early visitor to the Falls of St Anthony was Jonathan Carver, the son of a Colonial Governor, who saw them in 1776 and recorded his impressions in his volume of travels published in 1778. Thereafter a succession of European travellers made the journey to the Falls. See Lucille M. Kane, *The Waterfall that Built a City* (St Paul, 1966), pp. 66 ff.

9. Bryce Journal, 1870, p. 59.

10. *Ibid.*, pp. 62–3.

11. *Ibid.*, pp. 64–73.

12. See John Moses and Joseph Kirkland, *History of Chicago* (2 vols., Chicago, 1895), II: Chap. 2; Bessie L. Pierce, *A History of Chicago* (3 vols., New York, 1937–57), II: 390–402.

13. John H. Holmes, *Life and Letters of Robert Collyer* (2 vols., New York, 1917), I: Chaps. 5–7; II: Chap 11.

14. Bryce Journal, 1870, p. 64.

15. *Ibid.*, pp. 65, 72.

16. See pp. 84–6 below.

17. Bryce Journal, 1870, pp. 67–8.

18. Information on Charles Elliott from *Catalog of the Presbyterian Seminary*, published by the Seminary (Chicago, 1928). Although Dicey's diary of the 1870 trip has not survived, Rait, *Dicey*, pp. 66–7 suggests that Dicey was above all interested in the administration of justice in the United States, the position of the legal profession, and the methods by which its recruits were obtained.

19. Bryce Journal, 1870, pp. 70–1.

20. Alexander C. Flick, *Samuel Jones Tilden* (New York, 1929), pp. 205–12. See also Thomas A. Hendricks, *Life of Samuel Jones Tilden* (Boston, 1876), pp. 85–92, 108–12 ff. On Tammany Hall and the Tweed Ring in New York City, see Gustavus Myers, *The History of Tammany Hall* (New York, 1901), pp. 252–82.

21. Bryce Journal, 1870, pp. 76–7.

22. Hendricks, *Tilden*, pp. 108–12.

23. Bryce to his sister, Katherine Bryce, 18 October 1870, Bryce Papers.

24. Henry James, *Charles W. Eliot, President of Harvard* (2 vols., Boston, 1930), I: 236–48 ff., II: Appendix A, 335–42. See also Samuel Eliot Morison, *The Development of Harvard University, 1869–1929* (Cambridge, Mass., 1930), p. xlvii *et passim*.

25. Cf. Richard S. Barnes, 'German Influence on American Historical Studies' (Unpublished Ph.D. dissertation, Yale University Library, 1953), pp. 5, 10–17, 20 *et passim*.

26. Bryce to Katherine Bryce, 11 October 1870, Bryce Papers.

27. Bryce to Ralph Waldo Emerson, 15 October 1870, Emerson Papers, Houghton Library, Harvard.

28. Sarah Forbes Hughes, *Letters and Recollections of John Murray Forbes* (2 vols., Boston, 1899), I: 8, II: 206 *et passim*.

29. The literature on the history of American railroads is now vast. Two excellent studies on the political and social aspects of railroad development are Edward C. Kirkland, *Men, Cities and Transportation: A Study in New England History* (2 vols., Cambridge, Mass., 1948) and Gabriel Kolko, *Railroads and Regulation, 1877–1916* (Princeton, 1965).

30. On Simeon Baldwin see F. H. Jackson, *Simeon E. Baldwin* (New York, 1955), pp. 55–70.

31. Bryce to Eliot, 31 October 1870, Charles W. Eliot Papers, Harvard University Archives.

32. The Bryce–Eliot correspondence extends from 1871 to 1922 and is very full. The Bryce Papers, Bodleian Library, contain copies of most of the Bryce letters to Eliot except for the 1870 to 1879 period.

33. Bryce to Katherine Bryce, 18 October 1870, Bryce Papers.

34. A. V. Dicey to James Bryce, 12 February 1907, Bryce Papers.

CHAPTER SIX

1. James Bryce, *The Academical Study of the Civil Law* (Oxford, 1871). The lecture is reprinted in Bryce, *Studies in History and Jurisprudence* (New York, 1901), pp. 860–86. Another ed., (2 vols., Oxford, 1901, II: 475–503).

2. *Ibid*.

3. Holmes to Bryce, 17 May 1871, Bryce Papers. See also Howe, *Holmes*, Vol. II, *The Proving Years* (Cambridge, Mass., 1963), p. 92.

4. Howe, *Holmes*, I: 214 ff.

5. Holmes was also deeply influenced by Sir Frederick Pollock, of course. See Howe (ed.), *The Holmes–Pollock Letters* (2 vols., Cambridge, Mass., 1942), and more sceptically by Harold Laski. When Bryce died in 1922 Holmes wrote: 'Thus breaks one of the oldest associations I had with living men.' – Holmes to Pollock, 23 January 1922, *Holmes–Pollock Letters*, II: 87.

6. *Harvard Law Review*, 27 May 1871, pp. 777–8.

7. I am grateful to Professor F. H. Lawson of Lancaster University for some assistance on these points.

8. Fisher, *Bryce*, I: 132–3.

9. *Macmillan's Magazine*, XXV, No. 147 (January 1872), pp. 206–17.

10. Bryce also wished to introduce Law Schools at London, Oxford and Cambridge on the Harvard pattern, but there was no support for such a move.

11. *Macmillan's Magazine*, XXV, No. 148 (March, 1872), pp. 422–32.

12. *Ibid*., p. 428.

13. *Macmillan's Magazine*, XXV, No. 145 (November 1871), pp. 54–65.

14. *Cornhill Magazine*, XXVI (December 1872), pp. 704–16.

15. *Ibid*., pp. 706–7.

16. *Ibid*., pp. 707–8.

CHAPTER SEVEN

1. British Museum, Gladstone Papers. Add. Mss. 44770, ff. 5–14 and Add. Mss. 44786 ff. 75–9; 44787 ff. 179–85. See also Gladstone to Bryce, 1874–96 (84 letters), Bryce Papers, 'English Correspondents'.

2. Gladstone to Bryce, 26 April 1880. Bryce Papers.

3. Bryce, *Transcaucasia and Ararat* (London, 1877), p. 277.

4. Apart from topics on which Bryce could be expected to be knowledgeable, such as constitutional history and law, his articles in the *Nation* ranged from ancient and medieval history to modern biography.

5. Bryce to Mrs Margaret Bryce, 16 August 1881 and 27 August 1881, Bryce Papers.

6. Kouwenhoven (ed.), *Columbia Historical Portrait of New York*, pp. 356–7 ff.; New York Public Library, Pictures Collection; Bryce to Mrs Margaret Bryce, 31 August 1881, Bryce Papers.

7. Holmes to Bryce, 17 August 1879, Bryce Papers.

8. *Ibid.*

9. Morton White, *Social Thought in America* (New York, 1949), p. 13.

10. Bryce to Mrs Margaret Bryce, 11 September 1881, Bryce Papers.

11. Lewis C. Gandy, *The Tabors: A Footnote to Western History* (New York, 1934), pp. 182 and 186–96. (There is a useful woodcut of Leadville in 1879, p. 188.) See also W. F. Stone, *History of Colorado* (3 vols., Chicago, 1918), I: 267–70.

12. Bryce to Mrs Margaret Bryce, 21 September 1881, Bryce Papers.

13. *Ibid.*

14. *Ibid.*

15. Bryce to Mrs Margaret Bryce, 11 November 1881, Bryce Papers.

16. *Ibid.*

17. Daniel C. Gilman, 'The Johns Hopkins University, 1876–1891', *Johns Hopkins Studies in History and Jurisprudence*, IX (1891), pp. 183–217. See pp. 193–4. See also Daniel C. Gilman, *The Launching of a University* (New York, 1906), *passim*.

18. Bryce to Mrs Margaret Bryce, 24 November 1881, Bryce Papers.

19. See Henry Villard, *Memoirs of Henry Villard* (2 vols., Boston, 1904), II: 399 ff.

20. See C. M. Fuess, *Carl Schurz, Reformer* (New York, 1932), *passim*. See also Carl Wittke, *Refugees of Revolution: the Forty-Eighters in America* (Philadelphia, 1952), pp. 262–79 *et passim*.

21. Henry Villard, *Memoirs*, II: 339 ff.

22. The Bryce–Godkin correspondence at the Houghton Library, Harvard, and in the Bryce Papers is almost complete for the years 1882 to 1902. (Godkin died in 1902.) The Bryce–Villard correspondence (1883 to 1900) is also fairly complete.

23. Godkin to Bryce, 28 February 1882, Bryce Papers.

24. Bryce to Mrs Margaret Bryce, 6 December 1881, Bryce Papers.

25. Bryce to Mary Bryce, 11 December 1881, Bryce Papers.

26. Bryce to Mary Bryce, 16 December 1881, Bryce Papers.

27. A possible explanation of constraint between Bryce and Henry Adams may lie with an article Bryce wrote in 1882 in which he strongly criticised the pessimism of the novel *Democracy*. See James Bryce, 'Some Aspects of American Public Life', *Fortnightly Review*, XXXII (1882), pp. 634–55.

28. See George Bancroft to Bryce, 17 December 1881, Bryce Papers, suggesting books for Bryce to read. See also Bancroft to Bryce, 26 December 1881 – a covering letter for several books (unidentified) which Bancroft is sending to Bryce. On Bancroft see M. DeW. Howe, *Life and Letters of George Bancroft* (2 vols., New York, 1908).

29. Bryce to Thomas Wentworth Higginson, 11 December 1881, Higginson Papers, Houghton Library, Harvard.

30. Bryce to Mrs Margaret Bryce, 24 November 1881, Bryce Papers.

CHAPTER EIGHT

1. Villard to Bryce, 25 July 1883, Bryce Papers; Bryce to Villard, 7 August 1883 (in the files of the New York Historical Society). *Note*: Details of the 1883 Northern Pacific excursion are in the Villard Papers, Harvard. The guest list, route followed and a collection of press clippings make up a full account.

2. Bryce to Mary Bryce, 13 September 1883, Bryce Papers.

3. A vivid photograph of the scene at Bismarck is preserved at the North Dakota Historical Society, Bismarck, North Dakota, though the figure of James Bryce cannot be discovered.

4. Bryce to Mrs Margaret Bryce, 6 September 1883.

5. *Ibid*.

6. Henry Villard's son, Oswald Garrison Villard, provided a good description of this scene in his autobiography *Fighting Years – Memoirs of a Liberal Editor* (New York, 1939), pp. 47–59. Villard Junior was editor of the New York *Evening Post*, later (1918) of the *Nation*. He was also a friend and correspondent of Bryce.

7. Bryce to Mary Bryce, 13 September 1883, Bryce Papers.

8. Bryce to Mrs Margaret Bryce, 27 September 1883 (post card), Bryce Papers. Also Bryce to his uncle, William Bryce, 17 October 1883, Bryce Papers.

9. See Oscar Lewis, *San Francisco since 1872: A Pictorial History* (San Francisco, 1946). See also John S. Hittell, *A History of San Francisco* (San Francisco, 1878), Chap. 6, 'The Silver Era'.

10. Bryce to Katherine Bryce, 6 October 1883, Bryce Papers.

11. See the Hawaii travel diary and notebook, Bryce Papers. This notebook is available in one of the boxes (B.13, 'Travels') not yet catalogued.

12. Bryce to William Bryce, Bryce Papers.

13. Bryce, Hawaiian travel diary.

14. Mentioned in Richard Hofstadter, *Social Darwinism in American Thought* (New York, 1959), p. 173.

15. The Shaw Notebooks, on which my account of the Bryce seminar is based, are in the New York Public Library (Manuscripts Division).

16. Cf. Alexis de Tocqueville, *Democracy in America* (Reeve Text, ed. Phillips Bradley, 2 vols., New York, 1945), I: 56.

17. Albert Shaw quoting Bryce, Shaw Notebooks, New York Public Library.

18. Bryce to Mrs Sarah Whitman, 14 December 1882, Bryce Papers.

19. James Bryce, 'The Predictions of Hamilton and de Tocqueville', *Johns Hopkins Studies in Historical and Political Science*, Fifth Series, Vol. IX (Baltimore, 1887). The article also shows some of the fruits of the 1883 Johns Hopkins seminar.

20. Albert Shaw in *Review of Reviews*, LXV (1922), pp. 277–84.

21. Woodrow Wilson to Ellen Axson, 27 November 1883. Quoted in R. S. Baker, *Woodrow Wilson, Life and Letters* (8 vols., Garden City, New York, 1927–39), IV: 18.

22. Bryce to Mrs Margaret Bryce, 24 November 1883, Bryce Papers.

23. Mrs Daniel C. Gilman to Bryce, 1 December 1883, Bryce Papers.

24. Bryce to Katherine Bryce, 4 December 1883, Bryce Papers.

CHAPTER NINE

1. Fisher, *Bryce*, I: 175.

2. Justin McCarthy, *British Political Portraits* (New York, 1903), pp. 296–7. McCarthy, an Irish politician and amateur historian, remarks that he had 'many a time' heard Tories say, 'Bryce is up – I must go and hear what he has to say.' Others testified, McCarthy goes on, to Bryce's command over the House.

3. *Hansard's Parliamentary Debates*, CCCV (1886), cc. 1215–33.

4. *Ibid.*

5. The extent and the strength of this feeling among groups of Americans is difficult to gauge with precision and the evidence is scattered in the historical literature which touches on the subject. Cf. Carl Wittke, *The Irish in America* (Baton Rouge, 1956) *passim*; and Wittke, *Refugees of Revolution*, Chap. 8, 'German Fenianism', pp. 92–110. Needless to say the Irish American and German American press constantly attacked and excoriated successive British governments over their Irish policies.

6. Dicey to Bryce, 3 January 1885, Bryce Papers.

7. Andrew White to Edward Freeman, 19 May 1883 (copy in Bryce Papers).

8. Gladstone to Bryce, 3 October 1889, Bryce Papers.

9. Cf. Theodore Roosevelt, *The Naval War of 1812* (New York, 1882). See also Theodore Roosevelt, *Collected Works* (National Edition, 20 vols., New York, 1926), esp. Vols. VII–X.

10. Cf. Howard K. Beale, *Theodore Roosevelt and the Rise of America to World Power* (Baltimore, 1956), pp. 81–6 and 448–62. (Hereafter cited as Beale, *Roosevelt and the Rise of America to World Power*.)

11. Roosevelt to Bryce, 6 January 1889, Bryce Papers. This letter is printed in Elting Morison and John Blum, *Letters of Theodore Roosevelt* (8 vols., Cambridge, Mass., 1951–4), I: 134–5. (Hereafter cited as Morison, *Letters of T.R.*) *Note*: the above letter is incorrectly dated in Morison, *loc. cit.*, which shows the date as 6 January 1888.

12. Baker, *Woodrow Wilson, Life and Letters*, I: 310.

13. Woodrow Wilson, *Congressional Government* (Boston, 1885). The influence of Bagehot on Woodrow Wilson (revealed in this work) is a commonplace. Bryce was also a great admirer of Bagehot (see his tribute in a letter to A. V. Dicey, 16 April 1916, Bryce Papers). This shared enthusiasm was probably a continuing bond between Wilson and Bryce.

14. *Political Science Quarterly*, IV (1889), pp. 153–69. Woodrow Wilson's review was reprinted in a symposium celebrating the fiftieth anniversary of the publication of *The American Commonwealth*. See Robert C. Brooks (ed.), *Bryce's American Commonwealth, Fiftieth Anniversary* (New York, 1939).

15. Woodrow Wilson, *loc. cit.*, p. 169.

16. Edmund J. James, 'Bryce's American Commonwealth', *Publications of the American Academy of Political and Social Science* (Philadelphia, 1896), pp. 377–410.

17. James Smith (Secretary of the Plymouth Institute, Indianapolis) to Bryce, 4 February 1890, Bryce Papers.

18. The Library of Congress, Washington, D.C., holds the following editions in translation: French (4 vols., Paris, 1900–2); Italian (3 vols., Turin, 1913–16); Spanish (3 vols., Madrid, 1912–14); Portuguese (2 vols., Buenos Aires, 1929); Russian (3 vols., Moscow, 1889–90).

19. Jesse Macy to Bryce, 7 November 1889, Bryce Papers.

20. See Fisher, *Bryce*, I: 136.

CHAPTER TEN

1. On assistance to Tocqueville, see George W. Pierson, *Tocqueville in America* (abridged edition, New York, 1959), pp. 272–82, 439–45.

2. Sidgwick to Bryce, 22 January 1885, Bryce Papers.

3. Acton to Bryce, 6 September 1884, and Acton to Bryce, n.d. (probably 1884 from internal evidence and subsequent Bryce–Acton letters), Bryce Papers.

4. *English Historical Review*, IV (1889), pp. 388–96. Reprinted in Acton, *The History of Freedom and Other Essays* (London, 1919), pp. 575–87.

5. Acton, *Inaugural Lecture on the Study of History* (London, 1895) reprinted in Acton, *Lectures on Modern History* (London, 1906), pp. 1–30.

6. Cf. Gertrude Himmelfarb, Introduction to Acton, *Essays on Freedom and Power* (ed. Himmelfarb, New York, 1955), pp. 10–13 and 18 ff.

7. See Acton to Bryce, 25 March 1889 *inter alia*, Bryce Papers; and Acton Papers, Cambridge University Library, especially Acton's 'American Notes' (add. 4894–8). Acton's views on the 'Englishness' of the American revolution changed considerably between his visit to America in 1855 and the appearance of Bryce's work in 1888. Cf. Acton, 'The Political Causes of the American Revolution' (1861), in Himmelfarb. *op. cit.*, pp. 171–224 especially pp. 175–80; and Acton Papers, add. 4898, ff. 166, 223, 391, *inter alia*.

8. See Bryce *Studies in Contemporary Biography*, pp. 382–99.

9. Bryce, *The American Commonwealth* (1888 ed.), I: 620–35.

10. *Ibid.*, II: 335–53.

11. *Ibid.* (3rd ed., London and New York, 1895), II: 377–403.

12. The literature on reform movements and corrupt politics between (roughly) 1870 and 1900 is very extensive. Cf. Frank M. Stewart, *A Half-Century of Municipal Reform* (Berkeley, 1950); A. B. Sageser, *The First Two Decades of the Pendleton Act* (Nebraska U.P., 1935).

13. See Robert K. Merton, *Social Theory and Social Structure* (Glencoe, Illinois, 1957), p. 71.

14. Bryce, *op. cit.* (3rd ed.), II: 469–520.

15. *Ibid.*, pp. 496, 510.

16. For an interesting recent discussion of this classic problem of representative government see E. G. West, 'Liberty and Education: John Stuart Mill's Dilemma', *Philosophy*, XL (April 1965), pp. 129–42.

17. Bryce, *op. cit.* (3rd ed.), II: 506, 520.

18. It deserves to be stressed that *The American Commonwealth* is in an important sense a study in comparative government and institutions. Throughout the work there is constant reference to the early Greek, Roman, and the later European (especially the English and Swiss) models.

CHAPTER ELEVEN

1. The genealogies of the Ashton and Gair families are contained in a box marked 'Ashton Family' in the Bryce Papers.

2. Eliot to Bryce, 2 April 1889, Bryce Papers.

3. Bryce to Mrs Margaret Bryce, 11 August 1890, Bryce Papers.

4. Bryce to Mrs Margaret Bryce, 16 August 1890, Bryce Papers.

5. Eliot to Bryce, 2 April 1889, Bryce Papers.

6. Bryce gave a lecture on his Canadian travels when he returned home and this was soon in print. See James Bryce, 'A Recent View of Canada', *Transactions of the Aberdeen Philosophical Society*, II (1891), pp. 313–35. The article

shows that Bryce had a wary eye on the old annexationist sentiments across the Canadian border.

7. Bryce to Mrs Margaret Bryce, 27 September 1890, Bryce Papers.

8. On William M. Salter, see *Dictionary of American Biography*, VIII: 315–16.

9. Bryce to Edward Freeman, 4 November 1890, Bryce Papers. See also E. Wallace, *Goldwin Smith*, pp. 137–8, 270–8.

10. Cf. James Q. Dealey, *The Growth of American State Constitutions, 1776–1914* (Boston, 1915), pp. 89 ff.

11. *New York Times*, 5 November 1890, and Bryce to Edward Freeman, 4 November 1890, Bryce Papers.

12. See John D. Hicks, *The Populist Revolt* (Minneapolis, 1931), Chaps. 2–4.

CHAPTER TWELVE

1. Godkin to Bryce, 28 May 1886, Bryce Papers.

2. By 1890, the Fenian movement in the United States had more than twenty-five years of history behind it. In 1866 the Fenian Brotherhood organised raids across the Canadian border in attempts to promote annexation by the United States. Bryce made an appeal to moderates in American politics in 1883, when he deplored the activities of politicians using the Irish problem to whip up anti-British sentiment at election times. See Bryce, 'England and Ireland', *North American Review*, XXVI (1883), pp. 249–64.

3. Allan Nevins, *Grover Cleveland: a Study in Courage* (New York, 1934), p. 428.

4. *Ibid.*, p. 431.

5. *Ibid.*, p. 415.

6. Henry Cabot Lodge, 'England, Venezuela and the Monroe Doctrine' *North American Review*, CLX, No. 6 (June 1895), pp. 651–8.

7. *Ibid.*, p. 657.

8. See Samuel Flagg Bemis, *A Diplomatic History of the United States* (4th ed., New York, 1957), p. 418.

9. Quoted in A. L. P. Dennis, *Adventures in Diplomacy, 1896–1906* (New York, 1928), p. 29. This work uses the official documents and is most useful for tracing the precise steps in the Venezuela dispute. See also J. A. S. Grenville, *Lord Salisbury and Foreign Policy: the Close of the Nineteenth Century* (London, 1964), pp. 70 ff.

10. Godkin to Bryce, 6 January 1896, Bryce Papers. For Cleveland's Message of 17 December 1895, see James D. Richardson, *A Compilation of the Messages and Papers of the Presidents, 1789–1902* (11 vols., Washington, D.C., 1905–6), IX: 655.

11. Godkin to Bryce, 6 January 1896, Bryce Papers.

12. Bryce to Godkin, 24 January 1896, Godkin Papers.

13. Bryce to Theodore Roosevelt, 1 January 1896, Roosevelt Papers, Library of Congress.

14. Bryce to Henry Villard, 4 January 1896, Villard Papers. (Cited in Fisher, *Bryce*, I: 320, but shown incorrectly as 4 January 1886. Very probably a printer's error.)

15. In 1890 in the pages of the North American Review, James Gillespie Blaine, the American Secretary of State, engaged in a verbal duel with William Ewart Gladstone on the issue of Free Trade. See *North American Review*, CL, Nos. 398 and 399 (1890), pp. 1–54, 145–76.

16. James Bryce, 'British Feeling on the Venezuelan Question', *North American Review*, CLXII, No. 2 (1896), pp. 145–53.

17. *Ibid.*, p. 153.

18. J. L. Garvin, *The Life of Joseph Chamberlain* (3 vols., London, 1932–5), III: 96.

19. J. A. S. Grenville, *Lord Salisbury and Foreign Policy*, p. 72.

20. A. W. Ward and G. P. Gooch, *Cambridge History of British Foreign Policy, 1783–1919* (3 vols., Cambridge, 1922–3), III: 225.

21. See Andrew White, *Autobiography* (2 vols., New York, 1905), II: 122–4.

22. Bemis, *Diplomatic History of the U.S.*, pp. 420–2; Dexter Perkins, *The Monroe Doctrine, 1867–1907* (Baltimore, 1937), p. 235.

CHAPTER THIRTEEN

1. Eliot to Bryce, 30 July 1897, Bryce Papers.

2. See, for instance, the following: G. B. Adams, 'Why Americans Dislike England', *Independent*, 2 January 1896; R. I. Curtis, 'Hostility to England', *Independent*, 23 April 1896; Andrew Carnegie, 'Does America Dislike England?', *Contemporary Review*, LXXII (November 1897); and Goldwin Smith, 'American Anglophobia', *Saturday Review*, LXXXI (February 1896).

3. In March 1895 Lodge began to impress on his colleagues in the United States Senate and also in the House of Representatives the vital importance of sea power. See John A. Garraty, *Henry Cabot Lodge* (New York, 1953), pp. 152 ff. Roosevelt and Mahan were in close touch with each other soon after the publication of Mahan's lectures 'The Influence of Sea Power Upon History, 1660–1783' (1890). Roosevelt's published correspondence makes clear his reverence for Mahan. Cf. Roosevelt to Mahan, 1 May 1893, in Morison, *Letters of T.R.*, I: 315–16. Unpublished letters in the Lodge Papers show that Roosevelt lobbied Lodge and others in high places to gain appointment as Assistant Secretary of the Navy. Lodge strongly recommended his friend to McKinley the new Republican President, in a letter of 9 November 1896. (Lodge Papers, Massachusetts Historical Society.) Historians who incline to Carlyle's view of history may find much grist for their mill in the combined achievements of Lodge, Roosevelt and Mahan in altering the course of American history.

4. See Morison, *Letters of T.R.*, I: 723.

5. Roosevelt to Bryce, 10 September 1897, Morison, *Letters of T.R.*, I: 672.

6. See Garraty, *Henry Cabot Lodge*, Chaps. 9 and 11. See also Beale, *Theodore Roosevelt and the Rise of America to World Power*, esp. Chaps. 1 and 2.

7. See Bryce to Godkin, 6 January 1894, Godkin Papers.

8. Clipping from *Philadelphia Press*, 30 September 1897, Bryce Papers.

9. Quoted in Elie Halevy, *History of the English People in the Nineteenth Century* (6 vols., London, 1949–52), V: 9 (fn.).

10. Quoted in Bemis, *Diplomatic History of the U.S.*, p. 442, fn. 2.

11. *North American Review*, CLXII (1896), pp. 151–2.

12. James Bryce, 'The Policy of Annexation for America', *Forum* (New York), XXIV (1897), pp. 385–95.

13. *Atlantic Monthly*, LXXXI (1898), pp. 577–88.

14. The authorship of Washington's Farewell Address is still a subject of controversy, of course, owing to the undoubted influence of Hamilton and possibly John Jay in writing drafts for Washington.

15. *Atlantic Monthly*, LXXXI (1898), p. 588.

16. James Bryce, 'The Essential Unity of England and America', *Atlantic Monthly*, LXXXII (1898), pp. 22–9.

17. *Atlantic Monthly*, LXXXII (1898), pp. 433–40.

CHAPTER FOURTEEN

1. See Bryce to Gladstone, 24 March 1874, setting out 'in what respects the old Icelandic writings may be made to throw light upon Homer and the Homeric age', and Gladstone to Bryce, 25 March 1874, urging Bryce to publish an article on the subject; Bryce Papers and British Museum, Add. Mss., 44786–44789. The discussion on Homer and also on Dante continues into the Bryce–Gladstone correspondence of the 1880s and early 1890s, although by then more urgent discussions on Ireland and the Eastern Question take first place.

2. Bryce, *Studies in History and Jurisprudence* (2 vols., Oxford, 1901), I: 1.

3. *Ibid.*, I: 83 ff. The *Studies* was primarily a work on comparative government (replete with historical allusions, of course) and foreshadowed the main intellectual preoccupations of Bryce from 1901 to his death.

4. Bryce to Villard, 8 November 1898, Villard Papers, Harvard; Bryce to Godkin, 27 March 1899, Godkin Papers, Harvard.

5. The activities of the Anti-Imperialist League can be traced in a collection of pamphlets in Widener Library, Harvard. A journal, *The Anti-Imperialist*, was begun in 1899 but it expired soon afterwards. Godkin, Eliot, Carl Schurz and Andrew Carnegie were among the founding members of the League.

6. Marion Bryce to her mother, Mrs Thomas Ashton, 19 September 1901, Bryce Papers, Oxford. *Note*: the letters of Marion Bryce to her mother provide valuable information on the Bryces' travels and associations in America after 1900.

7. Marion Bryce to Mrs Thomas Ashton, 1 October 1901, Bryce Papers.

8. Marion Bryce to Mrs Ashton, 5 October 1901, Bryce Papers.

9. Bryce to Eliot, 7 February 1902, Eliot Papers, Harvard.

10. See Hermann Hagerdorn, *Leonard Wood* (2 vols., New York, 1931), I: 366–92; the Bryce visit to Cuba is recorded on pp. 374 ff. Bryce wrote on Cuba in the *North American Review* 174 (1902), pp. 445–56.

11. Eliot to Bryce, 14 March 1902, Bryce Papers.

12. Marion Bryce to Mrs Ashton, 17 November 1901, Bryce Papers.

13. Bryce to Godkin (in confidence), 8 November 1892, Godkin Papers, Harvard. Bryce was again Minister in Attendance at Florence in April 1893. 'I like Mr Bryce', said Queen Victoria on one occasion. 'He knows so much and is so modest.' – Fisher, *Bryce*, I: 295.

14. See the tribute from Sir Michael Sadler in Fisher, *Bryce*, I: 298–9.

15. Bryce to Eliot, 7 February 1902, Eliot Papers, Harvard. It need hardly be said that Bryce's thoughts were provoked not only by his visits to the Caribbean but also by long debate on Darwinism and the proselytisers of Social Darwinism.

16. Printed by the Clarendon Press, 7 June 1902. A copy is in the Bryce Papers.

17. See a catalogue published by Basil Blackwell in 1940, 'Books from the Library of Viscount Bryce, O.M.' (Catalogue No. 464, Oxford, 1940), p. 15. Although this printed catalogue represents only the remaining portions of Bryce's large personal library (Bryce made substantial gifts in his will to the libraries of Trinity College, Oxford, Lincoln's Inn, Oriel College and to the Bodleian Library), it is useful for evidence of Bryce's interests and the range of his reading. The 1,556 items in the Blackwell catalogue include many famous American works presented to Bryce, with personal greetings from their authors on the flyleaf.

18. See pp. 183–4 below.

CHAPTER FIFTEEN

1. Cf. Hofstadter, *Social Darwinism in American Thought*, Chap. 9, 'Racism and Imperialism'.

2. *Ibid.*, pp. 179–82.

3. Cf. Edward Westermarck, *Memories of My Life* (London, 1929), pp. 208 ff. See also *Proceedings of the Sociological Society* (London, 1905 *et seq.*), *Sociological Review*, I, No. 1 (London, 1908) and subsequent issues. (The *Review* replaced the *Proceedings* in 1908). Bryce would have regarded as truisms recent suggestions that historians should use the findings of social anthropologists and sociologists in their researches. (Keith Thomas, 'History and Anthropology', *Past and Present*, No. 24 (1963), pp. 3–24; and 'New Ways in History', *Times Literary Supplement*, 7 April 1966, and subsequent correspondence.)

4. Although Bryce's Harvard friends were responsible for choosing him as

first Godkin lecturer, nevertheless it was an unusual honour to accord to a non-American in 1904.

5. Marion Bryce to Mrs Ashton, 13 September 1904, Bryce Papers.

6. *St Louis Post Dispatch*, 24 September 1904.

7. Marion Bryce to Mrs Ashton, 25 September 1904, Bryce Papers.

8. James Bryce, Notes on 1904 trip, Bryce Papers.

9. Marion Bryce to Mrs Ashton, 1 October 1904 (written from the White House), Bryce Papers.

10. Bryce to Eliot, 5 October 1904, Eliot Papers, Harvard.

11. Marion Bryce to Mrs Ashton, 14 October 1904, Bryce Papers.

12. There are fifty-three letters from Murray Butler to Bryce in the Bryce Papers, covering the years 1891 to 1921. Germany is discussed at several points from 1905 onwards.

13. After his visits to Cuba and Jamaica in 1901 Bryce was, of course, newly aware of the social and economic benefits which wise colonial administration could bring. See several Bryce articles in the *Nation*, LXXIV (1901–2) and the *Nation*, LXXXI (1905), pp. 145–7.

14. See detailed reports in the *New York Times*, 11–22 October 1904, and a synopsis of the seven lectures in the Bryce Papers.

15. Marion Bryce to Mrs Ashton, 28 October 1904, Bryce Papers.

16. Cf. Bernard Crick, *The American Science of Politics* (Berkeley, 1959), Chap. 4, pp. 95–117 *et passim*.

17. James Bryce, 'The Study of Popular Governments' (Godkin Lectures, 1904), second lecture. The lectures were printed verbatim in the *Boston Transcript*, 25, 27 and 29 October, and 1 and 4 November 1904. Copies of the verbatim reports are preserved in Harvard University Archives.

18. See Munro's remarks in Brooks (ed.), *Bryce's American Commonwealth, Fiftieth Anniversary*, pp. 204–20.

19. James Bryce, *Modern Democracies* (2 vols., London, 1921), I: 16. The affinity between Bryce and Woodrow Wilson on scientism in political studies is worth remarking. 'I do not like the term "political science",' Woodrow Wilson said in 1911: 'Human relationships . . . are not in any proper sense the subject matter of science.' Cited in Crick, *op. cit.*, pp. 104–5.

20. Marion Bryce to Mrs Ashton, 28 October 1904, Bryce Papers.

CHAPTER SIXTEEN

1. The *Nation*, LXX–XC (1900–9), *passim*. Daniel C. Haskell's *Index* (New York Public Library, 1953), II: 67–8, lists the Bryce articles.

2. *Outlook* (New York), 25 March 1905, pp. 733–40, and 1 April 1905, pp. 846–55.

3. *Outlook*, 25 March 1905, p. 738.

4. Steffens' articles in *McClure's Magazine* were collected in his book *The Shame of the Cities* (New York, 1904) and were an important part of the

groundswell of Progressive reforms in city government and administration between 1904 and 1908.

5. *Outlook*, 1 April 1905, p. 846.

6. Bryce was biased against the Senate, but the facts lent support to his views. Cf. W. Stull Holt, *Treaties Defeated by the Senate* (Baltimore, 1933), pp. 165–77 and Chap. 9.

7. *Outlook*, 1 April 1905, pp. 854–5.

8. *Ibid.*, p. 854.

9. Bryce to Oliver Wendell Holmes, 25 December 1906, Holmes Papers, Harvard; Bryce to Eliot, 24 December 1906, Eliot Papers, Harvard.

10. See Roosevelt to Von Sternberg, 11 October 1901, Morison, *Letters of T.R.*, III: 172–3. See also, Theodore Roosevelt, *Autobiography* (1st ed., New York, 1913), p. 36.

11. Roosevelt to Whitelaw Reid, 27 June 1906, Morison, *Letters of T.R.*, V: 318–19. On Durand, see Sir Percy Sykes, *Sir Mortimer Durand* (London, 1926), p. 275.

12. See Stephen Gwyn (ed.), *The Letters and Friendships of Sir Cecil Spring-Rice* (2 vols., London, 1929), I: 51–5; II: 178 ff. See also Roosevelt to Whitelaw Reid, 6 November 1906, Morison, *Letters of T.R.*, V: 488.

13. Beale, *Theodore Roosevelt and the Rise of America to World Power*, p. 133. See also G. M. Trevelyan, *Grey of Fallodon* (London, 1937), pp. 204 ff. Gilbert Murray, *The Foreign Policy of Sir Edward Grey* (London, 1915), *passim*; Edward (Viscount) Grey, *Twenty-Five Years, 1892–1916* (2 vols., London, 1925), II: 83–7 ff.

CHAPTER SEVENTEEN

1. Barbara Tuchman has provided a graphic account of the failure of the Hague conferences and also portrays the feeling of an uneasy decade in *The Proud Tower* (New York, 1965, London, 1966).

2. Cf. Charles S. Campbell, *Anglo-American Understanding, 1898–1903* (Baltimore, 1957); A. E. Campbell, *Great Britain and the United States, 1895–1903* (London, 1960); Lionel Gelber, *The Rise of Anglo-American Friendship, 1896–1906* (Toronto, 1938). Each of these writers concludes that by *circa* 1903 Britain and the United States had achieved a firm basis of mutual understanding. It seems to me that this thesis greatly oversimplifies the pitfalls of electoral politics in the United States.

3. Quoted in a lecture by Professor Max Beloff in 1957. Whoever the source it seems apt enough to exist in its own right.

4. The illusion may owe something to the tendency of Anglo-American diplomatic historians to concentrate on the doings of ambassadors and chancelleries, to the partial neglect of the more brutish politics of the era. Most American Ambassadors to the Court of St James have been decidedly Anglophile (one of the reasons for choosing them, no doubt). But a consequence is

that their despatches have often belied the true condition of Anglo-American relations. Similarly, Ambassadors such as Sackville-West, Durand, and Spring-Rice were often deluded by the kindness of their friends in Washington. One of the less obvious advantages of the Bryce appointment to Washington was that he had learned to shed many illusions.

5. Quoted by Viscount Lee, 'Cromwell and Roosevelt' in Roosevelt, *Works* (National Edition), X: 176.

6. See Bryce to Eliot, 24 December 1906, Eliot Papers, Harvard.

7. Bryce despatch, n.d. (but ? 1907 from internal evidence), Bryce Papers.

8. See Julius Pratt, *The Expansionists of 1898* (Baltimore, 1936); Robert E. Osgood, *Ideals and Self Interest in America's Foreign Relations* (Chicago, 1961).

9. John B. Brebner, *North Atlantic Triangle: the Interplay of Canada, the United States and Britain* (Toronto and New Haven, 1945), pp. 245, 257–62.

10. Beale, *Theodore Roosevelt and the Rise of America to World Power*, pp. 126–9; Bemis, *Diplomatic History of the U.S.*, pp. 426–8; Thomas A. Bailey, *Diplomatic History of the American People* (6th ed., New York, 1958), pp. 507–10.

11. Beale, *loc. cit.*

12. Bailey, *op. cit.*, p. 510; see also Dennis, *Adventures in Diplomacy*, pp. 146 ff.

13. Bryce, 'A Recent View of Canada', *Proceedings of the Aberdeen Philosophical Society*, II (1891), pp. 314–35 (based on his address to the Society).

14. Earl Grey to Bryce, 20 March 1907, Bryce Papers. *Note*: most of the correspondence and copies of despatches during the Bryce Ambassadorship are contained in seven volumes of Embassy Papers in the main Bryce archive in the Bodleian Library. (Hereafter cited as Bryce Embassy Papers).

15. Grey's disquiet over the growth of German naval strength is revealed in a large number of letters (more than 200) which he sent to Ambassador Durand and Bryce between 1904 and 1911. Originals are in the Public Archives of Canada, Ottawa. Photostats are contained in the Albert (4th Earl) Grey Papers. The Prior's Kitchen, University of Durham. A number of Grey's letters to Bryce are in the Bryce Embassy Papers, Oxford, and others are in the Bryce Despatches (1907–13) in the Foreign Office Library, London. These separate sources are indicated hereafter.

16. *Toronto Globe*, 2 April 1907. Bryce and Sir Wilfred Laurier were in fact old friends. In 1904 Laurier asked Bryce to pay him a visit for informal talks, but the election campaign in Canada prevented the two friends from meeting. See Marion Bryce to Mrs Ashton, 1 October 1904, Bryce Papers.

17. *Toronto Globe*, 2 April 1907.

18. *Ibid.*

19. *Toronto Globe*, 4 April 1907; and see E. Wallace, *Goldwin Smith*, pp. 227 ff.

20. Roosevelt to Arthur Lee, 8 April 1907; Morison, *Letters of T.R.*, V: 644. King Edward VII also wrote personally to Bryce on 24 March 1907 to express his gratification at the reception Bryce had received from President Roosevelt This letter in Bryce Embassy Papers, Oxford.

21. See Philip C. Jessup, *Elihu Root* (2 vols., New York, 1938), especially II: 86–9 ff.

22. Elihu Root to Bryce, 10 April 1908, Bryce Papers.

23. Texts of the Fisheries Treaty and the Boundary Treaty are in the Bryce Embassy Papers: Cd. 4138 and 4139 (1908).

24. Cf. G. P. Glazebrook, *A History of Canada's External Relations* (Toronto, 1950), pp. 244–9 *et seq.*; and Brebner, *North Atlantic Triangle*, pp. 250–2 *et passim.*

25. Text of the Arbitration Convention is in the Bryce Embassy Papers: Cd. 4179 (1908).

26. Jessup, *Elihu Root*, II: 270–8. For texts of the Conventions, see *61 Cong 2 Sess. Senate Doc.* No. 357 (2 vols., Washington, D.C., 1910). Also *Foreign Relations of the United States (1908)*, Washington, D.C. (1912), *passim.*

27. It is equally true, of course, that Germany considered Britain her chief rival in naval matters and thus her most obvious adversary if war came. Cf. R. S. J. Hoffman, *Great Britain and the German Trade Rivalry, 1875–1914* (Philadelphia, 1933). This monograph modifies some of the accounts proceeding from British historians of the period.

28. Hardinge to Bryce, 2 December 1907, Bryce Embassy Papers.

29. Hardinge to Bryce, 26 February 1909, Bryce Embassy Papers.

30. Hardinge to Bryce, 4 June 1909, Bryce Embassy Papers.

31. See Edward Grey to Bryce, Bryce Embassy Papers, various dates and esp. 10 January 1909.

32. Bryce to Edward Grey, 3 March 1910, Bryce Despatches, Foreign Office Library, London.

33. Speech to the American Society for the Judicial Settlement of International Disputes, December 1910. See Henry Pringle, *Life and Times of William Howard Taft* (2 vols., New York, 1939), II: 738.

34. Texts of Knox–Bryce Conventions are in Bryce Embassy Papers: Cd. 4815 (1909); Cd. 5222 (1910); Cd. 5223 (1910); Cd. 5971 (1911); Cd. 6034 (1912); Cd. 6201 (1912): and in *Foreign Relations of the U.S., passim.*

35. Earl Grey to Bryce, 11 August 1911, Bryce Embassy Papers.

36. Elihu Root to Bryce, 30 March 1910, Bryce Papers. See also Sir Wilfred Laurier to Bryce, 15 June 1910, Bryce Embassy Papers.

CHAPTER EIGHTEEN

1. James Bryce, *University and Historical Addresses: Delivered During Residence in the United States as Ambassador of Great Britain* (New York, 1913) – hereafter cited as Bryce, *Addresses.*

2. Cf. Arthur Mann, 'The Progressive Tradition' in John Higham (ed.), *The Reconstruction of American History* (New York, 1962), pp. 157–79.

3. Bryce, *Addresses*, p. 10.

4. *Ibid.*, p. 14.

5. *Ibid.*, p. 22.

6. James Bryce, 'What Is Progress?', Address to the Phi Beta Kappa Chapter of Harvard University, 1907; printed in *Atlantic Monthly*, C, No. 2 (1907), pp. 145–56; also in *Harvard Graduates' Magazine*, XVI (1907), pp. 1–19.

7. For good historical reasons, the idea of Progress was subscribed to with more fervency in America than it was in Europe (with the possible exception of France) during the nineteenth century. Cf. A. A. Ekirch, *The Idea of Progress in America, 1815–1860* (New York, 1944), esp. Chaps. 2, 6, 7; and Charles Beard's Introduction to J. B. Bury, *The Idea of Progress* (New York, 1932). An odd congruence of American optimism and French positivism.

8. See Bryce, *Addresses*, pp. 33–40, 107–24, 317–38, 407–25.

9. James Bryce, 'The Relations of Political Science to History and to Practice', *American Political Science Review*, 3 (1909), pp. 1–19; issued as a special reprint, 1909 (a copy in Bryce Papers).

10. Memoir by Mr George Young, First Secretary of the Embassy during Bryce's tenure (cited by Fisher, *Bryce*, II: 25).

11. Correspondence in the Macmillan Company (New York) Papers, New York Public Library, Manuscripts Divn.

12. The *Nation*, LXXXIX–XCVI (1909–13), *passim*.

13. See several letters, Marion Bryce to Mrs Ashton, 20, 27 March and 2, 10 April 1909, Bryce Papers.

14. *San Francisco Chronicle*, 24 March 1909. See also Bryce, *Addresses*, p. 239.

15. Bryce, *Addresses*, pp. 244–5.

16. *San Francisco Chronicle*, and *San Francisco Examiner*, s.d.

17. The *Daily Californian*, 26 March 1909.

18. *Palo Alto Times*, 27 March 1909, and *Daily Palo Altan*, s.d.

19. James Bryce, *The Hindrances to Good Citizenship* (New Haven, 1909). Bryce reminded his Yale audience that mankind 'has not shown any moral improvement under democracy' (p. 12). The price of liberty, he suggested, was the recognition of duties over rights, together with self-control, hard work and conscience. (Yale's ambience seems to have induced a Calvinist mood in Bryce.)

20. Address by A. Lawrence Lowell to the Massachusetts Historical Society *Proceedings*, LV (1921–2), pp. 201–14. The British historian A. F. Pollard, who visited the United States as Bryce's Embassy closed, made a similar observation. 'He was, one was told on every hand, the first ambassador Great Britain had ever sent to the American people'; A. F. Pollard, appreciation of Lord Bryce in *History*, VII, No. 28 (1923), pp. 256–65.

CHAPTER NINETEEN

1. Copy of despatch from H.M. Minister in Montevideo, 1910, in Bryce Despatches (1910), Foreign Office Library, London, Vol. 3, Series 414.

2. Grey to Bryce, 10 August 1910, Bryce Embassy Papers, Oxford.

3. Brebner, *North Atlantic Triangle*, p. 245.

4. The best study for following the intricacies of the 1911 Reciprocity diplomacy is L. E. Ellis, *Reciprocity, 1911* (Toronto and New Haven, 1939) – a monograph with complete documentation; on Ridder and the Newspaper Publishers' Association, see pp. 191 ff. See also a pamphlet by Albert H. Walker, *Reciprocity of William H. Taft* (New York, 1912) which attempts to show that Taft struck a bargain with Ridder and his associates for their support in the 1912 elections. The pamphlet is rare, but a copy exists in Columbia University Library.

5. Pringle, *Taft*, II: 589.

6. Ellis, *op. cit.*, pp. 191 *et seq*. See also Albert H. Walker, *op. cit.*, pp. 25–32.

7. Brebner, *North Atlantic Triangle*, p. 268; also quoted in Bemis, *Diplomatic History of the U.S.*, p. 735.

8. The Canadian Reciprocal Trade Agreement (ratified, 14 May 1936) finally brought reciprocity.

9. Ellis, *op. cit.*, pp. 181 ff.; and Earl Grey to Bryce, 2 August 1911, Bryce Embassy Papers.

10. Bryce, *Addresses*, pp. 249–63.

11. See a document dated 4 August 1911 in Bryce Embassy Papers, headed 'World Peace Foundation' and listing 168 Boards of Trade and Chambers of Commerce in the United States endorsing President Taft's moves for unreserved arbitration treaties with Britain and France.

12. Edward Grey to Bryce, 3 April 1911 and subsequent instructions to Bryce, April to July 1911, Bryce Embassy Papers.

13. W. R. Thayer, *Life and Letters of John Hay* (2 vols., Boston, 1915), II: 293.

14. Edward Grey to Bryce, 12 September 1912, Bryce Embassy Papers. On 5 October 1912 Grey wrote: 'I despair of finding anyone to succeed you, who will be up to the American ideal of being outside the diplomatic service and of world wide renown.' – Bryce Embassy Papers.

15. Bryce to Edward Grey, 12 October 1912 (in draft), Bryce Embassy Papers.

16. Progressive Party Platform for 1912; printed in Kirk Porter and D. B. Johnson, *National Party Platforms, 1840–1956* (Urbana, 1956), p. 180.

17. In the 1912 election Woodrow Wilson received just over six million votes, Theodore Roosevelt just over four million, and Taft three and a half million votes. Republicans had some cause to feel that Woodrow Wilson was decidedly not the choice of the majority of the electorate.

18. R. S. Baker, *Woodrow Wilson, Life and Letters*, IV: 400.

19. See Bryce to Edward Grey (draft) on his final conversation with Wilson and Wilson's promise, 29 April 1913, Bryce Embassy Papers. Bryce instructed his successor Spring-Rice on the matter before departing.

20. Stephen Gwyn (ed.), *Spring-Rice*, II: 178. Gwyn states, *loc. cit.*, that Spring-Rice knew so little about Woodrow Wilson's mind and outlook that he sought instruction from Henry Adams; hardly, one imagines, the best possible source of enlightenment.

21. See a large number of press clippings from the American national press and weeklies, Bryce Papers (add. mss., 1965).

22. Bryce to Woodrow Wilson, 19 June 1914, Woodrow Wilson Papers. The letter is also published in R. S. Baker, *Woodrow Wilson, Life and Letters*, IV: 419.

23. Woodrow Wilson to Bryce, 6 July 1914, Bryce Papers.

CHAPTER TWENTY

1. Bryce to Low, 26 January 1914, Seth Low Papers, Columbia University.

2. It would be rash to assume any air of certainty about the state of opinion of the American people on the European war at any time between 1914 and 1917. Nevertheless three regular reviews of thought and opinion during the period give useful clues. They are: *Literary Digest* (New York) presenting reports on periodical literature; *Review of Reviews* (New York) – international in flavour, but devoting much space to American reportage; and *Street's Pandex of the News* (Chicago, 1909–), an excellent guide to American newspaper opinion.

3. The Bryce–Eliot correspondence between 1914 and 1921 is voluminous. The two men were in constant touch with each other. The Bryce–Lawrence Lowell and the Bryce–Murray Butler correspondence is also full. The Bryce–Henry Cabot Lodge correspondence is continuous, though less frequent, from December 1914 to January 1922.

4. See Bryce to Andrew White, 19 December and 29 December 1897, Andrew White Papers, Cornell University; White to Bryce, (?) December 1897, Bryce Papers. Bismarck died in July 1898, so the opportunity did not occur again. See also Villard's remarks on German aspirations and intentions in Villard to Bryce, 6 January 1899, Bryce Papers.

5. *New York Times*, 4 September 1914.

6. *Ibid*. (It should be noted that the *New York Times* had vigorously preserved an independent viewpoint for more than forty years. If it had any leanings, these tended to be towards moderate Republicanism. See Elmer Davis, *History of the New York Times, 1851–1921* (New York, 1921).

7. Eliot to Woodrow Wilson, 20 August 1914, Woodrow Wilson Papers, Library of Congress.

8. See many letters from Bryce to Eliot between 9 September 1914 and 30 January 1917, Eliot Papers, Harvard (copies of most of these letters in Bryce Papers).

9. *New York Times*, 22 September 1914.

10. Both Theodore Roosevelt and Alfred Thayer Mahan branded Germany as the aggressor as soon as war broke out. The celebrated – but also tragic – quarrel between Roosevelt and Wilson, soon extending to Cabot Lodge and Wilson, developed apace after August 1914.

11. Bryce to Eliot, 1 December 1914, Eliot Papers (copy in Bryce Papers).

Bryce urged Eliot (15 January 1915) to publish his letters to the *New York Times* in book form. Eliot took up the suggestion and his book *The Road Towards Peace* (Boston, 1915) was soon circulating.

12. Bryce to Eliot, 17 September 1914, Eliot Papers (copy in Bryce Papers).

13. English translation by J. Ellis Barker (London, 1914). An American imprint (translated by Allen H. Powles, New York, 1914) appeared shortly after the London imprint. Both translations taken from Bernhardi's *Unsere Zukunft: Ein Mahnwort an das Deutsche Volk* (Stuttgart, 1912).

14. *Daily Chronicle*, 5 October 1914, and *Review of Reviews* (New York), November 1914, pp. 612–14.

15. Bryce, *Neutral Nations and the War* (London, 1914). Supplies were quickly shipped to the United States. A note in Bryce's hand (Bryce Papers, add. mss. 1965) headed 'Neutr. Ntns.' carries a list of 28 eminent Americans to whom copies were sent. The list includes President Wilson, William Jennings Bryan, Elihu Root, Roosevelt, Holmes, Cabot Lodge and other Senators; also Borden and Laurier in Canada, together with the Lieut.-Governors of the Provinces.

16. Bryce, *Neutral Nations and the War*, pp. 23 ff.

17. *Ibid.*, pp. 29–30.

18. Bryce to Seth Low, (?) September 1914, Low Papers, Columbia University. Low replied (11 October 1914, Bryce Papers) that he doubted whether an American committee would be formed. Low's doubts were justified by events.

19. *Report of the Committee on Alleged German Atrocities, Appointed 15 December 1915* (London, H.M.S.O., 1915). It was later established that some of the evidence given by Belgian civilians was highly coloured; however, the gravamen of the main charges – extreme brutality against defenceless civilians – was substantiated.

20. Beginning in August 1914, demonstrations in New York City by German Americans were a regular occurrence. On 21 August 1914 the *New York Times* reported a vast German American meeting where the speakers denounced 'all but the Irish'. With the arrival of the new German Ambassador Count Bernstorff, on 25 August 1914, the German Embassy in Washington (assisted by Hermann Ridder's Staats-Zeitung) became a news agency for pro-German and anti-Allied propaganda. See Barbara Tuchman, *The Zimmerman Telegram* (New York, 1958), Chaps. 2–5.

21. The best published sources for tracing the exchanges between Wilson and the Allies from 1914 to 1917 are Charles Seymour (ed.), *The Intimate Papers of Colonel House* (4 vols., London, 1926–8) – hereafter Seymour, *House Papers;* and the definitive biography of Woodrow Wilson by Arthur Link, 5 vols. to date (Princeton, 1947–65), IV–V: hereafter Link, *Wilson*.

22. Diary of Edward House, 25 February, 3 June 1915 *et seq.*, Yale University.

23. Mentioned also in Seymour, *House Papers*, I: 390.

24. Diary of Edward House, 3 June 1915, Yale University.

25. Bryce to House, 26 August 1915, House Papers, Yale University.

26. House to Bryce, 12 August 1915, Bryce Papers, and Seymour, *House Papers*, II: 62–3. The letter argued the case for President Wilson's neutralism. House remarked that he wished many of the President's English and French friends would remember that the American nation 'is one of many nationalities, and that he [the President] has to recognise many diverse elements in our makeup'. This letter could be interpreted as a sign to Bryce to urge the Allied leaders to be patient; that Wilson could not move faster than American public opinion would allow – and certainly not decisively before the November 1916 elections.

27. Bryce to House, 26 August 1915, House Papers.

28. Page 121 above.

CHAPTER TWENTY-ONE

1. These letters are far too numerous to treat in detail here, but copies of the letters to Lawrence Lowell, Seth Low and Theodore Roosevelt are in the Bryce Papers and are calendared.

2. See reviews of German American press, especially the *New Yorker Staats-Zeitung* in *Review of Reviews* (New York), 1916 and *Current Opinion*, 1916–17.

3. *Review of Reviews*, November 1914, pp. 614–15. (Dernburg's article appeared first in the *New York Sun*, 11 October 1914.)

4. Translated by J. Ellis Barker (London, 1914; from Bernhardi's *Unsere Zukunft: Ein Mahnwort an das Deutsche Volk* (Stuttgart, 1912).

5. Link, *Wilson*, Volumes III, IV, V. See also Ernest R. May, *The World War and American Isolationism*, 1914–17 (Cambridge, Mass., 1959).

6. Bryce to House, 26 November 1915; see also Bryce to House, 19 February 1916, 31 May 1916 and 28 September 1916, House Papers.

7. Bryce also took care to enquire from his many friends the state of public opinion in the particular region – whether pro-German or anti-British, and if so, how vehement and widespread it seemed to be. Cf. Bryce to Seth Low in New York, 18 November 1915, and subsequent correspondence, Low Papers. See also Elihu Root to Bryce, 26 November 1915, Bryce Papers (a detailed survey of American opinion).

8. Seymour, *House Papers*, II: 74–6, 99–100, 108–9 *et passim*. Spring-Rice was something of an embarrassment to House and Wilson when he was not an irritant – especially when he signed notes to House 'With much love'. See House to Wilson, 21 December 1915, *ibid.*, II: 109. House discussed with Bryce in strictest confidence the difficulties with Spring-Rice in Washington and asked his advice. Bryce said that it would be exceedingly unwise for House to attempt to take the matter up in London – *ibid.*, II: 132–3.

9. House to Bryce, 10 December 1915, House Papers, Yale University.

10. House Diary, 13 January 1916, and Seymour, *House Papers*, II: 125.

11. Burton J. Hendrick, *Life and Letters of Walter Hines Page* (3 vols., New York, 1922–5), I: 391.

12. *Ibid.*, I: 392.

13. House Diary, 13 January 1916, House Papers, Yale University. Printed in part in Seymour, *House Papers*, II: 124.

14. See Link, *Wilson*, IV: 130–5.

15. Bryce to House, 31 May 1916, House Papers, Yale University.

16. Eliot to Bryce, 13 February and 2 March 1916, Bryce Papers. (During these months Eliot and Bryce were exchanging voluminous letters on the subject of American neutrality and Wilson's attitude to the belligerents. By now Eliot was willing to countenance armed American intervention on behalf of the Allies.)

17. Bryce to Eliot, 7 March 1916, Eliot Papers (copy in Bryce Papers).

18. *New Republic*, 20 May 1916, pp. 58–9.

19. *New York Times*, 19 May 1916. The editor must have secured an advance copy and rushed it into print before the weekly *New Republic* appeared next day. On May 21 the *New York Times Magazine* published another special article by Lord Bryce, entitled 'England's War Attitude'. In the article Bryce put forward the principles for which, he argued, England had gone to war. These included liberty, the right of self-determination, the maintenance of treaty obligations, the regulation of the methods of warfare in the interests of common humanity, and the cultivation of a pacific rather than a military type of civilisation. Bryce wrote the article at the suggestion of a Swiss editor – *New York Times Magazine*, 21 May 1916.

20. R. S. Baker, *Woodrow Wilson, Life and Letters*, VI: 217.

21. Seymour, *House Papers*, II: 295.

22. *Ibid.*, pp. 296–7.

23. See the complete draft of Wilson's speech and the House draft in Seymour, *House Papers*, II: 337–9.

24. *Ibid.*, 299.

25. Lawrence Godkin to Bryce, 14 January 1916, Lawrence Godkin Papers, Houghton Library, Harvard University. (No copy in Bryce Papers).

26. Bryce to Dicey, 22 October 1917, Bryce Papers. Bryce remarks: 'I knew all along he was in sympathy with us and felt that he was right in not showing his hand till he was sure he could carry the country with him . . .' (etc., etc.). This letter raises important questions about Wilson's 'neutralism', adequate. discussion of which would occupy much space. It may be noted that Bryce would have little cause to delude Dicey, his oldest and best friend. The present writer is exploring this puzzle as sources permit. Cf., fn. 30 below.

27. Kirk H. Porter, *National Party Platforms*, p. 196.

28. House to Bryce, 17 January 1917, House Papers, Yale University.

29. James B. Scott, *President Wilson's Foreign Policy: Messages, Addresses, Papers* (New York, 1918), p. 260.

30. The mystery is not wholly solved by the latest volume of Professor Link's definitive biography (Vol. V, *Confusions and Crises*, Princeton, 1965). Professor

Link suggests, p. ix, that Wilson was 'profoundly affected by considerations of long-range interest . . .'. But in the discussion which follows it is stated that Wilson 'could see no other way to protect American national rights and shipping . . . he [also] believed the war was in its final stages and American participation would hasten its end'. One would like to see a sharper distinction made between immediate policy objectives and 'considerations of long-range interest'. We are driven back to Barbara Tuchman's reminder: 'We still do not know at any level that really matters why Wilson took the fateful decision to bring the United States into the First World War.' – Tuchman, *The Zimmerman Telegram* (New York, 1958), vi (quoting the anonymous reviewer of George F. Kennan's *Russia Leaves the War* in *Times Literary Supplement*, 4 January 1957).

31. See Chapter 22 below and cf. Seymour, *House Papers*, I: 365 *et seq.*, II: 132 *et seq.*

CHAPTER TWENTY-TWO

1. John H. Latané (ed.), *The Development of the League of Nations Idea: Documents and Correspondence of Theodore Marburg* (2 vols., New York, 1932) – hereafter cited as Latané, *Marburg Documents*. See also R. J. Bartlett, *The League to Enforce Peace* (Chapel Hill, 1944) and Henry R. Winkler, *The League of Nations Movement in Great Britain, 1914–1919* (New Brunswick, 1952).

2. Latané, *Marburg Documents*, I: 15. See also Bryce to Eliot on the same day (15 January 1915) – 'By what means can a cooperation of the Great Powers be brought about to form a League of Peace for enforcing Treaties and averting war?' – Eliot Papers.

3. Latané, *Marburg Documents*, I: 19–20; see also Marburg's notes to Bryce, Bryce Papers. (The Bryce-Marburg correspondence in the Bryce Papers is fairly complete for the period May 1915 to July 1920.)

4. Latané, *Marburg Documents*, I: 20–1.

5. *New York Times*, 4 October 1914.

6. Latané, *Marburg Documents*, I: 26 ff.

7. *Ibid.*, I: 33.

8. *Ibid.*, I: 37–8.

9. *Ibid.*, I: 46 ff. The Bryce proposals later appeared in book form, *Proposals for the Prevention of Future Wars* (London and New York, 1917).

10. Bartlett, *League to Enforce Peace*, pp. 70–1.

11. See F. P. Walters, *A History of the League of Nations* (London, 1960), p. 19.

12. The Presidential Address, the British Academy, June 1915, and July 1916. Printed in *Proceedings of the British Academy, 1915–16* (London, 1919), pp. 1–36. Reprints in Bryce Papers.

13. Lord Bryce, 'War and Human Progress', the Huxley Lecture, Birmingham University, 1916: reprinted in *Atlantic Monthly*, CXVIII (1916), pp. 301–15.

14. Lowell to Bryce, 13 March 1917, Bryce Papers. See also Garraty, *Henry Cabot Lodge*, esp. Chaps. 18 and 19, for the development of the Lodge–Wilson vendetta.

15. Lowell to Bryce, 3 January 1917, Bryce Papers; and cf. Colonel House to Bryce, 17 January 1917, '. . . all you say has weight on this side of the Atlantic'. – House Papers, Yale University.

16. Although the *Proposals* first appeared in book form in 1917, they were circulating privately well before then. The Bryce preface in the book is dated February 1915.

17. Bryce to Lloyd George, 8 August 1917; copy in Bryce Papers.

18. Jan Smuts to Bryce, 27 October 1917, Bryce Papers.

19. Wilson to Marburg, 6 May 1918, Latané, *Marburg Documents*, I: 403–5 and 415; Marburg to Bryce, 7 May 1918, Bryce Papers.

20. Lord Phillimore, *Schemes for Maintaining General Peace* (printed for restricted circulation by H.M.S.O., 1917, and later published, London, 1920) See pp. 28–30 for the examination of the Bryce proposals.

21. Walters, *History of the League of Nations*, pp. 23–4, 29, 32. See also David Hunter Miller, *The Drafting of the Covenant* (2 vols., New York, 1928), I: 34–9.

22. Bryce to Lowell, 3 October and 25 November 1918, Lowell Papers.

23. Garraty, *Henry Cabot Lodge*, pp. 332, 345 ff.

24. Lowell to Bryce, 8 March 1919, Bryce Papers, and Bryce to Lowell, 18 June 1919, Lowell Papers.

25. Bryce to Lowell, 27 March 1919, Lowell Papers (and see many more letters passing between Bryce and Lowell in 1919).

26. Bryce to Charles Larned Robinson, 16 November 1918; Bryce Letters, New York Historical Society, New York City.

27. John Maynard Keynes, *The Economic Consequences of the Peace* (1st ed., London, 1919).

28. Bryce to Lowell, 4 November 1919, Lowell Papers.

29. There are almost as many theories as there are diplomatic historians on precisely why the Senate rejected the Covenant and the Treaty. Possibly John McC. Roots comes closest to it in an unpublished doctoral dissertation, 'The Treaty of Versailles and the U.S. Senate' (Harvard University Archives, 1925). Roots argues that the forces which combined to defeat the Treaty in the Senate were 'Personal and official antagonism', 'Political Opportunism' and 'Sincere opposition'. He finds it impossible to apportion relative weights to these three sets of causes – an honest and reasonable humility in the face of an infinitely tangled story.

CHAPTER TWENTY-THREE

1. *Report of the Lord Bryce Conference on the Reform of the Second Chamber:* Cd. 9038 (London, 1918), pp. 21 *et seq.*

2. James, Viscount Bryce, *Modern Democracies* (2 vols., London and New York, 1921), I: 23–56 and 57–78.

3. Charles Oman, review of *Modern Democracies* in *Quarterly Review*, CCXXXVI (1921), pp. 129–46.

4. Bryce Papers.

5. James, Viscount Bryce, *The Study of American History* (Cambridge, 1921) – the inaugural lecture of the George Watson Chair of American History, Literature and Institutions. See pp. 3–4 ff.

6. See M. J. Pusey, *Charles Evans Hughes* (2 vols., New York, 1951), I: 315 ff.

7. Hughes to Bryce, (?) June 1921 and 18 July 1921, Bryce Papers; and see Pusey, *op. cit.*, I: 189–90, II: 460.

8. James, Viscount Bryce, *The Study of International Relations* (New York, 1922), p. 4.

9. *Ibid.*, p. 256.

10. *Ibid.*, pp. 245–53.

11. *Ibid.*, pp. 261–2, 265.

12. *Harvard Crimson*, 28 September 1921. Information also obtained from members of the Harvard Class of 1924 and Harvard Class of 1925 (Harvard Faculty, 1965, and Harvard Alumni Office.)

13. Complete details, with printed greetings, are given in the brochure printed by the Sulgrave Institution, 1921. (A copy in New York Public Library, Manuscripts Division.)

14. Reported in the *New York Times*, 10 October 1921.

15. *Ibid.*

16. See Bryce to Moorfield Storey (a founder of the National Association for the Advancement of Colored People), 18 October 1921, and Bryce to J. A. Chambliss ('on the relation of the whites to the coloured population in the Southern States . . . one of the most important [subjects] that affects your nation'), 18 October 1921, Bryce Papers.

17. Marion, Lady Bryce, to James Ford Rhodes, 3 February 1922, Rhodes Papers, Massachusetts Historical Society.

18. Cited by Fisher, *Bryce*, II: 292 (the letter no longer extant): mentioned in *The Times*, 28 January 1922.

19. Lord Cecil of Chelwood, *ibid.*, II: 292. See also House of Lords, Debates, Vol. 49 (February 1922), cc. 16–17, cc. 19–20.

20. Proceedings of the Washington Conference on the Limitation of Armaments: reported in the *New York Times*, 24 January 1921.

21. Proceedings of the Ceremonies Attending the Unveiling of a Bust of James Bryce at the United States Capitol, 12 October 1922, *67 Cong.*, 4 Sess., Senate Doc. 298 (Washington, D.C., 1923).

Index

333